Integrative Views of Motivation, Cognition, and Emotion

Volume 41 of
the Nebraska Symposium
on Motivation

University of Nebraska Press
Lincoln and London 1994

Volume 41 of the Nebraska Symposium on Motivation

Integrative Views of Motivation, Cognition, and Emotion

Richard Dienstbier
William D. Spaulding

Series Editor
Volume Editor

Presenters
Herbert A. Simon

Professor of Computer Science and Psychology, Carnegie Mellon University

Muriel D. Lezak

Professor of Neurology and Psychiatry, Oregon Health Sciences University

Howard Gardner

Professor of Education, Harvard University

John A. Bargh

Professor of Psychology, New York University

Peter M. Gollwitzer

Privat Dozent, Universität Konstanz

Nancy Cantor

Professor of Psychology, Princeton University

William Fleeson

Postdoctoral fellow, Max Planck Institute for Psychological Research

Don C. Fowles

Professor of Psychology, University of Iowa

Integrative Views of Motivation, Cognition, and Emotion is Volume 41
in the series
CURRENT THEORY AND RESEARCH
IN MOTIVATION

International Standard Book Number
0-8032-4233-6 (Clothbound)
International Standard Book Number
0-8032-9221-X (Paperbound)

The paper in this book meets the minimum
requirements of American National Standard for
Information Sciences—Permanence of Paper for
Printed Library Materials, ANSI Z39.48-1984.

"The Library of Congress has cataloged
this serial publication as follows:"
Nebraska Symposium on Motivation.
Nebraska Symposium on Motivation.
[Papers] v. [1]–1953–
Lincoln, University of Nebraska Press.
v. illus., diagrs. 22cm. annual.
Vol. 1 issued by the symposium under
its earlier name: Current Theory and
Research in Motivation.
Symposia sponsored by the Dept. of
Psychology of the University of Nebraska.
1. Motivation (Psychology)
BF683.N4   159.4082   53-11655
Library of Congress

Preface

The volume editor for this 41st edition of the Nebraska Symposium, Professor William D. Spaulding, coordinated the evaluation of posters in addition to the usual volume-editor responsibilities of planning the volume, drawing together the contributors, and supervising the editing. My thanks to our contributors for excellent chapters developed and delivered in timely fashion, and to Will for his editorial excellence in seeing the volume through to its completion.

Under Will's direction, the changes in our procedures begun last year have continued. I mention them here to alert you, our readers and our future Symposium participants and attenders. To make your coming to the Symposium more rewarding, we have consolidated all Symposium activities into one session that spans several days. For this and the previous volume, we invited posters on topics relevant to the main theme of each volume. Abstracts of the posters accepted for this edition appear before the indexes.

The Symposium series is supported largely by funds donated in memory of Professor Harry K. Wolfe to the University of Nebraska Foundation by the late Professor Cora L. Friedline. This Symposium volume, like those of the recent past, is dedicated to the memory of Professor Wolfe, who brought the study of psychology to the University of Nebraska. After studying with Wilhelm Wundt, Professor

Wolfe returned to this, his native state, to establish the first under-graduate laboratory of psychology in the nation. As an undergraduate at Nebraska, Professor Friedline studied psychology under Professor Wolfe.

We are grateful to the late Professor Friedline for her bequest and to the University of Nebraska Foundation for continued financial support for the series.

RICHARD A. DIENSTBIER
Series Editor

Contents

Introduction

William D. Spaulding
University of Nebraska–Lincoln

One of my formative experiences as a graduate student came during a break in our afternoon-long first-year proseminar. We had been discussing the scope of psychology, or rather, listening to two professors debate the scope of psychology. Both the protagonists were clinical psychologists by training, but one had remained an empirically focused social learning theorist, while the other had pursued the study of Eastern religion, psychoanalysis, and transpersonal psychology. As the class milled about, the social learning empiricist sought some closure on the discussion. "Dick," he said to his transpersonal colleague, "it seems to me that we disagree because in your view, what I do isn't psychology, and in my view, what you do isn't science."

We tend to think of the preparadigmatic era of science as characterized by instability and ambiguity in the *nature* of explanatory paradigms. As that break revealed, however, we often seem to be as confused about *what* we are attempting to understand as *how* we should understand it.

Today many believe that over the past decade or so psychology has become a paradigmatic science (Baars, 1986). The new paradigm is an understanding of behavior in terms of cognitive representations, "the computational metaphor," and a view of biological organisms as heterarchically organized information-processing systems interacting with environmental exigencies. If psychology now has a paradigm, we might expect that the explanatory scope of psychology will be clarified by that paradigm. We might further expect that this clarification will come as new conceptualizations of ideas that have evolved over the hundred or so years of psychology's modern era.

Motivation, emotion, and *cognition* have all been superordinate ideas in psychology. Motivation refers to the meaning and purpose of behavior. Emotion refers to experiential and psychophysiological phenomena that accompany motivational processes. Cognition refers to organismic activity, not directly observable, which translates motivation and emotion into observable behavior. Psychological theory has traditionally attempted to explain events in one of these domains in terms of events in the other ones. Different theories have postulated different causal directions and relations between the domains. For example, specific motivational processes are hypothesized to give rise to specific emotional, cognitive, and behavioral events. The diversity of theories and lack of consensus about which ones have explanatory superiority are precisely the type of confusion to be expected in a preparadigmatic science. Similarly, lack of consensus about which processes in which domains constitute "psychology" illustrates the effect of a poorly defined explanatory scope. The benefits of a psychological paradigm should include a new, unified, and integrated understanding of the relationships between motivation, cognition, and emotion.

The cognitive revolution in psychology has fostered a particular view of cognition as the passing of information back and forth between perceptual, memory, and motor components of an integrated system. Can this view be systematically extended to phenomena that have traditionally fallen under the rubrics of motivation and emotion? This volume of the Nebraska Symposium on Motivation is a collection of views that address that question. Most generally, the contributions taken together stimulate a hypothesis that the cognitive paradigm has began to move psychology toward a "unified field theory" of behavior and experience.

The first contribution in this volume, by Herbert Simon, tests the limits of a pure information-processing paradigm. It is a basic tenet of information theory that information exists independent of the medium by which it is represented. By analyzing the information-processing capabilities of nonbiological systems, or "artificial intelligence," we may perhaps determine what aspects of motivation and emotion require consideration of the biological substrate of cognition and which do not. The second contribution, by Muriel Lezak, raises the same sort of question by focusing on the biological substrate itself and analyzing constraints and determinations that it imposes. The third contribution, by Howard Gardner, considers in tandem the medium and the information it processes and lays a conceptual foundation for making the facts of biological brain science congruent with the richness and diversity of human behavior and experience. The fourth contribution, by John Bargh and Peter Gollwitzer, elaborates on constructs that potentially incorporate key aspects of human functioning, such as social behavior and creativity, into a comprehensive, integrated, and cognitive view of motivation.

The final two contributions take the discussion out of purely theoretical context to address issues in clinical application. Psychopathology and the psychology of adjustment have traditionally provided a conceptual compass to theoretical psychology. We may learn about normal processes by studying the abnormal. This applies to abnormalities in the information-processing substrate, as Lezak's chapter so clearly illustrates, and to problems in the informational processes that are independent of the substrate. The fifth contribution to this volume, by Nancy Cantor and William Fleeson, describes an integrated cognitive theoretical perspective, which is potentially useful for understanding, among other things, the differences between effective and ineffective social functioning. The sixth contribution, by Don Fowles, presents a theoretical framework for understanding a diversity of severe psychopathology in terms compatible with an integrated cognitive, motivational, and emotional understanding of normal behavior.

Posters were invited for presentation at the symposium in Lincoln in October 1992. They represent diverse work on integrative views of motivation, cognition, and emotion. Abstracts of the poster presentations are included at the end of this volume.

Grateful acknowledgment is made to series editor Richard Dienstbier and the Nebraska Symposium on Motivation editorial committee, for their sponsorship and support. Additional thanks are extended to the contributors, who responded with diligence and alacrity to the demands of producing this volume, and to the poster session authors. Most important, special thanks are due to the faculty and students of the University of Nebraska–Lincoln Department of Psychology, whose scholarly energy inspired this volume and gave it its direction and focus.

REFERENCE

Baars, B. (1986). *The cognitive revolution in psychology.* New York: Guilford.

The Bottleneck of Attention: Connecting Thought with Motivation

Herbert A. Simon
Carnegie Mellon University

Classical learning theory provides an interesting insight into the uneasy relation that has existed throughout the history of modern psychology between the study of thought and the study of motivation. Central to learning theory was the idea that if certain responses of the organism in the presence of a stimulus were positively reinforced (rewarded) while others were negatively reinforced (punished), the organism would learn to respond to the former rather than the latter. Motivation, in this view, was a key factor in learning.

Latent Learning

The dispute about latent learning, that is, "learning without motivation," forced a revision of classical learning theory (Hilgard & Bower, 1975, pp. 134–36). Tolman and others showed that a hungry

This research was supported by the National Science Foundation under grant no. DBS–912 1027 and by the Defense Advanced Research Projects Agency, Department of Defense, ARPA Order 3597, monitored by the Air Force Avionics Laboratory under contract F33615-81-K-1539. Reproduction in whole or in part is permitted for any purpose of the United States government. Approved for public release; distribution unlimited.

rat could learn the location of water, even though it was motivated to search for food, and a thirsty rat could learn the location of food, even though it was motivated to search for water. From these experiments one could argue that the key factor was not reward and punishment but knowledge of results—that is, feedback connecting behavior with its consequences. If the rat followed a certain path and found water, then it could remember that this path led to water even if the initial discovery was not motivated by thirst and the rat did not stop to drink the water. But knowledge of results is a cognitive rather than a motivational mechanism.

Of course, this interpretation was too simplistic. The rat, when hungry, did not *always* learn where the water was. It was more likely to learn when thirsty and least likely to learn when *very* hungry. Motivation reentered the picture, but with the help of an intermediate mechanism. The alternative explanation was that the rat learned (obtained knowledge of results) about anything it *attended to*. While searching for food, but in not too hungry a state, it might attend to other interesting characteristics of its environment, for example, the location of water. But when the rat was very hungry, its attention would not be distracted by anything but food; water would go unnoticed, and hence its location unlearned.

Attention as the Mediator

Learning, in this revised version, derives from the following sequence:

motivation   → search
(e.g., hunger)   → noticing (attention to item of interest)
                    → knowledge of results (path to item)
                    → storage (of path-item relation)

Noticing, in turn, depends on the control of attention. A strong motive attracts attention to objects in the environment relevant to that motive. Under weaker motivation, attention could be distracted by other objects, that is, those relevant to motives not then active (and these motives could thereby be aroused). Hence, a theory of learning would have to encompass the laws of attention. Motivation reenters the theory in two ways. First, attention is itself a function of motivation. Second, motivation might initiate an activity that would encounter information relevant to a different goal, sometimes causing that information to be learned or even diverting attention and search to the new goal.

Another, evolutionary, line of thought leads to the same conclusion (Simon, 1956, 1967). A system that is capable of working on only one task at a time but that must, over some period of time, satisfy many goals or needs requires a mechanism that will allocate its activity among its several goals. If some of its needs have to be satisfied in "real time"—that is, now or never—the attention-directing mechanism must have the means for interrupting ongoing activity to give priority to the urgent needs.

Further, if the system's activities in the service of particular goals bring it in contact with information useful for the attainment of other, currently latent goals, it would be advantageous to store that information. But the key phrase here is "useful for the attainment of other goals." The system would need a mechanism for discriminating, at least roughly, between potentially useful information and uninteresting information.

We should not be surprised, therefore, if natural selection (in an organism that had to satisfy some needs in serial, one-at-a-time fashion) developed motivational mechanisms for signaling current urgencies among its many needs, noticing mechanisms for detecting and learning information of future interest to goals not currently active, and an interrupt mechanism to set aside currently active goals for more urgent or advantageous ones. Precisely such mechanisms appear to have emerged in the evolution of animals, including human beings.

Seriality and Parallelism

Before we return to the mechanism of attention as the linchpin between motive and emotion on the one hand and cognition on the other, let us pursue a little further the respective roles of seriality and parallelism in human processes and behavior. While the empirical evidence, both neurological and behavioral, on these roles is still highly incomplete, perhaps some light can be cast on them from the evolutionary viewpoint above.

SERIALITY AND PARALLELISM OF "HIGHER" FUNCTIONS

From the mid-1950s until the early 1980s, the formal psychological models that accompanied the "cognitive revolution" mainly described human thinking as a collection of processes executed in a serial, one-at-a-time fashion. Of course, it was understood that the principal sensory organs were parallel in structure and function and that there was a substantial degree of parallelism in motor action. However, the models of the more central parts of the nervous system were perceived as predominately serial.

This commitment to seriality rested on the clear and massive evidence that, at the level of "higher" nonautomatic functions (e.g., solving problems, generating meaningful linguistic strings, attaining concepts), a human being can only do one or at most a few things at a time. What little parallelism is evident in such behavior (e.g., pacing up and down while lecturing) can sometimes be explained away as time-sharing—that is, alternating attention between activities. Time-sharing would be expected when one or both of the shared activities require only a little attention. In the limit, one of the activities might be automatized through extensive practice and thus places no burden on cognitive capacity. But only activities requiring no processing of sensory stimuli can be fully automatized.

The severe limits on concurrent activity have been amply demonstrated in the psychological laboratory, but they are also evident in everyday experiences. One can carry on a conversation while driving a car, but the intensity and quality of the conversation deteriorates as traffic becomes heavier and the driving demands more attention. Once, in the dead of winter in Iowa, I maneuvered a car in which I was the passenger into a large snowbank by giving the driver (who was defending the case for cognitive parallelism) a mental imagery task to perform while driving. (I kept close watch over his foot on the accelerator to make sure the car was moving very slowly, but we should not be unwilling to make sacrifices for the progress of our science.)

PARALLELISM AND AUTOMATISM

Of course, if our observations begin on the neural end of the scale, we are just as strongly impressed by the evidence of parallelism— not only in the retina and the inner ear but also in the immense neuronal structures of the central nervous system. What are all these neurons doing if there is not a great deal of parallel activity going on?

Even here we must be careful in drawing conclusions. A classical von Neumann computer, the quintessence of seriality, has large banks of memory units, all in parallel. Since these units are "passive," that is, used only to record and retain information, we do not think of them as operating in parallel; we call the von Neumann machine a serial computer since all of its processes other than memory storage and retrieval are highly localized in a few units. It is quite possible that much of the apparent parallelism of the human brain also consists of passive memory units, with only a few units active in the processing sense at any moment. The decisive neurological evidence on this point is simply not yet available.

But the accumulated evidence of high degrees of automatism for many tasks acquired through extensive practice cannot be ignored (Shiffrin & Schneider, 1977). To the extent that such automatism is achieved, the organism's capacity for parallelism is increased.

A plausible explanation for the parallelism associated with the automatization of processes is that the sequence of "instructions" controlling such processes is gradually *compiled*. That is, instead of depending on sensory signals to initiate each new step in the process, the system gradually learns that the next step can safely be taken on completion of the previous one without new tests of appropriateness. Removal of these frequent tests both speeds up execution of the process and releases it from using scarce short-term memory capacity at intermediate points (Hayes & Simon, 1974).

For a skilled driver, operating an automobile is an example of a process that has become partly but not wholly automated (the driver must still occasionally obtain new sensory information about the current situation and cannot drive successfully with eyes closed or while processing other mental images). But as a result of the compilation of the process, the skilled driver makes far smaller demands on the senses and on short term memory than does the novice.

PARALLELISM IN SENSATION AND PERCEPTION

The existing evidence is *consistent* with the position that somewhere between the sense organs and the central system and between the central system and peripheral motor neurons are zones within which incoming signals are converted from parallel to serial encodings, and outgoing signals from serial to parallel. We have only the vaguest indications of exactly where these zones lie, and there is a broad no-man's-land in which it is not unreasonable to model the system as either parallel or serial.

In encoding from parallel sensory stimuli to serial symbols, a considerable compression of information occurs. The organism attends to only a small part of the information received by the sensors. The nature of this "filtering," for auditory stimuli, has been studied since World War II in a long series of experiments on dichotic listening by Cherry, Broadbent, Moray, Treisman, and many others (see Treisman, 1969).

In early experiments, it appeared that, when a message in one ear was being attended to, the message in the other ear was almost completely neglected, and little or no information about it was retained. Then more and more exceptions were found to this rule, such as the "cocktail party" phenomenon: when the name of the listener was spoken in the unattended ear, it was noticed rather than filtered out. Attention could switch "automatically" from one ear to the other if a meaningful continuous message was broken off in one ear and simultaneously taken up in the other. Even more troublesome to the theory of filtering, a word sounded in the unattended ear, synonymous with one meaning of an ambiguous word presented simultaneously to the other ear, could resolve the ambiguity in favor of the "unattended" synonym.

These experiments showed that, although attention was presumably focused at a given moment on the message in one ear, the message delivered to the other ear was also being processed, at least sufficiently to detect "interesting" content, which could then sometimes either divert attention from the previously attended ear or influence the processing of the message in the attended ear. The filtering of the unattended message was much less than complete. Later, I will consider mechanisms of attention that are compatible with this evidence of parallelism.

WHY SERIALITY?

But let me return to the issue of why there should be seriality at all. Isn't this highly inconvenient for the organism, and wouldn't the forces of natural selection gradually have replaced seriality with parallelism? To answer these questions, we must examine more closely the nature of the needs of the human organism, for example for air and for food.

Air is nearly ubiquitous in the human environment, and we breathe in parallel with our other activities. When breathing is interfered with in any way, however, the need for air becomes urgent, and the autonomic nervous system sends messages that take high priority in interrupting attention from other goals to satisfying this need. The urgency is related to our small capacity, in time units, for storing air for subsequent use. This small capacity in turn reflects the usual ready availability of air and the high cost of storing an item that is used in large volumes. The respiration mechanisms, including those that implement the "drive to breathe," seem well adapted, from an evolutionary standpoint, to the economies of the situation.

Food, particularly for hunting-and-gathering creatures, is not at all ubiquitous but is only obtained by arduous search and harvest processes. Inventory capacity must be amply provided to span the intervals between successful harvests. The body must signal when the inventory shows signs of depletion, but the arousal can be more gradual than in the case of air, and, even when aroused, hunger need not interrupt ongoing activity as imperiously as does the need to breathe. Again, evolution seems to have shaped the system in such a way as to relate inventory capacity in an efficient way to the costs of replenishment and to adapt the attention-interrupting system to the urgency of competing demands.

There are, of course, a whole host of requirements for survival and procreation beyond these two. Most of them, like hunger, are handled by systems of inventories and periodic replenishment, with corresponding drives to compete for the system's attention. This scenario still does not explain why the organism does not attend to many of these needs simultaneously, but the answer should now be evident. Because of the dispersion of need-satisfying situations in the environment, most needs can be satisfied only after extensive activity involving collaboration of sense and motor organs in pursuit of a specific goal. It is seldom either convenient or effective to make love, for example, while hunting for prey.

An effective division of labor is not achieved by segmenting the organism into components that each work toward satisfying one of these goals. It is much more efficient to divide labor by time segments—the resources of the entire organism being devoted, in turn, to satisfying successive goals, the priorities being established by the signaling and attention control mechanisms. Much more extensive parallelism and division of labor by functions reappear at the social level, at which independent, physically self-contained members of a society can be allocated temporarily, or even permanently, specialized tasks.

When we look at the organism's internal metabolic mechanisms parallelism reappears again on a large scale, and insofar as internal processes depend on neural control, they call for a corresponding measure of neurological parallelism. The regulation of the action of the heart and of breathing is the most obvious example of this internal activity that goes on in parallel with the regulation of external activities.

From all of these easily observed phenomena and the inferences we can draw from the requirements of evolutionary fitness, we conclude that there is no simple answer to the question: Is the nervous system serial or is it parallel? It is both—not haphazardly but in an organization that is responsive to the demands of survival and efficiency. The serial constriction imposed by the limits of short-term memory is itself a response to the structure of the environment and of the organs that sense and act on it. The parallel functioning that is observable in the sensory organs and in the control of internal processes is a response to the need to process information in real time, when it is presented and available, and to control processes that must operate continuously.

Unified Theories of Behavior

Currently the cognitive community is strongly interested in constructing unified theories of cognition, theories that aspire to describe and explain the whole cognitive person. For example, at Carnegie Mellon University alone there are at least four candidates for such a unified architecture. The Act* architecture of John Anderson is designed around the structure of semantic memory and the spreading-activation processes that operate in it. The Soar architecture, developed under the leadership of Allen Newell, places problem spaces, production systems, and learning through chunking in central positions. The connectionist architecture of parallel distributed processing is championed by Jay McClelland. And the slightly more ramshackle architecture that I espouse includes among its principal components EPAM (elementary perceiver and memorizer), GPS (general problem solver), and UNDERSTAND (a program for constructing problem spaces from problem descriptions in natural language).

These architects are all aware that behavior must be motivated and, consequently, that a unified theory of cognition must include a theory of motivation. Newell, in his magistral *Unified Theories of Cognition* (1990), is explicit on this point. In describing the ultimate scope of a unified theory (pp. 15–16), he places motivation and emotion fifth among the six areas to be covered (the ellipses at the end of his list remind us that there are others). But he then observes that this area is not yet part of any extant unified theory. Unification must proceed by stages, and in its first stages of development a unified theory must attend to problem solving, decision making, routine action, memory, learning, skill, perception, motor behavior, languages—a formidable list of topics before we arrive at motivation and emotion.

However, there is perhaps more motivation in these theories than immediately meets the eye, and we become aware of its role when we switch our own attention from the term "motivation" to the terms "attention" and "goals."

Goals and Motivation

In the description of experiments conducted in cognitive psychology laboratories, the motivation of subjects is usually mentioned only casually and in terms that already assume a theory of human motivation. We are told that the subjects were satisfying a course requirement in Psychology 100 or that they were paid $5.00 per hour. The assumption is that these conditions are sufficiently motivating that the subjects will address themselves to whatever cognitive task is presented. We are supposed to know enough about college sophomores to understand that these rewards are enough to gain their attention for some length of time—an hour, perhaps.

If we were trying, say, to secure the attention of a professional chess grandmaster or a practicing architect for half a day, we might have to say more about motivation in describing our experiments. The question also arises, especially in experiments concerned with decision making under risk and uncertainty, whether modest rewards of a few dollars produce behavior that is predictive of how people behave when the stakes are larger—a million dollars, say, or potential loss of an arm or leg. And appropriate motivation cannot be presumed for tasks that are aversive for subjects: very boring tasks protracted for hours, for example.

But in more common types of experiments, when measuring problem-solving skills or the use of language or visual imagery, we usually take motivation for granted, and not without reason. We have extensive experience with the fact that, within broad limits, people are very obliging about doing what researchers ask of them. Organizations could not otherwise exist: in them we pay people to accept authority, and as long as orders remain within their "areas of acceptance," they generally obey. Of course, they may obey with greater or less enthusiasm, and their performance may vary in quality and quantity accordingly.

Laboratory subjects likewise obey authority within an area of acceptance. In the cognitive psychology laboratory, we typically ask our subjects to perform some tasks as well as they can. Provided they direct their attention to the tasks and are not distracted, added increments of effort would not greatly alter their performance. The subjects are trying about as hard as they can to apply their knowledge and skills to solve the problems posed. (We should be less confident of this, the less well structured the tasks are.) In addition to the extrinsic rewards they will receive, their self-esteem is also enlisted. Within broad limits, trying harder would not alter their performance much.

But if we can assume in most circumstances that our subjects will be motivated to do what we ask of them, we must still be clear and precise in informing them exactly what the goal of the experimental task is. Explicit goals attach free-floating motives (the willingness to do what we ask) to specific tasks. They secure the subject's attention to the relevant things in the task situation.

Suppose that we present a column of numbers to a subject. If the instructions call for the sum of the column, then the subject will likely hold the running total in short-term memory and scan down the list, adding each successive number to this running total until reaching the bottom of the list. If, on the other hand, the instructions call for reporting the largest number in the list, the subject will likely hold in short-term memory the largest number noticed so far and, progressing down the list, will compare it with each new number, replacing it whenever the new number is larger. By specifying different goals, the same motive (doing what the experimenter asks) is enlisted for performing different tasks. In this example, both tasks attract attention to the same objects but extract different information from them.

In Stroop-like tasks, the conflict of attention is made explicit. One can attend to the shape of a color word or the color in which it is printed. The goal (of reporting the word or its color) attaches the motive to perform correctly one or the other of these tasks, although they are not of equal facility. It is easy to invent tasks in which different instructions cause the subject's eyes to attend to different locations in the stimulus. A chess player who is asked to describe the position around the black king will look at a different part of the board from someone asked to describe the position around the white king.

If unified theories of cognition are silent about motivations, they are quite explicit about mechanisms for controlling attention. Newell (1990, p. 257) provides an example in his discussion of how perception operates:

> The *attention operator* is the required active process. It can be executed, as can any other operator, by central cognition. It is given a search specification [i.e., a goal], and it finds an element satisfying this specification from anywhere in [the percept]. The result of the attention operator (if successful) is that it switches cognition to be at the place of the attended element.

ATTENTION CONTROL IN PRODUCTION SYSTEMS

In Soar, in my own eclectic architecture, and in architectures based on production systems in general, goals are the essential directors of attention. The basic component in production systems (sometimes inaccurately called "rule-based systems") is the structure known as a production, which has a striking resemblance, at least superficially, to the S $\rightarrow$ R connections of our behaviorist past. If we replace S and R by C (for "conditions") and A (for "actions"), respectively, then we have the production C $\rightarrow$ A, to be read, "Whenever the conditions, C, are satisfied, the actions, A, are carried out."

A production system is simply an unordered list of productions. If the conditions of more than one production are satisfied at the same time, then either some rules of priority must determine which will be executed or the system must be capable of executing them in parallel. In their pure form, production systems provide the possibility of anarchy, for every production in the entire system is potentially active at every moment: it is simply waiting, independent of the rest of the system, for the announcement that its conditions are satisfied. Indeed, production systems were first applied to cognitive simulation in reaction to the overly structured control imposed by hierarchies of routines and their subroutines. In the hierarchical schemes, a process can execute only if it is "called" by a superordinate process, and it retains control of attention until it terminates and returns control to the superordinate process. Production systems and hierarchical languages represent wholly different theories of attention, its persistence, and its shifting.

The pure production system proved to be too much of a libertarian good thing and was soon modified, in particular by the introduction of goals. Recall the example above of two arithmetic tasks performed on a column of numbers. Suppose we had two productions: If there is a column of numbers $\rightarrow$ find its sum; and: If there is a column of numbers $\rightarrow$ find the largest. If this system were presented with a column of numbers, even without specific instruction it would report both the sum of the column and the largest number. To limit the system's actions to the relevant goal, we create a symbol, S, for "sum" and place it in short-term memory if the task is to add the column. We create a different symbol, L, for "largest" and place it in short-term memory if the task is to find the largest number in the column. We amend the first production by adding the presence of S in short-term memory as another condition for its execution: "If there is a column of numbers, and if S is in short-term memory $\rightarrow$ . . ." Similarly, we amend the second production by adding the presence of L in short-term memory as another condition for its execution. Now, giving the system the appropriate goal, by placing S or L in short-term memory, will cause it to perform the desired task.

Having introduced goals, we can also easily provide for subgoals. If we have a goal, G_1, as one of the conditions of a production, and if its achievement requires the achievement of subgoals G_2, G_3, and so on, then we simply include among the actions of G_1 the placing of G_2, G_3, and so on in short-term memory. This will arm productions, otherwise inactive, that are relevant for attaining these subgoals.

In this way, motivation to achieve goals is propagated through the cognitive system to direct attention to relevant information and actions. In simple situations, presence of a goal permits recognition of conditions that invoke, through one or more productions, an immediate response that achieves the goal. This kind of response, often called "intuitive," is common in familiar matters, whether they be everyday affairs or the routine matters that constitute so much of professional activity. Intuitive responses are acts of recognition that are conditioned by goals that bring them within the focus of attention.

When goals cannot be satisfied through immediate and unreflective recognition, then more elaborate problem-solving schemes come into play. These schemes make considerable use of means-ends analysis: that is to say, the initial goal defines a situation not yet attained, and differences between the goal situation and the present situation evoke actions that may reduce or remove the difference, creating a new situation closer to the goal. At each step in this recursive process, removal of the perceived difference constitutes a new goal to connect the action with the original motive and final goal.

The typical "rule-based" expert systems that seek to emulate professional performance are largely based on a combination of these two procedures: problem solution by recognition and by heuristic search through means-ends analysis. For example, a chess-playing program designed to emulate human chess play would have stored in memory a large number of patterns (perhaps 50,000) that commonly appear on chess boards during games and that signal important features of the positions in which they occur. Skill in chess requires the recognition of these patterns when they occur, which in turn gives access in memory to information about their significance and the actions they call for. Every serious chess player will recognize the feature called an "open file" when it appears on the board and will be reminded to consider placing a rook on that file.

Chess players can play reasonably well using only their recognition capabilities, based on the patterns stored in memory (e.g., in speed chess, in which the time for each move is limited to a few seconds). But in more deliberate play, they also look ahead to possible sequences of moves, their own and their opponents', using means-ends analysis to guide the search. In this way they become aware of future contingencies that recognition of static features of the present position may not reveal.

Goal symbols in short-term memory create contexts within which certain actions are relevant and others irrelevant. In the absence of a particular goal symbol, productions that include that symbol among their conditions will simply not execute. Thus, despite the infrequency of mention of motivation, information-processing models of cognition are thoroughly impregnated with goals. They have motives as well as reasons for what they do.

I do not want to imply that goal symbols and recognizable stored features solve all of the problems of attention control in cognition. I have described their use in some detail to give a concrete picture of how attention control mechanisms might actually operate to connect thinking with motivation.

ATTENTION CONTROL WITH SPREADING ACTIVATION

In Act* and connectionist systems, attention control, and hence the link with motivation, is handled somewhat differently, that is, with the help of spreading activation or some nearly equivalent mechanisms. (In some versions, Act*, which is actually a whole family of related systems, uses goal symbols as well as spreading activation, but I consider here only the latter.)

In any system composed of nodes connected by links (and this describes almost all symbolic architectures), it is possible to attach numbers that represent levels of activation to the nodes and numbers that represent the strengths of connections to the links between them. Suppose now that an increase in the activation of one node increases the activation of the other nodes to which it is connected by strong links—the strength of the effect depending on the strength of the link. (We may also postulate *negative*, inhibitory, links that transmit a *decrease* in activation of the destination node when the activation of the source node is increased.)

If we now postulate that only when activation is above some threshold level will a node be "noticeable," we again restrict the activity of the system to interaction among nodes that lie in this focus of attention. We can think of the set of nodes that are above the threshold as constituting the system's short-term memory and the conditions of productions as referring only to symbols in short-term memory. Arousal of a node is roughly equivalent to linking it with the current goal.

Without searching out the details, we can see that activation can play the same general role in controlling actions in node-link systems as goal symbols in systems that do not employ activation levels. In both cases, mechanisms link more or less general or specific motivation to particular tasks and thereby direct the system's attention to the performance of these tasks rather than others.

We can also see how activation can account for some of the phenomena revealed by the dichotic listening experiments. If attention to the message in one ear largely inhibits the activation of other information, then the latter information will remain unnoticed. However, if some of the information in the unattended ear also has an additional independent source of activation, it may pass through the filter and gain attention. Consider here two phenomena mentioned previously: switching from one ear to another to perserve continuity of meaning and noticing the mention of one's name in the unattended ear.

Attention to a particular semantic context, evoked by a continuous message dealing with that context, activates nodes in long-term memory that belong to that context. (If the text deals with "Italian operas," activation arises in those parts of memory relevant to Italian operas, operas, or even music and Italy.) When the continuity of the message is suddenly interrupted in one ear but the same context is taken up by the other ear, the activation of the message in the latter ear may now be higher than in the former, with a consequent switch in attention. The role of a synonym in the unattended ear in influencing the interpretation of a word in the attended ear may be explained in a similar way.

To explain attention to one's name, we make a new assumption and also refer for the first time to emotion, which we have neglected up to this point. We assume that emotion, in various degrees, is associated with some nodes in long-term memory. Emotion raises the activation level of these nodes, making it easier to carry them above threshold and to divert attention to them. We will return to the topic of emotion and its relation to attention after some further consideration of the nature of the contexts that influence responses to stimuli.

Contexts and Situated Action

The notion of context has been recently brought into prominence in the literature of cognition by those who argue that real-world actions are *situated* and can only be understood in relation to the context in which they are embedded. The premise that actions are situated is sometimes taken to imply that thinking is therefore not symbolic, or not planned, or not represented inside the brain— there are many flavors of situated action and no single accepted party line. But I will not take up these issues here, since Alonso Vera and I (Vera & Simon, 1993) discuss them at length elsewhere. Instead, I consider here how cognitive systems can deal, as they must, with the context of action.

The general shape of my answer should be clear from the previous discussion of goals and their relation to motives. The cognitive system stores extensive knowledge about the world in its long-term memory and can gain additional knowledge through its sensory and perceptual processes. The voluminous knowledge in long-term memory relates literally to everything under the sun, most of which is unlikely to be relevant at any given moment. Moreover, because of the limits on the system's ability to operate in parallel, it can only make use of a small amount of information during any short interval of operation.

The problem of context is therefore twofold: both to gain access to the information that is relevant in the current context and to shield off the vast body of potentially available information that is irrelevant. In the earlier discussion of attention as the mediator, I argued that it is the structure of the real world in relation to the needs of the organism that makes it possible to meet both of these requirements. Fortunately, internal drives and external situations calling for action do not all press on the organism simultaneously. Except for those drives that are physiologically "wired" for parallel action, goals can usually be dealt with one at a time, and only knowledge and information relevant to the current goal—a tiny part of the total—need be evoked in order to deal with it. When a pressing real-time need presents itself while the system is engaged in another task, the interrupt mechanisms mentioned previously bring about the required shift of goals.

The mechanisms relating to attention that are important for creating the context of thought and action do not, of course, operate perfectly. Frequently, we are distracted by irrelevancies. Even more frequently, we fail to retrieve or perceive information that would be useful in dealing with the current situation—the well-known problem of transfer of training (or rather, failure to transfer). Thus, contexts may be defined by the cognitive system too broadly, too narrowly, or simply incorrectly. We can well apply to this system Dr. Johnson's comment on the dancing dog: "The marvel is not that it dances well—it doesn't—but that it dances at all."

Emotions

Apart from one previous mention of them, I have left emotions to the end of my discussion. My postponement reflects my feeling that I and perhaps my fellow psychologists understand emotions less well than we understand motivations or attention. In many ways, emotion seems an even less homogeneous category than motive. Motives can be connected with the goals they evoke, but they may or may not involve strong emotions.

Person A is motivated to kill B (he has been offered $10,000 for the deed) but will do it in cold blood, that is, with little or no emotion. Subject C is motivated to kill D because C is enraged with him.

In the latter case, but not the former, motive and emotion go cheek by jowl; in fact, the emotion seems to be the source of motivation.

To simplify matters, let us focus on just four of the common emotions and/or motives: hunger, fear, hate, and pleasure. Hunger is not always classified as an emotion, but it can be associated with intense feelings, and since emotions are usually defined in terms of the feelings they evoke, it is hard to see what criterion would rule hunger out.

Fear may be evoked not only by external events (e.g., a sudden noise) but also by a verbal stimulus (e.g., the word "cancer"). It is usually accompanied by arousal of the autonomic nervous system, and this arousal is often explained in evolutionary terms as preparing the organism for a response (e.g., flight). Hunger is usually evoked by internal stimuli, but it may also be aroused by the sight of a favorite food. As we have seen, it tends to turn the attention of the organism to seeking food.

Hate, like fear, may be aroused by the appearance of hated objects, but it may also be evoked by verbal stimuli that have become associated with that emotion. Pleasure is similar to hate and fear but seems somehow more general and diffuse than they. In some philosophies, pleasure and pain are taken as the ultimate sources of the motivational chain, from which all goals or motives are derived. Pleasure sets the task of maintaining the emotional status quo; pain the task of terminating it. Fortunately, our investigation here does not require us to decide whether this view is correct or not.

What kind of mechanisms can we propose to account for such diverse emotions (to say nothing of all the others we are ignoring) and for their effects on behavior? Since the phenomena themselves appear to be rather complex, there is no reason to suppose that the mechanisms are simple or that they may not be somewhat hybrid in structure.

First, we observe that there does appear to be some connection between the emotions and attention. The negative emotions tend to direct our attention to activities that might terminate them; the positive emotions to activities that might cause them to persist. Second, we observe that emotions may be associated with topics already stored in memory, so that mention of the topic arouses the corresponding emotion.

These considerations suggest the following metaphor (which is already part of the folk culture). Memory is not a uniform, grey network; parts of it are "colored" in varying intensities. When attention is directed to such a colored region of memory, evoking that memory activates the corresponding color—that is, the corresponding emotion. The emotion, in turn, has attention-directing and attention-interrupting capabilities, thereby modifying the organism's current motivation and actions. In the words of Robert Abelson, cognition may be color or it may be hot.

This account leaves the boundary between motivation and emotion in a rather fuzzy state, but it does provide a fairly unified account, in terms of arousal mechanisms and the focus of attention, of the nature of emotions and their operation. Items in memory with which emotion is associated are, ceteris paribus, more easily aroused than other items and hence more capable of directing attention or causing interruption of attention. They operate much like motives but are associated with perhaps less specific goals than motives usually are.

Conclusion

My goal in this chapter has been to look once more at the linkage between cognition on the one hand and motivation and emotion on the other. Professional specialization in the discipline of psychology has assigned responsibility for these two subsystems to two different groups of psychologists. As a consequence, the vital connection between them has sometimes been neglected.

I have argued here that the connection between motives (or emotions) and thoughts is in fact both strong and explicable. People have both motives and reasons for what they do. The motives define their goals, and the reasons connect those goals with particular courses of action for realizing them. Thinking begins with goals and cannot move without them. Emotions, when aroused from memory, interrupt action and redirect it to alternative motives that have become more pressing than the current one.

The general theory that postulates attention as the principal link between cognition and motivation is not new. Among physiological psychologists it goes back at least to the recognition of the functions of the reticular layers of the brain. If there is anything new on the present scene it is to be found in the concrete proposals for symbol-processing mechanisms that can account for the linkage and the phenomena it produces.

I have tried to provide a rough sketch of the main mechanisms that have been proposed for regulating the focus of attention and thereby enabling mental activity to be organized, appropriately situated, and motivated. Among them are attention-interrupting mechanisms, goal symbols, spreading activation, recognition mechanisms, and processes to guide heuristic search.

1. Attention-directing mechanisms act explicitly to distract attention from its current focus and direct it to some urgent task. The new direction may be influenced from the sensory source of the interrupter or from the nature of the motives or other contexts that have been activated in long-term memory.

2. If certain sets of productions are capable of firing only when appropriate goals are in activated memory, then goal symbols, by their presence or absence, limit the range of topics to which attention can be directed.

3. Spreading activation, by defining at each moment which part of memory is activated, defines a context that can influence the control of attention and the interpretation of the things attended to.

4. Recognition mechanisms activate particular contexts in memory as a function of the stimuli that are recognized. Most often, recognition directs attention to contexts that are already active and hence is a mechanism for continuity of behavior. But attention may sometimes be directed to the unexpected instead of the expected, with resultant surprise and the redirection of attention.

We are close to the time, if it has not already arrived, when we can aspire to construct models that will encompass these linking mechanisms and thereby elucidate a wide range of phenomena regarding attention, the elusive boundary between the parallel and serial components of mental processing, and the role of motivation and emotion in regulating behavior. Unified theories will rapidly give up their exclusive (if only apparent) preoccupation with cognitive processes and embrace also these other crucial aspects of the whole person.

REFERENCES

Hayes, J. R., & Simon, H. A. (1974). Understanding written problem instructions. In Lee W. Gregg (Ed.), *Knowledge and cognition* (pp. 167–200). Potomac, MD: Erlbaum.

Hilgard, E. R., & Bowers, G. H. (1975). *Theories of learning* (4th ed.). Englewood Cliffs, NJ: Prentice Hall.

Newell, A. (1990). *Unified theories of cognition.* Cambridge, MA: Harvard University Press.

Shiffrin, R. M., & Schneider, W. (1977). Controlled and automatic human information processing: II. Perceptual learning, automatic attending, and a general theory. *Psychological Review, 84,* 127–190.

Simon, H. A. (1956). Rational choice and the structure of the environment. *Psychological Review, 63,* 129–138.

Simon, H. A. (1967). Motivational and emotional controls of cognition. *Psychological Review, 74,* 29–39.

Treisman, A. M. (1969). Strategies and models of selective attention. *Psychological Review, 76,* 282–299.

Vera, A. H., & Simon, H. A. (1993). *Cognitive Science, 17,* 7–48.

Domains of Behavior from a Neuropsychological Perspective: The Whole Story

Muriel D. Lezak
Oregon Health Sciences University

Before beginning to address my topic I would like to offer a caveat that applies to the chapters presented in this volume. We symposium participants—and other psychologists working in different fields of our discipline—often talk about the same aspect of behavior but use different terms. Our somewhat idiosyncratic vocabularies make sense within our subdisciplines but get in the way of effective intercommunication until we work out the mutuality in our various constructs. I haven't worked them all out. I will use the terminology that I have found meaningful as a neuropsychologist. I hope that, where terminological differences occur, each reader can make the leap from one vocabulary to another. As one example of different terms for similar concepts, *implementation intention*, as used by Bargh and Gollwitzer (in this volume) covers major aspects of what I call *planning*.

Further, the discussion of terminology reminds me that I need to explain my understanding of the *executive functions* (Lezak, 1982a). In general, the executive functions involve capacities that initiate, direct, guide, manage, and modulate intentional behavior. They get activities—whether mental or overt—going, refine them, carry them out under supervisory control, and bring them to a halt. In this schema, the cognitive functions have to do with the *what* of behavior: attention and perception, speech and constructional activities, memory and skills, all of these provide the cognitive contents of behavior. Perhaps the emotions deal with the *why* of behavior—our interpretations of the attractions or repulsions of what we do, of what stimulates us. The executive functions concern the *how* of undertaking and carrying out activities, whether cognitive or emotional: how a person goes about constructing a block design, selling shoes, planning a menu, recoiling with fright, crying, or laughing. *Whether* a person undertakes an activity at all is also an executive issue. The two other major domains of psychology—cognition and emotion— have common definitions shared by all psychologists and do not need defining here.

The foundation of my thinking about executive functions comes from my clinical experience. Four major categories of executive functions can be conceptualized as discrete and distinctive aspects of executive behavior. Each of these is fully dissociable, although many kinds of brain damage will compromise more than one kind of executive behavior. *Volition* is dependent both on the capacity for self-generated initiation of goal-directed behaviors and on awareness of one's self and surroundings. Nothing happens without the self-generating capacity; and without the associated awareness of self and surroundings, at least at an early stage in the emergence of an activity, the behavior cannot be meaningfully or usefully goal directed. *Planfulness* involves a number of capacities including directed attention, memory search, and recall; ability to conceptualize sequences and hierarchies; ability to think about nonpresent situations, events, and persons and to take different points of view; the capacity to grasp a number of elements at once and juggle them conceptually; the ability to discriminate relevant from irrelevant in specific situations that may differ only slightly from other situations but contain a different set of irrelevancies; and other capacities as well. *Carrying out activities* has to do with being able to convert mental intentions and plans into actions and thus, to be effective, requires capacities to start, regulate, modify, modulate, and stop actions. *Self-monitoring* includes ongoing evaluation of one's activity with appropriate self-correction, what some workers call "quality control."

Introduction

Western thought has partitioned behavioral phenomena into three discrete categories, at least since Plato's time. Our language reflects this conceptual division in its many words for feeling behavior, many others for cognitive activities, and still others for behaviors that play an executive role. These conceptual habits are ingrained in academic psychology as well, with its typical bifurcation into cognitive and clinical domains. Cognitive psychology and cognitive psychologists focus on the information processing components of behavior; the emotions come under the aegis of clinical psychology and associated programs such as medical or abnormal psychology. Only now is the cognitive camp becoming aware of the executive functions, while clinicians have tended to assimilate them without a clear appreciation of either their distinctiveness or their importance. Thus, we have come to study and to treat the different dimensions of behavioral phenomena as though they occurred in isolation.

Earlier neuropsychological analyses supported this view of the disparateness of the different components of behavior by associating specific neuroanatomic regions with each of them. Thus, within this theoretical framework, the cerebral cortex becomes the engine of cognition, emotions arise within the limbic system, and those theoretical systems that included one or more of the executive functions found them in prefrontal structures (Luria, 1973). It follows then that the traditional examination of cortical functions entails tests of perceptual competency, learned skills, and acquired knowledge. The limbic examination rests mainly on observations and questionnaires for studying emotions and personality. The examination of executive functions in most instances consists of tests of complex aspects of expressive behavior, such as imitating finger movements, generating a series of similar but differentiable responses, or shifting responses appropriately and rapidly (e.g., Christensen, 1979). Within this conceptual framework each behavioral dimension retains its specificity and uniqueness relative to the conceptually compartmentalized functions of the brain.

The growing sophistication of neurobehavioral examiners and the development of increasingly sensitive examination techniques have contributed to an understanding of brain-behavior relations that goes beyond these older, rather rigidly demarcated views of cerebral geography. However, the techniques and tests, in themselves, only refine familiar observations and make new ones possible—they do not direct the purview of the observer. For example, deficits in any one or several important functions can be elicited by Ruff's elaborations of the Figural Fluency technique (Ruff Figural Fluency Test [Regard et al., 1982; Ruff et al., 1987]). This test requires subjects to make as many different patterns as they can within 1 min by drawing lines connecting any two or more of a five-dot pattern repeated 40 times on a page. Five sets of five-dot patterns are given one after the other (see Fig. 1). In addition to measuring visuomotor response speed, this test brings out problems in self-monitoring when subjects repeat designs at a greater than normal rate. Impaired self-monitoring shows up in persons whose mental processing is slowed, making it difficult for them to do two things at once (e.g., on the Figural Fluency Test both speed and nonrepetition are required; persons whose mental processing is slowed may focus on one of the requirements but be unable to keep up with both). Self-monitoring is also deficient in those persons whose brain injuries compromise self-awareness or appreciation of social standards of behavior. This test also offers subjects the opportunity for developing a strategy to enhance response speed and avoid repetitions, which requires constant self-monitoring. Strategy comes naturally to most intact persons; its absence in someone who demonstrates good visuospatial abilities on such structured tasks as the Block Design test (Wechsler, 1981) suggests an impaired capacity for planning, one of the executive functions. Problems with motor control or impulsivity may also be elicited. However, if the examiner is interested only in visuomotor response speed on a complex task, then other, often clinically valuable information may be overlooked.

Only fully comprehensive use of both observations and tests in the examination of persons who have sustained damage in one or another part of the brain will show us how any instance of brain damage can affect all aspects of behavior. Ideally such a set of observations include those made during the formal examination, those obtained in more casual or at least less structured encounters with the patient, and reports from persons who observe the patient in a natural setting, such as caregivers or relatives.

When all aspects or dimensions of behavior are taken into account, it appears that the behavioral alterations occurring with a dis-

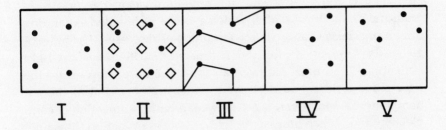

FIGURE 1. The dot patterns for each of the five trials of the Ruff Figural Fluency Test (Evans et al., 1985).

crete lesion or with damage within a single neuroanatomic system display a pattern that is both peculiar to that site or system and manifested in each dimension of behavior. The key word here is *pattern*, for the same kinds of distortions, disruptions, omissions, release phenomena, and compensatory responses will affect each major dimension of behavior to some degree. In illustrating this multifaceted nature of neurobehavioral aberrations I hope to show why awareness of it is so important for the behavioral scientist.

It is a truism to say that people only see what we look for or expect to find. Because of the discrete and delimiting nature of much neuropsychological research—both research inquiring into brain systems and subsystems and that teasing out specific, dissociable functions—many of neuropsychology's "facts" have their foundations in restricted or narrowly focused observations. As a result, neuropsychology's story may be only half told, with the most important—and often the most interesting—parts left out. Such circumscribed knowledge biases neuropsychological theory. Unfortunately, it also compromises the care of persons who have sustained brain damage since clinicians cannot help a patient with problems that they do not appreciate.

A striking example of how inappreciation of a behavioral deficit can affect a patient's care comes from a 1942 report by the pioneer Canadian neuropsychologist D. O. Hebb. Hebb contributed significantly to the development of both neuropsychological theory and examination techniques. However, in the late 1930s—when this examination took place—his focus was on cognitive functions or on, to use his term, "intelligence," and his tool was Terman and Merrill's 1936 edition of the Stanford-Binet scale. The patient was almost 16 yr old when tested after several neurosurgical cleansings of a right temporal brain abscess, after which a "huge right-sided expanding intracranial lesion" also required draining of abscesses. The radiologist and neurosurgeon together estimated that 40–50% of the right hemisphere had been removed and that pressure effects from the right-sided lesions had destroyed "at least 20 per cent of the left hemisphere." Moreover, the young man had become almost completely blind, which limited the scope of the examination. This fully oriented patient's performances on verbal skill and knowledge tasks and on digit span were *average* and better, although he failed several of the verbal reasoning tasks at age levels 10, 12, and 14. Hebb (1942) concluded that "the patient's psychological status appeared to be exceptionally good. . . . [I]n conversation he seemed normally alert and responsive and quite cooperative." However, being a keen observer, Hebb did note, almost as an aside, that "one defect, by informal observation was his inactivity, and apparent willingness to do nothing for rather long periods." Yet the latter observation of a significant lack of self-propelling behavior probably reveals more about what the future held for the patient than did the numbers obtained by testing, as we can expect that a person who is relatively bereft of the capacity for spontaneous and effective volitional behavior is probably doomed to a lifetime of social dependency. Moreover, without the patient's professional caregivers appreciating the nature or practical significance of this observation, we can conjecture that they were not able to help his parents understand their son's deficits or to plan realistically for a future dependent on the initiative-taking, planning, and organizing capacities of others.

Rather than trot out more reports of examinations in which one or another important aspect of behavior was overlooked or not appreciated, I will offer several examples of the multidimensional effects of brain damage. For this purpose I have chosen right hemisphere disease as it presents when a stroke damages the cerebral cortex and two conditions predominantly involving subcortical structures: Korsakoff's psychosis and Parkinson's disease. These three different brain conditions involve different etiologies, histories, and behavioral manifestations. By using as exemplar conditions several that differ from one another in many ways, I hope to show by implication that brain damage generally affects all three major categories of behavior to some extent and that to some degree, directly or indirectly, every functional brain system and subsystem plays into every aspect of awake behavior—and very likely sleep as well (Sergent, 1987). I also hope that this review may help to counteract the biased observation tendencies that have given neuropsychology its predominantly cognitive focus and thereby obscured both some of the most interesting behavioral phenomena and many of the socially relevant problems suffered by brain-damaged persons.

Right Hemisphere (Cortical) Stroke

The cognitive consequences of cortical damage are often striking, involving as they do such fundamental human abilities as verbal communication, computation, spatial orientation, and visual recognition. Stroke patients are desirable subjects for studies of cortical damage as the lesion is usually confined to one hemisphere, in which it typically follows a similar pattern for many patients (Anderson et al., 1990), and it can be relatively well visualized by recent generations of neuroimaging techniques (Damasio & Damasio, 1989). These studies have deepened our understanding of such phenomena as speech, reading, and other language behaviors; the dual nature of visual perception; the intricate and intimate relations between perception and memory; and the organization of the cortex— both in general and in its relation to subcortical structures and their interconnections. Moreover, the neuropsychological consequences of damage to the speech-dominant hemisphere—which in most instances is the left—differ greatly from the behavior distortions that arise from lesions in the right—or nonspeech-dominant—hemisphere (Corballis, 1983; Lezak, 1994). (Because the left hemisphere is dominant for speech in 95% or more of the population—among right-handers this percentage reaches 98–99% [Bryden, 1988; Corballis, 1983]—I refer to the speech-dominant hemisphere as the left and the nonspeech-dominant hemisphere as the right.) In addition, the neurobehavioral effects of cortical lesions differ according to their site relative to regions specialized for processing different kinds of information and organized along both longitudinal and lateral dimensions of the cerebral hemispheres (Goldberg, 1989, 1990; Luria, 1966; McCarthy & Warrington, 1990; McGlone & Young, 1986).

RIGHT HEMISPHERE STROKE AND COGNITION

Decades of study of these cortically lesioned patients have led to knowledge of the characteristic patterns of cognitive dysfunction for specific lesion sites. A review of the behavioral abnormalities associated with each cognitively differentiable site on the right side alone requires at least a book-length disquisition (see, e.g., Cutting, 1990; Joanette et al., 1990; Pimental & Kingsbury, 1989). Rather than devote this entire review to various aspects of cortical dysfunction and still only touch on a few of them, I will discuss just the behavioral alterations that occur with blockage to the territory fed by the right middle cerebral artery (MCA) (see Fig. 2).

The damage in this classic presentation of right hemisphere disease typically involves part of the posterior frontal lobe, including the section that subserves intentional control of the hand and arm, part of the auditory processing areas of the temporal lobe, and both somatosensory components and sites for processing and integrating complex sensory information located within the parietal lobe (Damasio & Damasio, 1989, pp. 34–35; Tranel, 1992). The limbs on the left side often sustain motor and sensory alterations, with the arm more affected than the leg, and weakened or paralyzed limbs the most obvious symptom. The most pronounced cognitive deficits are essentially perceptual in nature and include impaired visuospatial orientation that affects both constructional abilities and spatial knowledge. These deficits can show up in such bizarre behaviors as putting clothes on backwards or upside down, a condition called "dressing apraxia"; in impaired appreciation of one's deficits such that these patients may forget—or not realize from moment to moment—that they are paralyzed or have other neurobehavioral symptoms; in diminished awareness of stimuli occurring to the left of their midline; and in compromised ability to discriminate nonverbal sounds, including the tonal and rhythmic nuances of speech (Hier et al., 1983; Lezak, 1994; Pimental & Kingsbury, 1989).

RIGHT MCA STROKE AND EMOTION

Many of these patients also display characteristic emotional disturbances that appear acutely as blandness and indifference to their

Domains of Behavior from a Neuropsychological Perspective

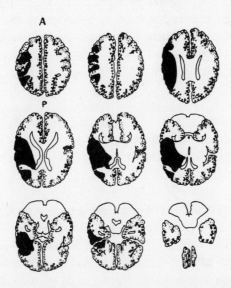

FIGURE 2. Templates of the computerized tomography (CT) scan of a 34-yr-old woman with left hemiplegia and severe left visuospatial inattention. She appeared unaware of her defects, denying left-sided paralysis. *A,* Anterior brain; *P,* Posterior brain. (Reprinted by courtesy of H. Damasio and A. R. Damasio and Oxford University Press. Copyright, 1989.)

plight—a not-unexpected reaction from persons who lack cognitive appreciation of their limb weaknesses or paralyses (Gainotti & Caltagirone, 1989; Starkstein & Robinson, 1992). However, the frequently seen bland indifference that may be coupled with unwarranted optimism contrasts eerily with serious physical disabilities that are so obvious to everyone else but these patients. In the long run, patients who are indifferent to their deficits in the immediate days and weeks after stroke onset will typically become depressed—often morbidly so—as they find themselves in situations of dependency, relative immobility, and loss of status without fully comprehending why (Finset, 1988; Ross & Rush, 1981). In addition, many of these patients become insensitive to affective expression in voice tone and gestures of others while losing their own capacity for appropriate nonverbal expression of emotion (Borod et al., 1986; Heilman et al., 1993; Joanette et al., 1990). These deficits can make persons with this characteristic pattern of depressed right hemisphere functioning difficult to live with. This is especially the case

INTEGRATIVE VIEWS OF MOTIVATION, COGNITION, AND EMOTION

for spouses, the natural primary caregivers of patients who no longer appear to care for them or seem interested in helping them with the enormous burdens of management and responsibility—and the emotional stress and isolation—that the patients' behavioral and physical alterations have placed on them.

HOW PROCESSING DIFFERENCES BETWEEN THE HEMISPHERES MAY ACCOUNT FOR BEHAVIORAL ANOMALIES ASSOCIATED WITH RIGHT MCA INFARCTS

When reviewed as a list of symptoms, except for the perceptual disorders, such behavioral distortions and incompetencies would seem to have little in common. However, knowledge of the processing characteristics of each hemisphere suggests one basis for comprehending these cognitive and emotional abnormalities (Bradshaw, 1989; Kinsbourne, 1978; Lezak, 1994). In brief, the left hemisphere appears to be organized to process detailed and time-bound—that is, linear—kinds of information best and is thus the hemisphere more profoundly involved with language and gestural acts that, whether in speech or in symbolic signs, require bit-by-bit processing. Configurational processing takes place in the right hemisphere and enables us to grasp a quantity of information at once, such as the instantaneous visual integration of the features in a face or landscape or auditory integration of chords in polyphonic music (see Table 1).

Processing differences between the hemispheres can account for many of the behavioral anomalies associated with right hemisphere disease. Strokes that affect the functioning of right-sided cortical areas involved in somatosensory, spatial, and auditory processing bring both losses and gains to the patient. On the one hand, the ability to process simultaneously all aspects of a complex stimulus is impaired, as is the ability to entertain mentally all aspects of a complex proposition or situation. On the other hand, reduced input from a damaged right hemisphere site may produce a release phenomenon giving relatively free rein to homologous areas in the left hemisphere that shows up in many patients as excess, often highly elaborated, verbiage that can be mistaken for cognitive competence (Lezak, 1982b; Moscovitch, 1979). The resulting effect, from the

Table 1

Hemisphere Processing Differences

	Left	*Right*
Type of processing	Linear: processes stimuli bit by bit	Configurational: grasps the whole stimulus complex
Processing feature	Time bound	Non-time bound; can be instantaneous
Stimuli processed best	Familiar material; details; speech; mathematical propositions; symbolic gestures	Novel situations; patterns; facial configurations; three-dimensional spatial relationships; tonal quality of voice and music

processing viewpoint, includes both a diminished ability to take in all of a situation or complex set of stimuli *plus* an exaggerated reliance on the piecemeal, bit-by-bit processing of the left hemisphere.

Spatial disorders. Thus, the appreciation and manipulation of spatial phenomena—which depend on the ability to grasp and integrate multifaceted stimuli—are compromised. These patients tend to become confused when attempting to copy designs with colored blocks (see Fig. 3), they may have difficulty in learning or recalling relationships between corridors and rooms in the hospital and even in homes in which they have lived a long time, and they may not be able to make heads or tails of a bathrobe or shirt.

Inattention. Moreover, clear awareness is often more or less restricted to left hemisphere activity as sensory stimuli coming from the left side of the body are muted or absent because of damage involving right hemisphere sensorimotor and perceptual processing centers (Bisiach, 1991). As information about the self and the surrounding environment is now processed primarily by the relatively more intact left hemisphere, that is, on a bit-by-bit, time-bound basis, and these processing limitations are further compounded by inability to assimilate many different stimuli simultaneously (Prather et al., 1992), it is not surprising that these patients' attention is better focused on or drawn by stimuli impinging on the intact side of the body such that left-sided stimuli—whether from within the

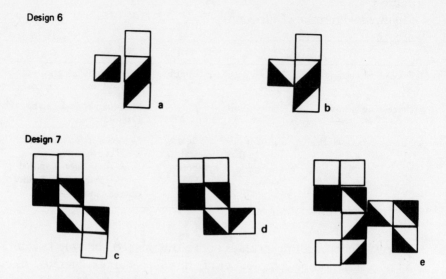

FIGURE 3. Copy sequences of a 2 × 2 (Design 6 a, b: chevron pattern) and 3 × 3 (Design 7: pinwheel pattern; solid black block is the pattern's center and was placed first) block pattern made by a 60-yr-old man with a right-sided stroke. Note visuospatial inattention exhibited in absence of lower left block in Design 6 and pile up of blocks to right of pattern's center in Design 7. (From Lezak, 1994.)

body or without—may not be integrated into awareness. Thus, many of these patients appear to have a weakened or even absent conscious awareness of the left side of their bodies or of what is happening in the space to their left (see Fig. 4). This restricted field of awareness is variously labeled left-sided neglect, inattention, or suppression and frequently accompanies strokes in the right MCA territory.

It has been hypothesized that the inattention phenomenon occurs more frequently with right than with left hemisphere damage because the right hemisphere has greater involvement in mediating arousal and attention (Heilman et al., 1993). The gestalt processing properties of the right hemisphere make it more sensitive to novelty and shifts in the attentional field and thus would also seem to contribute to the inattention phenomenon. However, hemispheric attentional preeminence alone is not sufficient to explain the discrete relations between the kinds of inattention displayed (visual, auditory, tactile, or some combination of these) and the associated

Domains of Behavior from a Neuropsychological Perspective

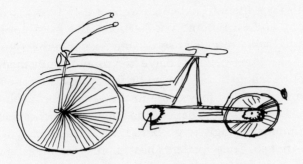

FIGURE 4. Bicycle drawn by 51-yr-old retired salesman with a right MCA stroke. Omissions on left of wheels, gear, and supporting rod are not simply due to carelessness as wheel and gear details faithfully document the amount of care taken by this man.

lesions situated at or near areas (or undercutting connections in the case of subcortical lesions) for primary processing of compromised sensory modalities. Nor can it account for the rarer phenomenon of right-sided inattention (Bisiach & Vallar, 1988) most commonly seen in the acute stages of left hemisphere stroke when right hemisphere function is reduced by virtue of metabolic and other brain responses to the damaging event.

Emotional alterations. The altered emotional behavior of these patients may also be understood in terms of their impaired capacity for configurational processing. First, it is important to note that, contrary to folklore holding that significant right cortical damage mutes emotionality, these patients can and do experience the full range of emotions. What they lack, however, is the ability to recognize the nonverbal emotional behavior of others: most of the emotional signals people send to one another—facial expressions, voice quality, posture—are nonverbal, and to decode these nonverbal stimuli requires the capacity for simultaneous processing of complex multi-dimensional stimuli. These patients not only have difficulty making sense of nonverbal signals, but they also do not appreciate that this ability has been compromised and that their social behavior and interactions are often inappropriate and maladaptive.

Further, their impaired capacity for configurational processing also curtails their ability to send meaningful nonverbal signals about their own emotional status. One may conjecture that their processing deficits keep them from being aware of their typically flat facial expressions and monotonic vocalizations and from appreciating that they no longer receive or send complex nonverbal signals. Unfortunately for these patients, naive friends and family members often feel hurt, rebuffed, or puzzled by the appearance of emotional indifference. They too may come to the same conclusion as have some clinicians, that these patients no longer experience normal human sentiments strongly (e.g., Borod, 1992; Heilman et al., 1985). But this is not so. These patients best express their feelings by verbalizing them and best understand others' verbalized feelings. Since most of us rely heavily on the nonverbal components of social communication, these patients become social outsiders and may be social outcasts within their families or living situations.

RIGHT MCA STROKE AND EXECUTIVE FUNCTIONS

Right hemisphere disease due to stroke in the MCA territory tends to affect executive functions radically, particularly those involving judgment and planning capacities. (The defective judgment associated with right hemisphere stroke contrasts sharply with the pattern of behavioral impairments when the damage is in a similar position on the opposite side of the brain, for these latter patients, although more or less severely compromised in their abilities for verbal communication and thinking, will most usually retain their capacity for practical judgment.) Except when overtaken by depression, otherwise-healthy patients with predominantly right-sided cortical damage typically retain their volitional capacity, as evidenced by their normal initiative-taking and goal-directed motivation. As many of these patients retain—and even seem to improve on—their verbal adeptness and many display excellent memories for verbalizable events, often reporting them in excruciatingly fine and circumstantial detail, on superficial examination they give the impression of being mentally intact. Their elaborate verbiage can serve as a smoke screen, making them look bright and obscuring their planning and judgmental deficits from naive observers. At home, their demands and actions bewilder their families, leaving spouses and children conflicted about how to deal with their now often glib, not infrequently willful patient. While these patients may sound knowledgeable and even competent, their requests and conclusions—about their physical capacities, work potential, financial capabilities, and so on—can range from silly to outrageous to dangerous.

Commonly occurring examples of these patients' poor judgment are insistence on driving despite diminished awareness of the left side of space (left visuospatial inattention); determination to handle the bills and keep budget records when spatial defects interfere with the ability to add, subtract, and carry numbers correctly; and poor cooperation in physical therapy for weakened or paralyzed limbs, since they are sure that the problem will go away soon, or when they get home, or when the pain stops (I have heard these explanations and more for noncompliance in physical therapy). Poor appreciation of their deficits contributes obviously to many of these judgmental problems. Faulty planning shows up repeatedly. One patient demands to return to his third-story walk-up apartment despite a massive left-sided paralysis that confines him to a wheelchair. Another spends all of his pension money riding around in taxis the first week of the month, leaving nothing for the rent that is due at the month's end. A retired police officer with a long-standing left hemiplegia secondary to right-sided MCA stroke talks about renewing his driver's license while recovering from a serious suicide attempt and asks to return to his wife's home on the Oregon coast so she can drive him daily to a rehabilitation program on Puget Sound, some 150 mi away. These may seem to be glaring examples, but they are typical of the defective planning problems of stroke patients.

These blaming and judgment defects make sense when viewed as the product of the fragmented—that is, piecemeal, time-bound, "sausage string"—thinking that gives us our wondrous speaking, reading, and writing skills but that is particularly unsuited to conceptually encompassing a host of disparate details all at once (see, e.g., Fig. 5). Thus, patients with right hemisphere damage have difficulty with integrating simultaneously awarenesses of the presence *or absence* of somatosensory and visual stimuli with stored experiential data and the immediate situation in all of its social and physical complexities; yet without this kind of simultaneous integration of all relevant facets of a situation in which they are personally involved, they are unable to develop reasonable judgments or make appropriate social adaptations. Inability to work out the relations among all

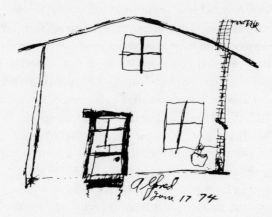

FIGURE 5. This 54-yr-old college graduate began his drawing at the lower left corner, proceeded to the roof line, and then drew the chimney and the "brick" wall on the right, stating, as he drew it, that the house needed a fireplace, which he added complete with hook, cooking pot, and fire. He then completed the ground line and added the door and windows. As he composed this house in a strictly linear manner, he never appreciated that his drawing included both inside and outside house structures.

these elements hinders their efforts to develop an effective scheme for action, regardless of how highly motivated or verbally clever they might still be. These problems frequently do not come to clinicians' attention, since the familiar social structures and routinized activities of hospitals, rehabilitation units, and doctors' offices provide little opportunity for bad judgment and disordered or unrealistic planning to become apparent (Lezak, 1982a). Their problems have thus remained a secret from many clinicians who see these patients only in the acute stages, and then only in structured settings, and from family members who cannot understand why living with the patient has become so difficult.

Knowing the cognitive, emotional, and executive limitations that right hemisphere disease can impose on its victims, how subtle its effects can be, particularly when sensory or motor disturbances are not apparent, and the patients' lack of appreciation of these limitations, I have often thought about the role right hemisphere disease may have played in world affairs. I cannot help but wonder, for example, whether our world might have been a better place but for the mild right-sided stroke suffered by Menachem Begin soon after taking over the highest office in Israel—or whether there would not have been an Irangate but for Central Intelligence Agency chief William Casey's right-sided brain tumor.

The Korsakoff Syndrome

A quite different example is provided by the prominent memory deficits of Korsakoff patients in whom both new learning and efficient retrieval of previously stored information appear to be severely compromised (Butters, 1985; Talland, 1965; Victor et al., 1971). The Korsakoff syndrome, or Korsakoff's psychosis as it has also been called, usually occurs in persons with a long history of very heavy alcohol intake (Kapur, 1988; Lishman, 1987; Reuler et al., 1985). It typically appears in its florid and easily diagnosed state following a very heavy and protracted bout of drinking during which the patient has eaten little if anything, thus sustaining a relatively prolonged condition of severe thiamine deficiency. On autopsy the critical lesions show up in limbic system structures, particularly in the thalamus and other lower forebrain (diencephalic) nuclei with known involvement in memory processing and retrieval (Butters & Stuss, 1989: Jernigan et al., 1991; Lhermitte & Signoret, 1976; Salmon & Butters, 1987) (see Fig. 6).

Many medical textbooks have described this condition as a memory disorder, with no recognition of its multidimensional character (e.g., Franklin & Frances, 1992; Lishman, 1987). Yet it is not the memory disorder alone that makes most Korsakoff patients fully dependent, nor is impaired memory the only striking behavioral anomaly in this disease. A comprehensive examination of these patients quickly shows that all aspects of their behavior are compromised by a profoundly impaired capacity for generating and sustaining volitional behavior. This impairment affects their every act—or, rather, produces a pattern of relative inactivity punctuated by the short-lived appearance of stimulated behavior. Almost complete absence of self-propelling motivation leaves them totally dependent and socially isolated.

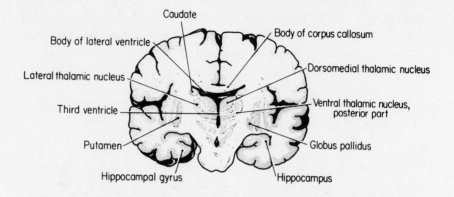

FIGURE 6. Coronal section through the human brain. The dorsomedial nucleus of the thalamus and the mammilary bodies are the diencephalic structures typically implicated in the Korsakoff syndrome (Butters & Stuss, 1989). (Reprinted by courtesy of N. Butters.)

COGNITIVE FUNCTIONS IN THE KORSAKOFF SYNDROME

At first blush the classic textbook descriptions of the Korsakoff syndrome as a memory disorder appear to be validated, as these patients seem to have lost their ability to learn new facts or retain memory of ongoing experiences, while preserving habits, skills, and previously stored information that enable them to perform at near-normal levels on many mental abilities tests, such as the Wechsler Intelligence Scales. However, by substituting various kinds of recognition and other arousal techniques for the usual tests of new learning that require recall of the target material, a careful examiner can demonstrate that these patients have learned at least some of the material they cannot recall spontaneously (Butters, 1985; Mayes, 1988; Parkin, 1982). Sophisticated testing of these patients thus suggests that passivity and inability to sustain a memory search may contribute as much or more to the retrieval problem as loss of old memories and inability to acquire new ones (see Talland, 1965). Some investigators suggest that defective encoding accounts for the Korsakoff retrieval problem (Butters, 1985; Ryan & Butters, 1986; Salmon & Butters, 1987), but much old information known to have been properly encoded is subject to the same kind of haphazard and grossly insufficient retrieval processes (Butters & Cermak, 1986; Lezak et al., 1983). Moreover, as in learning studies, a recognition format facilitates remembering information acquired prior to onset of the Korsakoff condition, again demonstrating that retrieval is a significant part of the Korsakoff memory problem (Kopelman, 1989).

EMOTION IN THE KORSAKOFF SYNDROME

Passivity, or greatly diminished self-generation of activity, character-izes each of the other major behavior dimensions (Butters, 1984; Butters & Stuss, 1989; Lezak, 1994). That these patients retain a capacity for emotion becomes evident when they are emotionally stimulated. Thus it is possible to elicit anger, anxiety, delight, and so forth by ap-plying the appropriate stimulation. The patient who is frustrated or crossed will become angry, maybe even hotly so; a tender-hearted man reminded of his mother may burst into tears or express re-morse; a patient offered something pleasant will react with plea-sure—*while the arousing stimulus is present and for a few minutes thereaf-ter*. Unless the stimulus is sustained, the emotion will dissipate rather quickly—just as the awareness of new information disap-pears from available recall in a matter of minutes.

EXECUTIVE FUNCTIONS IN THE KORSAKOFF SYNDROME

Executive functions, of course, are gravely compromised. This ren-ders these patients socially dependent. Among their executive defi-cits are diminished abilities to profit from mistakes, to recognize and use cues (Oscar-Berman, 1984), and to solve problems that require hypothesis generation and testing (Butters, 1985; Laine & Butters, 1982). If only long-term memory were affected and patients appreci-ated their problem and could generate the idea of making plans or keeping notes, they could still use their intact short-term memory to keep a record of relevant events and make notes about their goals and plans; they could then conduct themselves with relatively greater self-sufficiency. However, this same passivity, or loss of ca-pacity for generating behavior—whether ideas or actions—makes volitional behavior virtually nonexistent except as it appears reactively or reflexively.

For example, when one enters a Korsakoff patient's room, the patient may be seated, doing nothing, but will immediately become responsive and often even quite lively when addressed and for as long as a conversation or activities are stimulated by the examiner. However, as soon as the examiner leaves, the seated patient becomes quiescent again, remaining so until restimulated either externally or by internal sensations. The same holds for the restless Korsakoff patient who will pace without direction until stopped and stimulated, only resuming the habitual and directionless pacing when external stimulation ceases. Most Korsakoff patients that I have examined in a hospital setting when aroused will express a strong—sometimes quite passionate—desire to leave, to return home, or to get a lawyer to get them out. I have shown them where the exit is or pointed out the telephone booth, inviting them to do what they have said they wanted to do. None carried out their determination, since the generation of all aspects of behavior dissipated—including their desire—before they could get around to doing what they desired. These observations demonstrate that the Korsakoff syndrome is not simply a memory disorder but a condition in which the characteristic dysfunctions affect each of the major domains of behavior.

Parkinson's Disease

The usual studies of disorders involving the brain have focused on the most prominent, bizarre, or apparently incapacitating symptoms, giving neuropsychology its strong cognitive bias and a sensory-motor bias to the study of neuropathological phenomena. Thus, in the case of Parkinson's disease, typical textbook descriptions dwell on motor or sensory symptoms with little or no recognition of the importance—much less the presence—of neuropsychological dysfunction. Yet neuropsychological impairments can be among the most handicapping consequences of Parkinson's disease. As part of the disease pattern these impairments are probably always present, although they can be quite subtle.

The growing awareness of the neuropsychological alterations characteristic of Parkinson's disease has earned it a place among the relatively new category of central nervous system diseases affecting cognition, the *subcortical dementias* (Albert, 1978; Cummings, 1986, 1990). Although some cortical involvement may occur in Parkinson's disease, particularly in later stages, the universally implicated lesion site is the *substantia nigra,* a small, normally darkish-appearing body located high in the brain stem that synthesizes the neurotransmitter dopamine (see Fig. 7). Symptoms of parkinsonism appear when dopamine levels drop below 30% of normal (Koller et al., 1991; Wooten, 1990).

The motor symptoms of this disease have been known and well-described since the early 19th century (Stacy & Jankovic, 1992; Wooten, 1990). They include the "resting tremor," a rhythmic shaking that can affect the limbs, jaw, and tongue, which diminishes or disappears with voluntary movement; muscular rigidity; and difficulties initiating movement and motor slowing, resulting in an expressionless, unblinking gaze, dysarthric speech, and loss of grace, agility, and fine motor coordination. Walking, although difficult to start, may proceed with little steps in a slow, shuffling gait that becomes difficult to stop. By and large two subgroups of these patients have been identified: those whose outstanding symptom is tremor and those who are motorically slowed with the concomitant problems of starting, stopping, agility, speech, and expression. Only recently, however, has much attention been paid to behavioral alterations, and then it has most often focused on the cognitive or emotional problems occurring with this disease (e.g., Freedman, 1990; Huber & Cummings, 1992) while executive disorders have been mainly overlooked.

Many Parkinson patients also display behavioral alterations characteristic of Alzheimer's disease, a dementing process that primarily involves the cerebral cortex (Boller et al., 1980; Mortimer, 1988; Rajput, 1992). Obviously, this greatly complicates the symptom picture. For clarity, this discussion will focus on the majority of Parkinson patients who have only Parkinson's disease.

COGNITIVE DYSFUNCTION IN PARKINSON'S DISEASE

Patients disabled by motor slowing and muscular rigidity are those most likely to display the cognitive defects that are now recognized

INTEGRATIVE VIEWS OF MOTIVATION, COGNITION, AND EMOTION

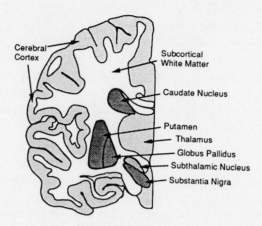

FIGURE 7. Diagram of the principle structures of the basal ganglia. The substantia nigra is the critical lesion site for Parkinson's disease. (From Shepherd, 1990. Reprinted by courtesy of Oxford University Press.)

as characteristic of Parkinson's disease. Most aspects of cognition can be affected (Brown & Marsden, 1988; Huber & Cummings, 1992; Mortimer et al., 1985; Passafiume et al., 1986).

Attention and memory. Problems tend to show up on complex tasks requiring shifting or sustained attention, such as mental calculations. Free recall, whether of visual or verbal material, recent or remote memory, tends to be impaired (Beatty, 1992; Taylor et al., 1986; Weingartner et al., 1984). However, except in dementing patients, learning itself is essentially unaffected as demonstrated in intact orientation and normal recall when patients are given such memory aids as cues or a recognition format (Beatty, 1992; Flowers et al., 1984; Harrington et al., 1990). Learning takes place more slowly than normal, since impaired recall in the short term may be enhanced with delay (Corkin et al., 1989). Moreover, sequencing and ordering requirements make learning much more difficult (Vriezen & Moscovitch, 1990; Weingartner et al., 1984).

Verbal functions. While vocabulary, grammar, and syntax remain essentially intact (Bayles, 1988; Brown & Marsden, 1988; Sullivan et al., 1989), word finding and retrieval problems are common and, as may be expected, Parkinson patients do poorly on fluency tasks that require both easy verbal retrieval and quick response (Gurd & Ward, 1989; Lees & Smith, 1983). Speech output is reduced (Bayles et al., 1985; Cummings & Benson, 1990), and its quality is impaired because of articulatory defects and impaired control over melodic intonation, volume, and speed of delivery (Bayles, 1988; Freedman, 1990). Alterations in writing parallel changes in speech production, as it becomes cramped, jerky, and may be greatly reduced in size (Hart & Semple, 1990; Tetrud, 1991).

Visuoperception and construction. What seem to be disordered spatial perceptions and judgments consistently show up in poor performances on tests of visuoperceptual functions including spatial orientation (Brown & Marsden, 1988; Cummings, 1986; Mortimer et al., 1985; Passafiume et al., 1986). Deficits on all kinds of construction tasks are frequently documented (Hovestadt et al., 1987; Pirozzolo et al., 1982; Riklan et al., 1962).

Reasoning and concept formation. Parkinson patients are typically realistic about their condition and situation (Brown et al., 1989; Flowers & Robertson, 1985; McGlynn & Kaszniak, 1991). They perform normally on well-structured abstraction items and on reasoning questions involving familiar issues (Loranger et al., 1972; Portin & Rinne, 1980) but tend to do poorly on more open-ended conceptual tasks involving problem solving, judgment, and concept formation (Bowen, 1976; Huber et al., 1986; Matthews & Haaland, 1979; Pillon et al., 1989).

EXECUTIVE FUNCTION DISORDERS IN PARKINSONISM

Patients' defective performances on tests of cognitive functions—whether they be verbal or visuospatial, involve attention or memory, or require reasoning and concept formation—may usually be understood as the products of disordered executive functions. The nature of the cognitive deficits in Parkinson's disease has probably been best demonstrated for visuospatial functions. When carefully analyzed, impaired performances on tasks with a significant visuospatial component can be accounted for by reduced mental flexibility that shows up as difficulty in *shifting* attention or set (Bowen, 1976; Ogden et al., 1990), in *monitoring* ongoing movements or performing two motor tasks simultaneously (Girotti et al., 1988) and in dealing with *novel or unfamiliar material* (Loranger et al., 1972). *Planful organization* of percepts is also affected by this disease (Mortimer, 1988; Ogden et al., 1990; Sullivan et al., 1989), and, of course, *response slowing* occurs due to slowing of both mental processing (Agid et al., 1987; Haaland & Harrington, 1990; Mahurin & Pirozzolo, 1985) and motor activity. Thus, except for patients with predominantly left-sided motor symptoms that implicate a lateralized disease process, visuospatial functions are not likely to be significantly impaired in Parkinson's disease despite poor performances on many visuospatial tests.

These problems of self-regulation—including starting and stopping as well as shifting, of planfulness, and of slowing in all aspects of behavior—affect other cognitive activities in similar ways. For example, these patients tend to fail tests of conceptual abilities that also involve mental shifting and/or maintaining a set (Cronin-Golomb, 1990; Huber et al., 1986; Pillon et al., 1989; Taylor et al., 1986a). However, as noted above, Parkinson patients perform normally on straightforward tests of verbal abstractions. Deficiencies in verbal retrieval and verbal fluency follow naturally from both slowed mental processing—including slowed memory scanning (Wilson et al., 1980) and mental inflexibility, which precludes appropriately responsive shifts in sets and contents (Flowers & Robertson, 1985). In fact, all of their cognitive deficits may be comprehended as effects of a central programming impairment that results in defective behavioral regulation (Brown & Marsden, 1988; Haaland & Harrington, 1990; Stern et al., 1984).

Depression in Parkinson's disease. Reports of the incidence of depression in Parkinson's disease range from 20 to 90% (Cummings, 1986; Kaszniak et al., 1985), with most estimates suggesting that depression troubles about half of all Parkinson patients (Lohr & Wisniewski, 1987; Sano et al., 1989; Santamaria & Tolosa, 1992). The nature of depression in Parkinson's disease remains somewhat of a mystery. Given the crippling effects of this disease with its bitter social and economic consequences, depression would seem to be a not-unexpected reaction and therefore essentially psychogenic. Yet while it tends to be associated with the severity of cognitive impairments, depression appears to be unrelated to the degree to which the disease is physically handicapping. Further complicating this question is the appearance of depression in patients with reduced levels of motor activity, facial impassivity, and general slowing, and the unreliability of self-reports by cognitively impaired patients.

However, a possible clue to the likelihood of organic contributions to depression in Parkinson patients shows up in descriptions of prodromal personality characteristics that include emotional and moral rigidity, introversion, seriousness, and restricted affective expression (Koller et al., 1991; Lohr & Wisniewski, 1987). Personality differences reflecting these prodromal characteristics have even been reported in twin pairs discordant for Parkinson's disease (Duvoisin et al., 1981). It is reasonable to conjecture that these personality characteristics may be among the earliest pathological effects of a disease process evolving for years and perhaps decades before the classical motor symptoms appear.

Further, the pattern of cognitive/executive function impairment is similar to that which accompanies depression of psychiatric proportions (Weingartner et al., 1984). This suggests that perhaps the mental slowing, mental rigidity, and diminished capacity for mental anticipation that show up in the cognitive impairments of Parkinson's disease are experienced subjectively as mental sluggishness and stickiness, experiences akin to those of depressed persons. Having many of the mental symptoms of depression may well become the experiential equivalent to feeling depressed—much as many persons recovering from a debilitating illness feel depressed until their normal energy level and mental alertness return.

Perhaps the descriptions of this condition as a motor system disease are not too far-fetched, since the same pattern of pathological alterations of movement appears to affect each of the major domains of behavior. The motor dysfunction of parkinsonism is characterized by sluggishness, rigidity, and a breakdown in the organization of complex movements. The cognitive dysfunctions most commonly associated with Parkinson's disease result from mental sluggishness, diminished mental flexibility, and poor planning—all reflecting deterioration in the capacity for appropriate responsiveness. The emotional and attitudinal rigidity and affective sluggishness manifested in their prodromal personality and certainly contributing to the high incidence of depression in parkinsonism—if not actually constituting its experiential base—are also symptoms of reduced responsiveness. And appropriate responsiveness is a central component of executive functioning. The overriding impairment in Parkinson's disease may be conceptualized as a reduced capacity for responsiveness, whether to stimuli from without or motivations from within, and it involves all aspects of behavior, including motor activity.

Conclusion

The salient proposition that has informed this review is that the great domains of behavior—cognition, emotionality, and executive functions—share the same brain substrate and reflect its functional status in similar ways. This proposition has been tested and supported by examining the effects of brain damage on three neuropsychological symptom complexes that differ in their etiology, site of damage, and neurobehavioral consequences, but it is no more verifiable in the general case than that which holds that all ravens are black—an exception could always be lurking just around the corner. However, knowing that the proposition of the multidimensional character of brain function is possibly valid—and my experiences have led me to believe that it probably is—should encourage scientists and practitioners alike to look at all dimensions of behavior whether they are examining a neuropsychologically impaired person, designing a neuropsychological research program, or constructing a theory of human behavior.

REFERENCES

Agid, Y., Ruberg, M., Dubois, B., & Pillon, B. (1987). Anatomoclinical and biochemical concepts of subcortical dementia. In S. M. Stahl, S. D. Iversen, & E. C. Goodman (Eds.), *Cognitive neurochemistry* (pp. 248–271). Oxford: Oxford University Press.
Albert, M. L. (1978). Subcortical dementia. In R. Katzman, R. D. Terry, & K. L. Bick (Eds.), *Alzheimer's disease: senile dementia and related disorders* (pp. 173–180). New York: Raven.

Anderson, S. W., Damasio, H., & Tranel, D. (1990). Neuropsychological impairments associated with lesions caused by tumor or stroke. *Archives of Neurology, 47,* 398–405.

Bayles, K. A. (1988). Dementia: the clinical perspective. *Seminars in Speech and Language, 9,* 149–165.

Bayles, K. A., Tomoeda, C. K., Kaszniak, A. W., Stern, L. Z., & Eagans, K. K. (1985). Verbal perseveration of dementia patients. *Brain and Language, 25,* 102–116.

Beatty, W. W. (1992). Memory disturbances in Parkinson's disease. In S. J. Huber & J. L. Cummings (Eds.), *Parkinson's disease. Neurobehavioral aspects* (pp. 49–58). New York: Oxford University Press.

Bisiach, E. (1991). Extinction or neglect: Same or different? In J. Paillard (Ed.), *Brain and space.* New York: Oxford University Press.

Bisiach, E., & Vallar, G. (1988). Hemineglect in humans. In F. Boller & J. Grafman (Eds.), *Handbook of neuropsychology* (Vol. 1, pp. 105–222). Amsterdam: Elsevier.

Boller, F., Mizutani, T., Roessmann, U., & Gambetti, P. (1980). Parkinson disease, dementia, and Alzheimer disease: Clinicopathological correlations. *Annals of Neurology, 7,* 329–335.

Borod, J. C. (1992). Interhemispheric and intrahemispheric control of emotion: A focus on unilateral brain damage. *Journal of Consulting and Clinical Psychology, 60,* 339–348.

Borod, J. C., Koff, E., Lorch, M. P., & Nicholas, M. (1986). The expression and perception of facial emotion in brain-damaged patients. *Neuropsychologia, 24,* 169–180.

Bowen, F. P. (1976). Behavior alterations in patients with basal ganglia lesions. In M. D. Yahr (Ed.), *The basal ganglia* (pp. 169–177). New York: Raven.

Bradshaw, J. L. (1989). *Hemispheric specialization and psychological function.* Chichester: Wiley.

Brown, R. G., & Marsden, C. D. (1988). "Subcortical dementia": The neuropsychological evidence. *Neuroscience, 25,* 363–387.

Brown, R. G., MacCarthy, B., Jahanshahi, M., & Marsden, C. D. (1989). Accuracy of self-reported disability in patients with Parkinsonism. *Archives of Neurology, 46,* 955–959.

Bryden, M. P. (1988). Cerebral specialization: clinical and experimental assessment. In F. Boller & J. Grafman (Eds.), *Handbook of neuropsychology* (Vol. 1, pp. 143–159). Amsterdam: Elsevier.

Butters, N. (1985). Alcoholic Korsakoff's syndrome: some unresolved issues concerning etiology, neuropathology, and cognitive deficits. *Journal of Clinical and Experimental Neuropsychology, 7,* 181–210.

Butters, N., & Cermak, L. S. (1986). A case study of the forgetting of autobiographical knowledge: implications for the study of retrograde amnesia. In D. Rubin (Ed.), *Autobiographical memory* (pp. 253–272). New York: Cambridge University Press.

Butters, N., & Stuss, D. T. (1989). Diencephalic amnesia. In F. Boller & J. Grafman (Eds.), *Handbook of neuropsychology* (Vol. 3, pp.107–148). Amsterdam: Elsevier.

Christensen, A.-L. (1979). *Luria's neuropsychological investigation. Text* (2nd ed.). Copenhagen: Munksgaard.

Corballis, M. C. (1983). *Human laterality*. New York: Academic Press.

Corkin, S., Growdon, J. H., Desclos, G., & Rosen, T. J. (1989). Parkinson's disease and Alzheimer's disease: differences revealed by neuropsychologic testing. In T. L. Munsat (Ed.), *Quantification of neurologic deficit* (pp. 311–325). Stoneham, MA: Butterworth.

Cronin-Golomb, A. (1990). Abstract thought in aging and age-related neurological disease. In R. D. Nebes & S. Corkin (Eds.), *Handbook of neuropsychology* (Vol. 4, pp. 279–304). Amsterdam: Elsevier.

Cummings, J. L. (1986). Subcortical dementia: neuropsychology, neuropsychiatry, and pathophysiology. *British Journal of Psychiatry, 149*, 682–697.

Cummings, J. L. (1990). Introduction. In J. L. Cummings (Ed.), *Subcortical dementia* (pp. 3–16). New York: Oxford University Press.

Cummings, J. L., & Benson, D. F. (1990). Subcortical mechanisms and human thought. In J. L. Cummings (Ed.), *Subcortical dementia* (pp. 251–259). New York: Oxford University Press.

Cutting, J. (1990). *The right cerebral hemisphere and psychiatric disorders*. Oxford: Oxford University Press.

Damasio, H., & Damasio, A. R. (1989). *Lesion analysis in neuropsychology*. New York: Oxford University Press.

Duvoisin, R. C., Elderidge, R., Williams, A., Nutt, J. & Colne, D. (1981). Twin study of Parkinson disease. *Neurology, 31*, 77–80.

Evans, R., Ruff, R., & Gualtieri, C. T. (1985). Verbal and figural fluency in bright children. *Perceptual and Motor Skills, 61*, 699–709.

Finset, A. (1988). Depressed mood and reduced emotionality after right hemisphere brain damage. In M. Kinsbourne (Ed.), *Cerebral hemisphere functions in depression* (pp. 51–64). Washington, D. C.: American Psychiatric Press.

Flowers, K. A., Pearce, I., & Pearce, J. M. S. (1984). Recognition memory in Parkinson's disease. *Journal of Neurology, Neurosurgery, and Psychiatry, 47*, 1174–1181.

Flowers, K. A., & Robertson, C. (1985). The effect of Parkinson's disease on the ability to maintain a mental set. *Journal of Neurology, Neurosurgery, and Psychiatry, 48*, 517–529.

Franklin, J. E., Jr., & Frances, R. J. (1992). Alcohol-induced organic mental disorders. In S. C. Yudofsky & R. E. Hales (Eds.), *Textbook of neuropsychiatry* (2nd ed., pp. 563–583). Washington, D. C.: American Psychiatric Press.

Freedman, M. (1990). Parkinson's disease. In J. L. Cummings (Ed.), *Subcortical dementia* (pp. 108–122). New York: Oxford University Press.

Gainotti, G., & Caltagirone, C. (Eds.). (1989). *Emotions and the dual brain*. Berlin: Springer.

Girotti, F., Soliveri, P., Carella, F., Geminiani, G., Aiello, G., & Caraceni, T. (1988). Role of motor performance in cognitive processes of parkinsonian patients. *Neurology, 38*, 537–540.

Goldberg, E. (1989). Gradient approach to neocortical functional organization. *Journal of Clinical and Experimental Neuropsychology, 11*, 489–517.

Goldberg, E. (1990). Higher cortical functions in humans: the gradiental approach. In Goldberg (Ed.), *Contemporary neuropsychology and the legacy of Luria.* Hillsdale, N.J.: Laurence Erlbaum Associates, pp. 229–276.

Gurd, J. M., & Ward, C. D. (1989). Retrieval from semantic and letter-initial categories in patients with Parkinson's disease. *Neuropsychologia, 27*, 743–746.

Haaland, K. Y., & Harrington, D. L. (1990). Complex movement behavior: toward understanding cortical and subcortical interactions in regulating control processes. In G. R. Hammond (Ed.), *Advances in psychology: Cerebral control of speech and limb movements* (pp. 169–200). Amsterdam: Elsevier North Holland.

Harrington, D. L., Haaland, K. Y., Yeo, R. A., & Marder, E. (1990). Procedural memory in Parkinson's disease: impaired motor but not visuoperceptual learning. *Journal of Clinical and Experimental Neuropsychology, 12*, 323–339.

Hart, S., & Semple, J. M. (1990). *Neuropsychology and the dementias.* London: Taylor and Francis.

Hebb, D. O. (1942). The effect of early and late brain injury upon test scores, and the nature of normal adult intelligence. *Proceedings of the American Philosophical Society, 85*, 275–292.

Heilman, K. M., Bowers, D., & Valenstein, E. (1993). Emotional disorders associated with neurological diseases. In K. M. Heilman & E. Valenstein (Eds.), *Clinical neuropsychology* (3rd ed.) (pp. 461–498). New York: Oxford University Press.

Hier, D. B., Mondlock, J., & Caplan, L. R. (1983). Behavioral abnormalities after right hemisphere stroke. *Neurology, 33*, 337–344.

Hovestadt, A., de Jong, G. J., & Meerwaldt, J. D. (1987). Spatial disorientation as an early symptom of Parkinson's disease. *Neurology, 37*, 485–487.

Huber, S. J., & Cummings, J. L. (Eds.). (1992). *Parkinson's disease. Neurobehavioral aspects.* New York: Oxford University Press.

Huber, S. J., Shuttleworth, E. C., Paulson, G. W., Bellchambers, M. J. G., & Clapp, L. E. (1986). Cortical vs. subcortical dementia. *Archives of Neurology, 43*, 392–394.

Jernigan, T. L., Schafer, K., Butters, N., & Cermak, L. S. (1991). Magnetic resonance imaging of alcoholic Korsakoff patients. *Neuropsychopharmacology, 4*, 175–186.

Joanette, Y., Goulet, P., & Hannequin, D. (1990). *Right hemisphere and verbal communication.* New York: Springer.

Kapur, N. (1988). *Memory disorders in clinical practice.* London: Butterworth.

Kaszniak, A. W., Sadeh, M., & Stern, L. Z. (1985). Differentiating depression from organic brain syndromes in older age. In G. M. Chaisson-Stewart (Ed.), *Depression in the elderly: an interdisciplinary approach* (pp. 107–160). New York: Wiley.

Kinsbourne, M. (Ed.). (1978). *Asymmetrical function of the brain.* Cambridge: Cambridge University Press.

Koller, W. C., Langston, J. W., Hubble, J. P., Irwin, I., et al. (1991). Does a long preclinical period occur in Parkinson's disease? *Neurology, 41* (Suppl. 2), 8–13.

Kopelman, M. D. (1989). Remote and autobiographical memory, temporal cortex memory and frontal atrophy in Korsakoff and Alzheimer patients. *Neuropsychologia, 27,* 437–460.

Laine, M., & Butters, N. (1982). A preliminary study of the problem-solving strategies of detoxified long-term alcoholics. *Drug and Alcohol Dependence, 10,* 235–242.

Lees, A. J., & Smith, E. (1983). Cognitive deficits in the early stages of Parkinson's disease. *Brain, 106,* 257–270.

Lezak, M. D. (1982a). The problem of assessing executive functions. *International Journal of Psychology, 17,* 281–297.

Lezak, M. D. (1982b). Specialization and integration of the cerebral hemispheres. In *The brain: Recent research and its implications* (pp.79–102). Eugene: University of Oregon College of Education.

Lezak, M. D. (1994). *Neuropsychological assessment* (3rd ed.). New York: Oxford University Press.

Lezak, M. D., Howieson, D. B., & McGavin, J. (1983). *Temporal sequencing of remote events task with Korsakoff patients.* Paper presented at the 11th annual meeting of the International Neuropsychological Society, Mexico City.

Lhermitte, F., & Signoret, J.-L. (1976). The amnesic syndrome and the hippocampal-mammillary system. In M. R. Rosenzweig & E. L. Bennett (Eds.), *Neural mechanisms of learning and memory* (pp. 49–54). Cambridge, MA: MIT Press.

Lishman, W. A. (1987). *Organic psychiatry* (2nd ed.). Oxford: Blackwell Scientific.

Lohr, J. B., & Wisniewski, A. A. (1987). *Movement disorders.* New York: Guilford.

Loranger, A. W., Goodell, H., McDowell, F. H., Lee, J. E., & Sweet, R. D. (1972). Intellectual impairment in Parkinson's syndrome. *Brain, 95,* 405–412.

Luria, A. R. (1966). *Higher cortical functions in man.* New York: Basic.

Luria, A. R. (1973). *The working brain* (B. Haigh, Trans.). New York: Basic.

Mahurin, R. K., & Pirozzolo, F. J. (1986). Chronometric analysis: clinical applications in aging and dementia. *Developmental Neuropsychology, 2,* 345–362.

Matthews, C. G., & Haaland, K. Y. (1979). The effect of symptom duration on cognitive and motor performance in parkinsonism. *Neurology, 29,* 951–956.

Mayes, A. R. (1988). *Human organic memory disorders.* New York: Cambridge University Press.

McCarthy, R. A., & Warrington, E. K. (1990). *Cognitive neuropsychology: A clinical introduction*. San Diego: Academic Press.

McGlone, J., & Young, B. (1986). Cerebral localization. In A. B. Baker (Ed.), *Clinical neurology* (chap. 8, pp. 1–74). Philadelphia: Harper & Row.

McGlynn, S. M., & Kaszniak, A. W. (1991). Unawareness of deficits in dementia and schizophrenia. In G. P. Prigatano & D. L. Schachter (Eds.), *Awareness of deficit after brain injury: Clinical and theoretical issues* (pp. 84–110). New York: Oxford University Press.

Mortimer, J. A. (1988). The dementia of Parkinson's disease. *Clinics in Geriatric Medicine, 4*, 785–797.

Mortimer, J. A., Christensen, K. J., & Webster, D. D. (1985). Parkinsonian dementia. In P. J. Vinken, G. W. Bruyn, & H. L. Klawans (Eds.), *Handbook of clinical neurology: Vol. 2. [46] Neurobehavioral disorders* (pp. 371–384). Amsterdam: Elsevier.

Moscovitch, M. (1979). Information processing and the cerebral hemispheres. In M. S. Gazzaniga (Ed.), *Handbook of behavioral neurobiology: Vol. 2. Neuropsychology*. New York: Plenum.

Ogden, J. A., Growdon, J. H., & Corkin, S. (1990). Deficits on visuospatial tests involving forward planning in high-functioning Parkinsonians. *Neuropsychiatry, Neuropsychology, and Behavioral Neurology, 3*, 125–139.

Oscar-Berman, M. (1984). Comparative neuropsychology and alcoholic Korsakoff disease. In L. R. Squire & N. Butters (Eds.), *Neuropsychology of memory* (pp. 194–202). New York: Guilford Press.

Parkin, A. J. (1982). Residual learning capability in organic amnesia. *Corex, 18*, 417–440.

Passafiume, D., Boller, F., & Keefe, N. C. (1986). Neuropsychological impairment in patients with Parkinson's disease. In I. Grant & K. M. Adams (Eds.), *Neuropsychological assessment of neuropsychiatric disorders* (pp. 374–383). New York: Oxford University Press.

Pillon, B., Dubois, B., Cusimano, G., Bonnet, A.-M., Lhermitte, F., & Agid, Y. (1989). Does cognitive impairment in Parkinson's disease result from non-dopaminergic lesions? *Journal of Neurology, 52*, 201–206.

Pimental, P. A., & Kingsbury, N. A. (1989). *Neuropsychological aspects of right brain injury*. Austin, TX: Pro-ed.

Pirozzolo, F. J., Hansch, E. C., Mortimer, J. A., Webster, D. D., & Kuskowski, M. A. (1982). Dementia in Parkinson disease: A neuropsychological analysis. *Brain and Cognition, 1*, 71–83.

Portin, R., & Rinne, U. K. (1980). Neuropsychological responses of Parkinsonian patients to long-term levodopa treatment. In U. K. Rinne, M. Klinger, & G. Stamm (Eds.), *Parkinson's disease: Current progress, problems and management* (pp. 271–304). Amsterdam: Elsevier North Holland.

Prather, P., Jarmulowicz, L., Brownell, H., & Gardner, H. (1992). Selective attention and the right hemisphere: A failure in integration, not detection. *Journal of Clinical and Experimental Neuropsychology, 14*, 35 (abstract).

Rajput, A. H. (1992). Prevalence of dementia in Parkinson's disease. In S. J. Huber & J. L. Cummings (Eds.), *Parkinson's disease. Neurobehavioral aspects* (pp. 119–131). New York: Oxford University Press.

Regard, M., Strauss, E., & Knapp, P. (1982). Children's production on verbal and non-verbal fluency tasks. *Perceptual and Motor Skills, 55,* 839–844.

Reuler, J. B., Girard, D. E., & Cooney, T. G. (1985). Wernicke's encephalopathy. *The New England Journal of Medicine, 312,* 1035–1039.

Riklan, M., Zahn, T. P., & Diller, L. (1962). Human figure drawings before and after chemosurgery of the basal ganglia in Parkinsonism. *Journal of Nervous and Mental Disease, 135,* 500–506.

Ross, E. D., & Rush, A. J. (1981). Diagnosis and neuroanatomical correlates of depression in brain-damaged patients. *Archives of General Psychiatry, 38,* 1344–1354.

Ruff, R. M., Light, R. H., & Evans, R. W. (1987). The Ruff Figural Fluency Test: a normative study with adults. *Developmental Neuropsychology, 3,* 37–52.

Ryan, C., & Butters, N. (1986). Neuropsychology of alcoholism. In D. Wedding, A. M. Horton, & J. S. Webster (Eds.), *The neuropsychology handbook,* pp. 376–409. New York: Springer.

Salmon, D. P., & Butters, N. (1987). The etiology and neuropathology of alcoholic Korsakoff's syndrome: Some evidence for the role of the basal forebrain. In M. Galanter (Ed.), *Recent developments in alcoholisms* (Vol. 5, pp. 27–58). New York: Plenum.

Sano, M., Stern, Y., Williams, J., Coté, L., Rosenstein, R., & Mayeux, R. (1989). Coexisting dementia and depression in Parkinson's disease. *Archives of Neurology, 46,* 1284–1286.

Santamaria, J., & Tolosa, E. (1992). Clinical subtypes of Parkinson's disease and depression. In S. J. Huber & J. L. Cummings (Eds.), *Parkinson's disease. Neurobehavioral aspects* (pp. 217–228). New York: Oxford University Press.

Sergent, J. (1987). A new look at the human split brain. *Brain, 110,* 1375–1392.

Shepherd, G. M. (Ed.). (1990). *The synaptic organization of the brain* (3rd. ed.). New York: Oxford University Press.

Stacy, M., & Jankovic, J. (1992). Clinical and neurobiological aspects of Parkinson's disease. In S. J. Huber & J. L. Cummings (Eds.), *Parkinson's disease. Neurobehavioral aspects* (pp. 10–31). New York: Oxford University Press.

Starkstein, S. E., & Robinson, R. G. (1992). Neuropsychiatric aspects of cerebral vascular disorders. In S. C. Yudofsky & R. E. Hales (Eds.), *Textbook of neuropsychiatry* (2nd ed., pp. 449–472). Washington, DC: American Psychiatric Press.

Stern, Y., Mayeux, R., & Rosen, J. (1984). Contribution of perceptual motor dysfunction to construction and tracing disturbances in Parkinson's disease. *Journal of Neurology, Neurosurgery, and Psychiatry, 47,* 983–989.

Sullivan, E. V., Sagar, H. J., Gabrieli, J. D. E., Corkin, S., & Growdon, J. H. (1989). Different cognitive profiles on standard behavioral tests in Parkinson's disease and Alzheimer's disease. *Journal of Clinical and Experimental Neuropsychology, 11,* 799–820.

Talland, G. A. (1965). *Deranged memory.* New York: Academic Press.

Taylor, A. E., Saint-Cyr, J. A., & Lang, A. E. (1986). Frontal lobe dysfunction in Parkinson's disease. *Brain, 109*, 845–883.

Tetrud, J. W. (1991). Preclinical Parkinson's disease: Detection of motor and nonmotor manifestations. *Neurology, 41* (Suppl. 2), 69–72.

Tranel, D. (1992). Functional neuroanatomy: Neuropsychological correlates of cortical and subcortical damage. In S. C. Yudofsky & R. E. Hales (Eds.), *Textbook of neuropsychiatry* (2nd ed., pp. 57–88). Washington, DC: American Psychiatric Press.

Victor, M., Adams, R. D., & Collins, G. H. (1971). *The Wernicke-Korsakoff syndrome*. Philadelphia: Davis.

Vriezen, E. R., & Moscovitch, M. (1990). Memory for temporal order and conditional associative-learning in patients with Parkinson's disease. *Journal of Clinical and Experimental Neuropsychology, 12*, 24 (abstract).

Wechsler, D. (1981). *WAIS-R manual*. San Antonio, TX: Psychological Corp.

Weingartner, H., Burns, S., Diebel, R., & LeWitt, P. A. (1984). Cognitive impairments in Parkinson's disease: Distinguishing between effort-demanding and automatic cognitive processes. *Psychiatry Research, 11*, 223–235.

Wilson, R. S., Kaszniak, A. W., Klawans, H. L., Jr., & Garron, D. C. (1980). High speed memory scanning in Parkinsonism. *Cortex, 16*, 67–72.

Wooten, G. F. (1990). Parkinsonism. In A. L. Pearlman & R. C. Collins (Eds.), *Neurobiology of disease* (pp. 454–468). New York: Oxford University Press.

The Stories of the Right Hemisphere

Howard Gardner

*Harvard Graduate School of
Education and Boston University
School of Medicine*

As a student in developmental psychology with a special interest in artistic development, my scholarly life changed decisively about a quarter century ago. Steeped in the writings of Piaget, while almost totally ignorant of work on the brain, I happened to meet the eminent neurologist Norman Geschwind, then at the height of his creative powers. Approaching artistry from a determinedly cognitive perspective, I had been pondering the ways in which artistic activities may be organized in the fluent practitioner. I had become frustrated, however, in my efforts to unravel the complex skills of the artist. Professional artists are so fluent that their skills prove difficult to dissect: consider a cello performance by Pablo Casals or the brushstrokes of Pablo Picasso at his easel. Matters were not helped by the fact that many artists do not like to be observed at all—and certainly not by philistine fledgling psychologists in search of research findings and publications.

Geschwind convinced me, and my colleagues at Harvard Project Zero, that there existed a world that cried out for investigation.

The research in this article was supported by grants from the National Institute of Neurological Diseases, Communication Disorders, and Stroke (11408, 06209), the Veterans Administration, and Harvard Project Zero. I thank Hiram Brownell for his comments on an earlier draft.

That world, which he did so much to elucidate, was the world of the brain-damaged patient—the once-"normal" individual who had the misfortune of suffering damage to his or her brain and who now exhibited an unexpected profile of severe intellectual deficits and islands of preserved competence. Not only were the cases described by Geschwind fascinating in themselves (in a way that we have come to associate with the writings of Oliver Sacks [e.g., 1990]), but they also held promise of illuminating the nature of artistry. Geschwind (1974) described instances of famous artists—like the French composer Maurice Ravel and the French painter André Derain— whose work had been altered as a consequence of injury to the brain. In broader terms, he held forth the hope that, just as studies of aphasia have helped to explain normal language, sustained study of such brain-injured musicians and painters could help to reveal the nature of artistic capacities.

It took me only a few weeks to decide that I wanted to undertake postdoctoral study in the area of neuropsychology under the tutelage of Geschwind and his colleagues Harold Goodglass, Edith Kaplan, and Frank Benson at the Boston Veterans Administration (VA) Medical Center. When I first arrived at the VA, it appeared as though my wildest phantasies would be realized. The first patient I saw at grand rounds was described as a singer, the second as a painter. Alas, these patients did not live up to their advance billing: the singer had sung only in his high school chorus, while the painter had restricted his talents to houses and commercial buildings.

While my immediate research questions seemed unlikely to be answered, I found myself increasingly intrigued by the phenomena of the neuropsychological ward. Before long, I was writing standard psychological papers on aphasia, alexia, agnosia, and other clinical conditions. Interesting cases occasionally came to my attention, but the supply of artists who made their way to the wards of the Boston VA was meager indeed.

After a while, however, I realized that I could nonetheless continue my research interest in the arts. Instead of investigating the decomposition of highly complex skills in expert artists, I could look at the kinds of artistic and arts-related abilities possessed by ordinary individuals at this hospital—in this case, in the middle 1970s, nearly all of them male veterans of World War II. In working with this population I could see how these skills and abilities were or were not affected by various kinds of brain injury, especially strokes. And thus, over the years, I probed the capacities of brain-injured patients to draw, to sing, to tell stories, and to carry out other kinds of art-related activities.

As one who worked at an aphasia research center, most of my studies dealt in some way with language and language disturbances. In such studies, it was common to employ a brain-damaged control group. Since most aphasics have sustained damage to the left hemisphere of the brain, my research typically used as a control group individuals who had sustained damage to comparable areas in the right hemisphere. And indeed, when it came to tasks like syntactic processing, detecting word meaning, reading, writing, and naming, right-hemisphere damaged (RHD) patients responded much more like normal individuals than like individuals who had sustained pathology in the left hemisphere of the brain.

However, this was not always the case. My associates and I began to notice that sometimes the RHD patients behaved in ways that were quite anomalous. For instance, in a study of sensitivity to jokes and cartoons, RHD patients exhibited rank orderings of understanding and of appreciation that differed more from those of normal controls than did the performances of left-hemisphere-injured (LHD) patients (Gardner et al., 1975). In a study of sensitivity to word connotation, RHD patients resisted participating in the experimental paradigm and, when they did, proved far better at matching words to their denotations than to connotations; LHD patients exhibited no such dissociations (Gardner & Denes, 1977). And in a study of story production, the RHD patients not only had difficulty in following the fate of specific characters but also often seemed to miss the point of the story (Gardner et al., 1983; Wapner et al. 1981).

To my knowledge these difficulties exhibited by RHD patients had not been much discussed in the experimental literature. The right hemisphere was known to be important in spatial processing and, possibly, in emotional processing, but its linguistic capacities and deficits were just beginning to be noticed. However, as is not infrequently the case, the clinicians had been there before. Geschwind (1976) had noted the proclivities of such patients to confabulation, their circumlocutoriness, and their emotional inappropriateness. Another neurologist, Edwin Weinstein (Weinstein & Kahn, 1955), had detected irregularities in the humor of such patients as well as a strong attraction to inappropriate metaphoric expressions. It was re-assuring to know that, even if my findings had not been much antic-ipated in the pages of the experimental journals, they were by no means at odds with what sensitive clinical observers had noted pre-viously.

At about the time that I was beginning to think that the behavior of the RHD patient might be bizarre in the linguistic or emotional realm, a well-publicized political event reinforced my speculations. Supreme Court Justice William O. Douglas suffered a right hemi-sphere stroke on New Year's Eve in 1974 (Gardner, 1982, chap. 29; Woodward & Armstrong, 1979). As is often the case in such matters, the press and the Court spokes-person tended to downplay the se-verity of the stroke. Yet, as I read the reports from Douglas's physi-cians and observed him occasionally on television news programs, I found his conformity to the emerging "RHD patient profile" to be quite telling.

Douglas could speak well enough but a good bit of what he said did not make much sense. It seemed on target for a while but then veered away. He sought to make light of his own injury even as he failed to appreciate the underlying intent of questions that were posed to him. Later, it turned out that Douglas caused enormous difficulty for his "brethren" on the Court. Not only did he fail to real-ize his own deficits and instead insist that he was fit to serve, but his understanding of new legal cases and his ability to draw appro-priately on his years of experience were clearly impaired. To valida-tion from the clinical laboratory I could now add fresh evidence from the daily news.

When encountering a new phenomenon, one is tempted to de-termine its limits. Thus, in the following years, my colleagues and I probed and documented a whole ensemble of difficulties exhibited by RHD patients in language and language-related tasks (for re-views, see Gardner et al., 1983; Kaplan & Gardner, 1989; Molloy et al; 1990; Weylman et al., 1988). In addition to the problems with conno-tation and humor noted above, RHD patients turn out to have diffi-culty appreciating figurative language—metaphors as well as sar-castic and ironic statements—comprehending indirect speech acts (e.g., requests made by implication), organizing sentences into a co-herent paragraph, drawing inferences rather than responding to di-rect assertion from one sentence to another, monitoring and correcting deviant conversations, and understanding several other spheres as well. For a while it looked as though RHD patients had difficulty with almost any aspect of language beyond simple denotative reference at the sentence level. Moreover, my colleagues and I documented a special complex of problems with stories. Once a story went beyond a familiar, canonical member of the genre, RHD patients proved unable to handle these texts. They could not reproduce coherent texts on their own, and when given a text written by someone else, they exhibited special problems with determining reference, coping with surprise, and discerning underlying morals.

Curious about whether these difficulties pertained to all kinds of stories, my colleagues and I sought to examine narratives that contained specific kinds of content. These studies revealed that, if the content could be expressed entirely in words and there was no apparent need to construct some kind of visual model of the action, patients could handle the texts reasonably well. Once a story seemed to require some kind of visual imaging, however, RHD patients were not successful. We also found that, if emotional content could be captured in words alone, patients would understand a scene that was discussed, but if patients had to infer the emotions or impute them to characters on the basis of situational or personality traits, then they were often at a loss to make sense of the story. Finally, they experienced great difficulty with stories that did not confirm to already-mastered genres, such as a script or joke format. If a story contained unfamiliar materials, subjects would either treat them as familiar or ignore them altogether (Ostrove et al., 1990, in press; Rehak et al., 1992; Roman et al., 1987).

When a set of problems obtains across a range of tasks, it is both easy and difficult to ferret out underlying causes: easy in the sense that general accounts can apply to many disparate symptoms and difficult in that one is hard-pressed to isolate the particular factor at work and to eliminate rival accounts. In the scientific literature as well as the popular press, there have been attempts to characterize the right hemisphere in the most general way—for example, as the gestalt hemisphere, the creative hemisphere, the intuitive hemisphere, and the artistic hemisphere. Each of these characterizations can be applied to some instances, but none suffices to describe the linguistic difficulties exhibited by patients with any degree of specification. Other efforts to characterize the province of the right hemisphere with respect to specific kinds of contents have described it as spatial, as musical, and as concerned with emotional content. From my point of view, these latter characterizations represent a productive development. From an evolutionary point of view I find it dubious that a hemisphere of the brain might be exclusively concerned with intuition or analysis, with wholes or with parts, with art or with science. Indeed, depending on the particular content, one hemisphere might be quite capable of analysis of, say, linguistic syntax but incapable of analyzing musical syntax or pictorial organization. It is for this reason that I favor a division of labor between the hemispheres that takes into account the *contents* of the materials that are being engaged (Gardner, 1983).

Yet even here a simple analysis in terms of content alone does not suffice. If one considers the left hemisphere to be the language hemisphere, then how can one account for the various linguistic capacities that are impaired in patients with intact left hemispheres? If one considers the right hemisphere to be concerned with spatial matters, then why is it that left hemisphere damage also impairs certain spatial operations? Moreover, when individuals are asked about spatial information in linguistic terms, how are they able to handle such questions adequately? By the same token, while it is clear that the right hemisphere has various emotional analyses as its province, it is not accurate to deem them as exclusive to the right hemisphere. Indeed, just as RHD patients tend to interpret matters in too positive or Pollyannaish a light, LHD patients tend similarly to interpret matters in too negative a light (Gainotti, 1972). Moreover, as in the case of spatial matters, RHD patients can often answer questions about emotional issues as long as the emotional issues have been lexicalized. Thus, for example, when asked how a target individual would feel in a certain situation, RHD patients often give an answer that is logically defensible, although, owing to the particulars of the case, it is likely that the target individual in question would have had a different emotional reaction to the situation.

If, then, neither a general process like analysis nor a specific content like space or emotion adequately qualifies the problem faced by RHD patients, can we go beyond an ad hoc characterization and offer an explanation that accounts for the range of difficulties exhibited on linguistic and language-like tasks? In my view, it is probably unrealistic to expect that any single characterization, no matter how broad or sharply delineated, could be completely adequate. Ockham's razor does not always cut as finely as one would wish. Yet our understanding is likely to advance, in Popperian fashion, if we can offer a characterization that is original and that seems on the face of it to account for much of the accumulated data.

With this caveat, I propose that, in the processing of language, the right hemisphere plays a specific role: that of monitoring the message at the level of emotional continuity and discontinuity. That is, it is the province of the right hemisphere to encode linguistic messages not in terms of the semantic content but rather in terms of the emotional weight attached to actions, to descriptions, and to the relations among them.

Let me provide some background to this claim. When an individual processes any kind of extended discourse, such as a story, a joke, a vignette, and so on, the individual must be able to follow syntax, phonology, and literal word meaning. All such monitoring is handled comfortably by the left, or linguistic, hemisphere. Moreover, to be able to follow the discourse, the individual must be able to appreciate the genre in which it is encoded: a short story, a shaggy dog joke, a legal deposition, and so forth.

Contrary to what one might have supposed, RHD patients seem capable of appreciating instances of a genre, such as a script (Roman et al., 1987). Moreover, they can both create and appreciate canonical instances of that genre. Thus, to the extent that an extended passage of prose follows the usual script, such patients are able to perform quite normally. In this context, it is worth noting that Justice Douglas, while unable to render judgments about new cases, was able to characterize old cases with considerable acuity, going well beyond strictly memorized utterances.

Where, then, does the RHD patient exhibit deficits? I contend that, under normal situations, individuals shadow discourse in parallel in two distinct ways: in terms of overt content (in which the left hemisphere performs a serviceable job on its own) and in terms of the conformities to and deviations from normal expectations within the genre. When there is a deviation of some sort from expected content or ordering, the right hemisphere registers this discrepancy as an emotional jag or anomaly—with accompanying surprise, laughter, or grimace of disappointment. In works of art, such deviations can be quite complex, as an ensemble of emotions comes to accompany a particular character, scene, or tableau and changes in accord with the fate of that element. A work of art may harbor its own emotional landscape, with a characteristic anatomy and physiology.

What happens to the individual who—wholly or in part—loses the ability to shadow discourse at this emotional level? To begin with, the individual may note a deviation from expectation but not know what to make of it. In the absence of an appropriate interpretation or categorization, it is difficult to store the bit of information, and the individual instead reports something as being anomalous or, more likely, reverts to the canonical version, the only one that he or she can still deal with. The more severe the impairment, the less likely that the deviation will be detected and registered, let alone processed appropriately. Such appropriate encoding, storage, and processing seems to require intact emotional monitoring.

How can this characterization account for the data on the comprehension of discourse? As noted, we find in our studies that RHD patients are able to process and remember script and scriptlike entities. When it comes to jokes or stories with a surprise ending, they are able to appreciate that something is noncanonical, and yet, when asked to reconstruct a stimulus item or continue it in some way, such patients are unable to do so. When dealing with conversation, they are unable to appreciate the reasons someone might have violated a canon of discourse (Grice, 1975), and thus they end up acquiescing to any kind of conversational move. By the same token, when attempting to understand indirect discourse, the individual does not appreciate the reasons underlying certain requests or statements and again falls back on the most canonical explanation (Rehak et al., 1992; Weylman et al., 1989).

One may ask how this pattern of behavior relates to patients' own linguistic production. This is a difficult question. Right-hemisphere-damaged patients usually speak in a comprehensible way, yet they also tend to go off on tangents, to be inappropriately jocular, and to embrace metaphors that may be inappropriate or even nonsensical. I believe that this strange manner of speaking may be related to the putative difficulty I have hypothesized. It seems to me that RHD patients, in a manner reminiscent of schizophrenic speakers, are susceptible to intoxication by the associations between one phrase or word and another. If they are consciously aware of them, normal speakers censor such associations because they know that others will find them bizarre. Bereft of an emotional shadower, lacking an emotional gyroscope to keep them on course, RHD patients are unable to appreciate the effects of a deviation and so they continue speaking blithely in a linguistically fluent manner.

When it comes to pathology, it is often useful to see whether a reported condition can be related to one's own phenomenal experience. Let me illustrate the role that the right hemisphere apparently plays for me in contexts such as these. Not infrequently, and more so the older one gets, one begins a book or attends a movie without knowing that this particular instance of the genre has already been encountered. Sometimes, of course, one recognizes the work of art, and the contents of the work emerge intact. At other times, however, the work exudes a certain familiarity and one struggles to figure out whether it has in fact been encountered previously. In such instances, I find that emotional encoding is often more reliable than semantic coding. That is, I recognize and can anticipate the mood of the piece, including wide shifts in tone, well before I know exactly which characters will appear and what will happen to them. This experience seems to model the role of the right hemisphere—the supplying of a kind of emotional glue that helps to confer coherence on unfamiliar narrative discourses. Or, as Nelson Goodman (1976) has put it, the emotions are functioning cognitively.

One may wonder whether this account conforms in particulars to children's linguistic development. It has been well documented that, in early childhood, youngsters develop powerful scripts about familiar events in the world (Nelson, 1986). Every normal 3- or 4-yr-old in our society can describe the highlights of a familiar birthday party, a meal at a restaurant, or an outing to the grocery store. These scripts become well consolidated; new stories or jokes are defined in reference to, or as deviating from, these well-entrenched scripts. Such scripts have a characteristic feeling tone or set of feeling tones. Once established, they exert a powerful hold over children's minds, and in early life, children tend to assimilate new and irregular instances to their canonical accounts (Gardner, 1991).

With time, however, the scripts become sufficiently consolidated so that a youngster can appreciate deviations from them. At first, a sheer deviation will be noticed and considered humorous or frightening, depending on its type and degree of deviation. Soon enough, youngsters become able to register the kinds of deviation

from chronic scripts and to hold onto these deviations with some fi-
delity (Mandler & Johnson, 1977; Stein, 1978). I maintain that they
are able to do so because of this dual coding, in which changing
emotional tone is a distinct and important feature of narratives, requiring separate encoding, storage, and reproduction. The ability to
monitor the emotional landscape seems to remain, and perhaps to
deepen, throughout life, except, as argued above, when the capacity for emotional shadowing becomes compromised, perhaps as a
consequence of damage to the brain.

While the domain of linguistic regularity, deviation, and anomaly is usually deemed the special province of the arts, I submit that
this territory of emotional nuance actually pervades much of our existence. Political candidates, for example, compete with one another
to convey stories that are convincing to the electorate. Usually they
simply manipulate classical scripts, hoping to convince the electorate that their script is the most faithful to beliefs and wishes that are
already widely held. However, the more adventurous leader is able
to boost the stock of stories or scripts that have not been appreciated
for some time and bring them to the fore; such, I believe, were the
accomplishments of such disparate leaders as Margaret Thatcher
and Franklin Roosevelt. Unless listeners can detect and draw proper
inferences from these deviations, they will either be missed entirely
or misinterpreted.

Such forces are even at work in the sciences. Those who attempt
to explain human or natural phenomena begin with the accounts
that are already prevalent in the literature and toy with them in various ways. Thus, in this very presentation, I began with a capsule
story of my own professional development—one not familiar to the
reader but presumably not too discrepant from other researchers'
accounts. I then shifted the narrative to an account of a set of empirical discoveries, reviewing the usual explanations that have been offered. Following this presentation, I then introduced a new line of
analysis that holds promise of explaining some proportion of the
disparate literature on linguistic processing in RHD patients. As one
encounters this novel idea, I suggest, not only must its literal meaning be processed but also the idea must be located emotionally: that
is, as something liked or disliked, something that is or is not consistent with one's belief system, something that seems promising for
suggesting new experiments or something that is limited or even

already falsified. Such dual coding is not simply a luxury: rather it contributes measurably to the comprehensibility and to the memorability of the particular explanatory account that I have introduced here.

Should this explanation be suggestive, one might ask which implications it entails. From an experimental point of view, one can investigate the generality of this hypothesized phenomenon. For example, does the right hemisphere participate in dual coding for linguistic messages only, or, as examples from film or cartoons suggest, is it also relevant for materials encoded in other systems of symbols? Are there certain kinds of emotional messages or connections that are more readily processed by such patients? For instance, our studies of story comprehension suggest that, when emotional charges are very potent, RHD patients are more likely to be able to process them (Rehak et al., 1992). The findings to which I refer suggest that the *degree* of emotional potency is relevant; it is possible, however, that certain emotional states (e.g., positive ones) may be more readily apprehended by RHD patients.

There are also clinical and therapeutic implications. In trying to communicate with RHD patients, it may be prudent to recognize that they are unlikely to be able to present, or to follow, a set of emotional associations, and so one must pay attention chiefly to the literal content of what they say. Finally, to the extent that such patients can benefit from therapeutic interventions, it may be advisable to help them appreciate the emotional implications of what they are saying—either by making these explicit, by infusing contents with greater-than-normal emotional weight, or by reacting to linguistic output with specific emotional signals. For the rest of us, such excessive reactions are not necessary. And so I would ask you to mute your reaction to this article, unless, of course, it is wholly positive.

REFERENCES

Gainotti, G. (1972). Emotional behavior and hemispheric side of the brain. *Cortex, 8,* 31–55.

Gardner, H. (1982). *Art, mind, and brain.* New York: Basic.

Gardner, H. (1983). *Frames of mind: The theory of multiple intelligences.* New York: Basic.

Gardner, H. (1991). *The unschooled mind.* New York: Basic.

Gardner, H., Brownell, H., Wapner, W., & Michelow, D. (1983). Missing the point: The role of the right hemisphere in the processing of complex linguistic materials. In E. Perecman (Ed.), *Cognitive processing in the right hemisphere* (pp.169–191). New York: Academic Press.

Gardner, H., & Denes, G. (1977). Connotative judgments by aphasic patients on a pictorial adaptation of the semantic differential. *Cortex, 9*, 183–196.

Gardner, H., Ling, P. K., Flamm, L., & Silverman, J. (1975). Comprehension and appreciation of humor in brain-damaged patients. *Brain, 83*, 399–412.

Geschwind, N. (1974). *Selected papers.* Dodrecht: Reidel.

Geschwind, N. (June 1976). *Approach to a theory of localization of emotion in the human brain.* Paper presented to the International Neuropsychology Symposium, Roc-Amadour, France.

Goodman, N. (1976). *Languages of art.* Indianapolis: Hackett.

Grice, P. (1975). Logic and conversation. In P. Cole & J. Morgan (Eds.), *Syntax and semantics: 3 Speech acts* (pp.41–58). New York: Academic Press.

Kaplan, J., & Gardner, H. (1989). Artistry after unilateral brain disease. In F. Boller & J. Grafman (Eds.), *Handbook of neuropsychology* (Vol. II, pp. 141–155). Amsterdam: Elsevier Science.

Mandler, J. & Johnson, N. S. (1977). The remembrance of things parsed: Story structure and recall. *Cognitive Psychology, 9*, 111–151.

Molloy, R., Brownell, H., & Gardner, H. (1990). Discourse comprehension by right hemisphere damaged patients: Deficits of prediction and revision. In Y. Joanette and H. Brownell (Eds.), *Discourse ability and brain damage: Theoretical and empirical perspectives* (pp.113–130). New York: Springer.

Nelson, K. (1986). *Event knowledge: Structure and function in development.* Hillsdale, N.J.: Erlbaum.

Ostrove, J., Kaplan, J., Brownell, H., & Gardner, H. (in press). The components of linguistic discourse: Lessons from neuropsychology. In P. Gryzbyk (Ed.), *Semiotic studies.*

Ostrove, J., Simpson, T., & Gardner, H. (1990). Beyond scripts: A note on the capacity of right hemisphere-damaged patients to process social and emotional content. *Brain and Language, 12*, 144–154.

Rehak, A., Kaplan, J., & Gardner, H. (1992). Sensitivity to conversational deviance in right hemisphere damaged patients. *Brain and Language, 42*, 203–217.

Rehak, A., Kaplan, J., Weylman, S., Kelly, B., Brownell, H., & Gardner, H. (1992). Story processing in right hemisphere brain-damaged patients. *Brain and Language, 42*, 320–336.

Roman, M., Brownell, H., Potter, J., Seibold, J., & Gardner, H. (1987). Script knowledge in right hemisphere damaged and in normal elderly adults. *Brain and Language, 31*, 51–70.

Sacks, O. (1990). *The man who mistook his wife for a hat.* New York: Harper Perennial.

Stein, N. (1978). The comprehension and appreciation of stories. In S. Madeja (Ed.), *The arts, cognition and basic skills* (pp.231–249). St. Louis: CEMREL.

Wapner, W., Hamby, S., & Gardner, H. (1981). The role of the right hemisphere in the apprehension of complex linguistic materials. *Brain and Language, 14*, 15–33.

Weinstein, E., & Kahn, R. (1955). *Denial of illness.* Springfield, IL: Thomas.

Weylman, S., Brownell, H., & Gardner, H. (1988). "It's what you mean, not what you say": Pragmatic language use in brain-damaged patients. In F. Plum (Ed.), *Language, communication and the brain* (pp.229–234). New York: Raven.

Weylman, S., Brownell, H., Roman, M., & Gardner. H. (1989). Appreciation of indirect requests by left and right brain damaged patients: The effects of verbal context and conventionality of wording. *Brain and Language, 36*, 580–591.

Woodward, R., & Armstrong, S. (1979). *The Brethren.* New York: Simon & Schuster.

Environmental Control of Goal-directed Action: Automatic and Strategic Contingencies between Situations and Behavior

John A. Bargh
New York University

Peter M. Gollwitzer
Universität Konstanz

My thinking is first and last and always for the sake of my doing.
—William James

All thought paralyzes action.

—Jean Cocteau

What is the relation between thought and action? Does thought exist in the service of action, as James (1890) contended? Or is the realm of thought somewhat separate from that of action, as implied by Cocteau—not to mention the experimental psychologists of his era, who considered thought to be epiphenomenal to responses to the environment (e.g., Guthrie, 1952; Skinner, 1953; Spence, 1950).

Our aim in this chapter is to address the links between environmental events and the actional responses to them. We focus on the issue of whether there is direct environmental control over behavior, in the form of behavioral responses automatically triggered by features of the current situation in which one finds oneself. We focus also on the mediating role of thought or cognition in this process and

Preparation of this chapter was supported in part by the Max Planck Research Award from the Humboldt Foundation and the Max Planck Society to the authors and by grant MH 43265 from the National Institute of Mental Health to J. A. B.

argue that a certain form of thought—termed *implementation intentions*—has a unique role in the environment-to-action sequence.

We argue that goal-directed action can be triggered directly by environmental stimuli, without the need for conscious involvement. Given a specific set of situational features, an individual may behave in ways he or she did not consciously choose or intend or may not be aware of the reasons for that behavior at the time.

The critical phrase in the above description is "at the time," because, as we will show, these direct environment-action links are dependent on intentions developed in the past. There are two basic types of environmental control. One form results from the repeated satisfaction of an enduring goal in a certain situation by certain behaviors. We propose that chronic situation-to-goal links develop from the frequent and consistent pairing of the features of a situation with goal-directed behaviors. That is, the individual chronically has the same goal in that situation so that the association between the mental representation of that situation and the representation of the respective goal-directed behaviors eventually becomes automatized. This principle, derived from the auto-motive model of environmentally directed behavior (Bargh, 1990), will be discussed in the first part of this chapter.

There is another route to direct control of action by the environment via the formation of specific implementation intentions (e.g., Gollwitzer, 1990, 1993). This route is strategically employed by the individual to attain desired goals in circumstances in which the person anticipates difficulty in attaining desired ends and so intentionally turns to environmental control to further goal achievement. Implementation intentions, in effect, create a contingency between a future (usually the short-term or immediate future) set of circumstances and the behavior one has decided to enact when those circumstances occur.

For instance, one may have to pick up one's daughter from kindergarten earlier than usual one afternoon. To make sure one remembers to do so, an implementation intention can be made that morning, such as "when my office clock strikes 3, I will leave the office for the kindergarten immediately." Note that this implementation intention is different from the goal intention to pick up one's daughter from school—it specifies the precise environmental circumstances or cues that provoke the desired behavior. Note also that this strategic use of environmental contingencies by implementation intentions would not have been necessary if the parent had to pick up his or her daughter from school at the usual time (say, at 4:30). In that case, the parent could have relied on the auto-motive or habitual control of the goal intention to pick up the daughter from kindergarten.

These two ways in which environmental control over goal-directed action can occur are each mixtures of the intentional and the unintentional, of the automatic and the controlled. It may seem paradoxical that a habitually automatic process could be intentional, in a sense, because a defining feature of automatic processes is their unintended nature (see Bargh, 1989; Shiffrin & Schneider, 1977). Yet a hallmark of learned, habitual, automatic processing abilities such as skills (e.g., driving, typing) is that they were once effortful and intentional and only slowly, with considerable experience, become efficient and reflexive (see Miller et al., 1960; Newell & Rosenbloom, 1981). In the same way, the auto-motive control of behavior originates in intended, consciously chosen behavioral responses that only become habitual after frequent and consistent employment.

In the case of the strategic route to environmental control, the resultant behavior is much more clearly intentional. After all, the strategic form is the result of a single mental act—the formation of an implementation intention (i.e., "I intend to perform behavior X when situation Y occurs."). However, this behavior is also automatic, because at the time of behaving, the effect of the triggering environmental features is direct and immediate and requires no intervening conscious choice, intention, or awareness at that time.

There are parallels to this model in the impression-formation, attitudes, and self-perception research literatures, all of which contain evidence of a direct, autonomous effect of the environment that can occur via either chronic or temporary means. There has been considerable research into the notion of trait-construct accessibility as an important determinant of social perception (e.g., Bruner, 1957; Higgins, 1989; Higgins & King, 1981; Wyer & Srull, 1989). Specifically, people's behaviors are said to be categorized or interpreted in terms of trait concepts (e.g., "That is an honest thing to do"; "She is being too pushy") relevant to the behaviors.

One factor in determining how a behavior is understood—especially considering the general ambiguity of social behavior (in that

any given act can be understood in several ways; see Bruner, 1958)—
is the relative accessibilities of the various trait constructs relevant to
that behavior. In other words, a person (say, a suspicious person)
can be mentally more ready to understand a behavior in terms of
manipulativeness than in terms of friendliness (e.g., "He just wants
me to do a favor for him in return someday."). How "perceptually
ready" (Bruner, 1957) a person is to understand a behavior in terms
of one relevant concept over another is a function of many factors,
such as the person's goals, but the factors we focus on here are how
recently and how frequently the concept has been used in the past.

An individual chronically invokes a certain limited set of trait
constructs in understanding behavior, and there are wide individual
differences in the particular constructs a person uses chronically
(Higgins et al., 1982). For present purposes, what is important is that
these frequently used constructs become capable of automatic activation by the presence of relevant behavior in the environment.
Trait terms related to one's self-relevant or other-relevant chronic
constructs, compared with one's nonchronically used constructs,
become active without an individual's awareness given the presence
of relevant stimuli (Bargh, 1982), when attention is overloaded and
in short supply (Bargh & Thein, 1985; Bargh & Tota, 1988), and even
when one is trying to ignore such trait terms as irrelevant to one's
task (Bargh & Pratto, 1986). Thus, these chronically employed mental representations of types of social behavior exhibit all four defining features of automatic, environmentally triggered cognition (see
Bargh, 1989, 1994): they become active on the mere presence of the
relevant environmental event, with no need for an individual's
awareness of that event, without the individual intending to think
about the event in that way, when conscious attention is devoted
elsewhere at the time, and even when the person is trying to ignore
or prevent the activation.

Such automatic activation of mental constructs can also occur
when the construct is made accessible temporarily through recent,
deliberate conscious use. Higgins et al. (1977) were the first to demonstrate such "priming" effects in the context of social judgment.
Subjects believed they were participating in two unrelated experiments. In the first experiment they were exposed to trait words as
part of a "memory test," and in the second they read about a target
person's behavior. The behaviors were ambiguously relevant to the

traits primed by the first task, and the results showed that subjects were more likely to interpret or categorize the target person's behavior in terms of the primed trait than in terms of the unprimed alternative trait. For example, subjects' opinion of a person who sailed across the Atlantic Ocean by himself was more positive if they had been presented earlier with "adventurous" traits in the memory experiment than if they had seen "reckless" traits instead.

Higgins et al. (1977) took great care to ensure that subjects had no awareness of the relation between the two tasks, as did subsequent contextual priming experiments. The first task, in which subjects are unobtrusively exposed to the critical priming stimuli, is usually some kind of simple mental task, such as memorizing words, naming their color, or making sentences out of them. Thus, the priming task is designed to have nothing in common with the second task, so there is no carryover of the goal or processing strategies of the first task to the second. This design also ensures that subjects do not become aware of how the first task might have affected their responses on the second task, nor are the results on the second task attributable to priming effects. Numerous experiments with this basic paradigm have confirmed that subjects are not aware of or intend this interpretational influence of temporarily accessible trait constructs (e.g., Bargh & Pietromonaco, 1982; Srull & Wyer, 1979).

Thus, just like chronically accessible trait constructs, primed or temporarily accessible constructs exert their influence automatically, without the perceiver's awareness or intent. Moreover, it has been demonstrated that these chronic and temporary forms of accessibility behave similarly within the same experiment (Bargh et al., 1986, 1988), both causing more extreme trait ratings of ambiguously relevant behaviors. In fact, in line with the theoretical notion that chronic and temporary construct accessibility are manifestations of the same underlying mechanism (i.e., amount of construct activation; see Higgins et al., 1985), Bargh et al. (1986) found that the two sources of accessibility combined additively.

The construct-accessibility results are consistent with the present conceptualization because they show that automatic activation of mental representations by relevant environmental events can occur through both the chronic and the temporary readiness of that construct to become active. But evidence of these two varieties of automaticity in social perception and cognition is not limited to trait-construct activation. Racial and gender stereotypes, attitudes, and self-concepts are among the social knowledge structures that have been shown to have characteristics of automatic activation by environmental features (see reviews by Bargh, 1989, 1994). One set of research demonstrates automatic activation of mental representations in the mere presence of the relevant object or event in the environment (e.g., stereotype activation given the corresponding physical features of the stereotyped group; see Devine, 1989), while the other form has the additional necessary condition of recent conscious activation (i.e., priming) of the representation for the effect to occur (e.g., recently expressing one's attitude increases its subsequent influence over behavior toward the attitude object; see Fazio et al., 1982).

To summarize, we argue in this chapter that direct control over behavior by the environment can and does occur. This delegation of control to the environment can either develop out of the repeated, chronic pursuit of the same goal in the given situation or be caused by a strategic creation of an environment-action contingency. In either case, behavior is triggered automatically—immediately, reflexively, efficiently, and without the interpolation of a conscious choice or decision—at the occurrence of the relevant environmental event.

Automatic Behavior through Auto-motive Control

Langer (1978) first raised the possibility that social behavior may not always be based on conscious deliberation and choice but instead could be a "mindless" reaction to situational features. This hypothesis was derived from script theory (e.g., Abelson, 1976), which posits that people develop representations of frequently experienced social interaction situations that generate expectations for what will happen in that routine situation. These expectations can become so strong with experience that one may react as if the expected feature were there when in fact it was not (see Langer et al., 1978).

It is an often-observed characteristic of knowledge structures, such as scripts, person prototypes (Cantor & Mischel, 1977, 1979), schemata (Markus, 1977; Spiro, 1977), and stereotypes (Hamilton, 1981; Pratto & Bargh, 1991), that one fills in missing features of an experience, allowing expectations or predictions about nonpresent elements to be made in default of relevant individuating information (Fiske & Neuberg, 1990). Often, as in the case of racial or gender stereotypes, people may then react as though the expected feature was really present (Neuberg, 1988; Snyder & Swann, 1978), sometimes eliciting the expected behavior as a self-fulfilling prophecy (e.g., Jussim, 1986; Rosenthal & Jacobson, 1968).

In a study most directly relevant to our hypotheses, Carver et al. (1983) proposed that priming effects on impression formation might also explain modeling effects, in which witnessing the behavior of another individual makes one more likely to engage in that behavior oneself. Carver et al. (1983) hypothesized that there would probably be associations between the information in memory as to how to perceive or recognize a given kind of behavior (e.g., aggressiveness) and the information in memory that enables us to act aggressively ourselves. Thus, priming of the perceptual representation as in impression-formation studies may also result in heightened activation of the behavioral-production representation, because of the semantic relatedness of the two sets of information. Carver et al. (1983) showed that the same hostile-priming manipulation (from Srull & Wyer, 1979) caused subjects both to rate a target person who behaved in an ambiguously hostile way as more hostile than did control subjects (Experiment 1 in Carver et al., 1983) and to administer electric shocks of greater intensity to another subject (in reality a confederate who was not actually shocked) in a learning experiment (Experiment 2 in Carver et al., 1983).

By arguing that contextual priming could have behavioral consequences, Carver et al. (1983) were the first to predict that behavior can be influenced by situational features outside awareness and without intention. However, there is an important theoretical difference between the present model and that put forward by Carver et al. (1983). We hypothesize that enduring goals or motives become activated directly by the environment, whereas Carver et al. (1983) posit a more cognitive, informational basis for the effect. We will return later to a comparison and several experimental tests of the motivational versus cognitive explanations.

There is also an important methodological difference between the Carver et al. (1983) study and our own: in their Experiment 2, subjects were instructed to (i.e., given the goal to) shock the other subject, and the hostile priming served to augment the conscious, intentional goal-directed behavior. In our experiments, on the other hand, we did not give subjects an explicit conscious goal but rather sought to activate those goals without subjects' awareness or intention and then to see the effect of those automatic goals on behavior.

There is precedence in these various findings, therefore, for the idea that situational features can activate mental representations corresponding to them and that these representations can then serve as the informational basis for further behavior in that situation (e.g., toward a stereotyped individual, such as waiting for a yet-un-seen waiter to bring the menus in a restaurant). The central tenet of the auto-motive model (Bargh, 1990) is similar, except that it posits that latent enduring goals or motives are directly activated by situational features, not only informational knowledge structures. That is, previous work on the behavior-mediating quality of mental representations assumes that these representations serve as a supplemental knowledge base, with intentional, consciously made decisions about how to behave toward the other person or in that situation then made on the basis of this internal source of information. The process of automatic activation of one's enduring goals, on the other hand, bypasses the conscious choice stage entirely—it is these choices or goals themselves that are said to be automatically activated by the environment, according to the auto-motive model.

This feature of the model is critical for the proposal of direct environmental control over behavior. By "direct," we mean without the necessity of conscious, intentional intervention between the occurrence of the triggering environmental features and the engagement of the automated behavioral response. It is assumed that the habitual serving of a goal within a given situation not only connects the goal with the situation but also those goal-directed behaviors that have been effective in satisfying the goal in the past. Of course, any given goal can be reached by different lines of action, some of these being more effective than others and thus more readily used. This implies that the activation of the goal spreads to various goal-directed courses of action, with those most successful in the past being more strongly activated and thereby more likely to be employed in the present situation. This part of the model is reminiscent of Hull's (e.g., 1943, 1952) notion of response hierarchies.

What kind of goal striving can become habitualized? Habitualization of goal attainment requires frequent and consistent serving of this goal in the same situational context (e.g., Shiffrin & Schneider, 1977), which implies that the person must feel committed to this particular goal over time; for example, being a good mother, a high achiever, or a moral person (see Cantor & Kihlstrom, 1987; Emmons, 1989; Gollwitzer & Wicklund, 1985). We distinguish this type of goal, which cannot be reached by a single act or on a single occasion, from those that can—a distinction captured, for example, by the difference between wanting to affiliate and wanting to be affiliative. It is this latter type of goal that we mean when we refer to "enduring goals." Motives are similar to enduring goals, as they describe a class of incentives (e.g., power-related incentives) that a person finds particularly attractive and, therefore, chronically strives for (McClelland, 1953, 1985).

THE CASE AGAINST AUTOMATIC (ENVIRONMENTALLY DIRECTED) BEHAVIOR

The theoretical heritage of the auto-motive model is seen in the considerable evidence of preconscious processing of social information that has been gathered over the past 15 yr (see reviews in Bargh, 1989, 1994). This form of automatic processing requires only the presence of the relevant social stimulus object or event—person, type of behavior, situational setting—to occur; no intention that it occur or awareness of the process, or devotion of conscious attentional resources, is necessary. Thus, given the presence of a female job applicant, for example, the personnel manager's stereotypic conception of women will become active without the manager's intention or awareness and will possibly influence the hiring decision. In another example, a person with chronically accessible mental constructs for rudeness and intelligence will pick up those features of people (if they are present) at a busy cocktail party and possibly not much else. However, the operation of these preconscious processes was found to be limited to the selection and interpretation of social information and not to extend to the making of judgments and decisions themselves (see Bargh, 1989; Higgins & Bargh, 1987). Impressions, for example, were not formed unless the perceiver had the goal or intention of forming one and the attentional resources (i.e., no distractions or concurrent demands on conscious attention) to do so (see Bargh & Thein, 1985; Bassili & Smith, 1986).

Second, a legion of motivational influences on the judgment process have been found that enable a person to overcome or override these automatic input effects. Making a person feel more accountable for his or her judgment (in that the subject believes he or she will later have to justify the reasons for it to others; see Tetlock, 1985), having one's outcomes dependent on the other person about whom one is forming an impression (creating a pragmatic need to be more accurate; see Erber & Fiske, 1984), and possessing strong values, such as not to be prejudiced (Devine, 1989), have all been shown capable of attenuating if not eliminating preconscious influences. Of course, the individual has to be aware of the influence or at least the potential for being influenced for the motivational correction to occur (see Bargh, 1992), but it is not uncommon for a person to feel that he or she may have been influenced (e.g., by gender or skin color) without actually being aware of the (automatic) influence itself.

With these two research conclusions—that social judgments and decisions are not made automatically but only when the individual has the goal of making them and that goals or motivations are capable of overriding automatic input analyses—it seemed clear that a person's current goal determined responses to the environment. To the extent that these goals or intentions were generated or put into play by conscious processes, direct environmental control over behavior (through behavioral choices or decisions) would not be a possibility.

THE CASE FOR AUTOMATIC BEHAVIOR

However, the fact that such mental representations as stereotypes and chronically accessible trait constructs had been shown to be directly activated by the environment meant that it was possible for other forms of representations to develop such automatic links to the environment. The content or purpose of the representation should not matter, so long as the same conditions needed to produce the automatic association held. Those conditions are the same as for the development of any mental association, the (literally) ancient principles of how two ideas become associated with each other in memory: through frequent and consistent pairing of the two mental representations caused by their being active in memory at the same time (see historical review by Anderson & Bower, 1973; see also James, 1890; Hebb, 1948; Schneider & Fisk, 1982; Shiffrin & Schneider, 1977). In the case of automatic activation of racial or gender stereotypes, certain physical features are frequently and consistently paired with representations of beliefs and traits; in the case of automatic activation of attitudes (see Bargh et al., 1992; Fazio et al., 1986), the representation of the attitude object is paired with its evaluation as good or bad. Eventually, this associative link becomes "unitized" (Hayes-Roth, 1977) or "compiled" (Anderson, 1983) such that the mere presence of the physical features of the person or object in the environment is sufficient to activate the stereotype or attitude because there is an automatic link between the relevant sensory feature representations and the person-type or object category and now an automatic link between the person or object category and the stereotypic or evaluative features.

Once such theoretical groundwork is laid, it becomes a relatively trivial matter to advance the proposition that enduring goals or motives should be capable of developing automatic associative links to environmental features in the same way. Certainly goals are represented in memory just as are stereotypes and attitudes and chronically accessible trait constructs. Indeed, there is good evidence that we represent others' behavior in terms of their goals and purposes and form impressions of them on the basis of their perceived goals (see Brewer & Dupree, 1983; Read et al., 1990; Trzebinski, 1985). What then should occur if a person pursues the same goal over time within a given situation? The mental representation of that particular set of situational features (e.g., of a party, an office meeting, a church service) will be repeatedly and consistently activated in memory at the same time that specific goal representation is active. By the associative principle of contiguous activation (Hebb, 1948), therefore, automatic links should develop between representations of social situations and those of goals the individual chronically pursues within them: this hypothesis is the core premise of the auto-motive model.

From this initial premise that these enduring goals will become activated automatically when the individual enters into the relevant situation (i.e., in the mere presence of the triggering situational features), several hypotheses follow. The first of these is that the automatically activated goals will then guide behavior within the situation, without the individual choosing or intending that particular line of action. The issue of volition is a tricky one here, and it is important to be precise. In one sense, as we argued earlier, this behavior is intentional in that it was repeatedly and deliberately selected in the past. Eventually, we postulate, this selection or choice becomes just another routine and invariant feature of the situation to the mental system, and is thus bypassed. The same principle of routinization can be found in models of skill acquisition (Anderson, 1987; Fitts & Posner, 1967; Newell & Rosenbloom, 1981), proceduralization of knowledge (Anderson, 1983, 1992), and script operation (Abelson, 1981). Therefore, it would be appropriate to say that automatic behavior due to the operation of enduring goals or motives is unintentional at the time but intentional in the sense that the choice of the behavior was made in the past, not in the present.

Because the goal that guides behavior is activated automatically and operates without the need for conscious attention or guidance, we can further hypothesize that a person will have no phenomenal experience of choosing that line of behavior or any consequent memory for the reasons or factors that entered into that choice. Accordingly, the person may misattribute the reasons for his or her behavior to causes that seem reasonable or logical on the basis of his or her theories of what must have caused the behavior (see Nisbett & Wilson, 1977).

Thus, if the hypothesis of direct environmental control over behavior is valid, we should be able experimentally to activate situational goals without the subject's awareness or intention and then observe both goal-directed behavior by the subject and evidence that he or she was not aware of the cause of the behavior. We now turn to several recent experiments testing these hypotheses.

The Priming of Goal-directed Behavior

THE INTERRUPTION STUDY

Can goals become activated without intention or awareness to then guide behavior? In our first experiment, we tested this possibility using the same priming methodology that has been employed in impression-formation research. In those studies, certain trait constructs are activated unobtrusively in one setting and are found to exert an influence over impression formation—specifically, the interpretation of relevant behavioral information—in what subjects believe to be a totally unrelated second study.

We (Bargh et al., 1993a, Experiment 1) placed subjects in a goal-conflict situation, after first priming one or the other (or neither) goal using the scrambled-sentence technique (see Srull & Wyer, 1979). Subjects were informed that they would be participating in two short "mini-experiments." They were shown into a room and told that the first study had to do with language ability and were then given the scrambled-sentence test to complete. There were 20 items, each of which consisted of five words in a "scrambled" order (e.g., "worked the clown hard laughed"). For each item, subjects were to write down a grammatically correct four-word sentence (e.g., "The clown laughed hard.") as quickly as they could. After they finished this task, they were to leave the room and go down the corridor to find the experimenter, who would be preparing the second experiment for them.

The three versions of the scrambled-sentence tests were identical except for eight words interspersed across the 20 items. These words were all either related to the goal of assertive behavior, polite behavior, or neither (in the control condition). In this way, we intended to activate the goal of assertiveness or politeness (or neither one) in subjects before their entry into the goal-conflict situation that followed.

After finishing the priming task, subjects went down the hall and around a corner, where they saw the experimenter standing in a doorway about 30 ft away. The experimenter was talking to another subject (who was actually a confederate) seated in that room. The actual subject, coming down the hall, could only see the experimenter and could hear but not see the confederate. When the experimenter saw the subject come around the corner, he made a signal to the confederate, who started a stopwatch.

The goal-conflict situation was created by having the confederate continually asking questions of the experimenter, not understanding much of what she was supposed to do, and generally keeping the experimenter continuously occupied by her questions. The experimenter had his attention focused on the confederate and did not break off and look at the subject after he or she had arrived. The subject knew that the second part of the experiment was to be brief, and if he or she could just get started on it, the experiment would be completed and they could leave. But the experimenter and confederate kept up their conversation, forcing the subject to interrupt the experimenter if he or she wished to proceed with the second experiment. Our dependent measure was simply the number of seconds that passed before the subject attempted to interrupt the experimenter.

The subject was thus put in a situation in which he or she wanted to interrupt but also wanted to be patient and polite (a goal generated from the social norm for the situation; see Bargh, 1990) and thus not interrupt while the experimenter was answering the questions of the hapless "preceding subject." Which path would subjects take? The power of our goal-priming manipulation was striking: those subjects primed for the goal of acting assertively interrupted the experimenter after about 5.5 min of waiting. Subjects in the "polite" goal-priming condition, on the other hand, did not interrupt until after waiting more than 9 min. The mean for the neutral-priming condition was between the two goal-priming condition means and closer to the polite than to the assertive mean.

The considerable difference in time-to-interrupt between the assertive and the polite conditions could well have been even greater, had we not placed a 10-min (600-s) limit on making the subject wait for the next part of the experiment. Given this self-imposed ceiling on the dependent measure, we evaluated the data in terms of the percentage of subjects in each condition who did interrupt during the experimenter-confederate conversation. Less than 20% of the subjects in the polite condition interrupted at all, compared with nearly 40% in the neutral condition. However, over 60% of the subjects in the assertive condition interrupted the experimenter to get the materials for the second mini-experiment.

These results strongly support our hypothesis that goals could be activated by situational features so that this goal would then direct behavior in a subsequent goal-relevant situation, without the subject consciously choosing or intending the behavior. This result constitutes a priming effect on behavior in the absence of an experimentally supplied goal to the subject to behave in that way (cf. Carver et al., 1983). The priming manipulation was an experimental simulation of situational features that would directly activate those goals and the respective associated behaviors of being assertive or polite.

THE ACHIEVEMENT-VERSUS-AFFILIATION STUDIES

In our second experiment, we sought to replicate this goal-priming phenomenon in a different goal-conflict situation based on a common classroom experience. Often a student knows the answer to a teacher's question and raises his or her hand to answer it. Doing this too often, however, runs the risk of incurring the ostracism of one's classmates, who think they are being shown up by a know-it-all. This is a classic goal-conflict situation: one wishes to achieve and perform well academically in class, but one also wants to have friends and be well liked by classmates. Pursuing one of these goals is often done at the expense of the other.

In our second and third experiments (Bargh et al., 1993a) we created such an achievement-versus-affiliation conflict by having the subject work as a team with another subject (who was actually a confederate) on a series of word-search puzzles, 11 × 11 matrices of letters in which words relating to a common theme (e.g., bugs, colors, fruits), presented above each puzzle, were embedded. The "teams" were to work together to find as many words as possible within the 3 minutes allocated for each puzzle.

Before working on these puzzles with their teammates, subjects had completed a "practice" version by themselves. This practice puzzle constituted the priming task. A list of words to be found in the puzzle was presented at the bottom of the page. These words were related to achievement (e.g., "achieve," "succeed") or affiliation (e.g., "friendship," "support") or were neutral words (e.g., "turtle," "lamp").

In the experimental situation, the confederate performed poorly by design on the word-search task, having evident trouble with it and becoming more and more withdrawn from the task over the five trials. He or she became somewhat frustrated and a little embarassed at his or her lack of ability. (The confederate on the average circled one word for every three found by the subject.) By finding a lot of words, the subject would thus fulfill the achievement goal but would also be making the confederate feel worse about himself or herself (and perhaps resentful toward the subject); by "dumbing down" and not getting as many words as he or she could, the subject would help to minimize the difference in the numbers of words circled between them (each used pens with different colors, so this discrepancy was salient) and so pursue the affiliation goal by performing at a more similar level to that of the confederate and preventing the confederate from feeling too bad.

Again, we obtained a sizable difference in performance on the word-search task as a function of which goal had been primed. Achievement-primed subjects found significantly more words on the first two word-search puzzles than did subjects in the affiliation- or neutral-priming conditions. All three groups performed similarly on the final three puzzles. The finding of priming effects early on that dissipate over time is consistent with several studies in the trait-construct-priming literature, which show such priming effects to decrease over time (e.g., Bargh et al., 1988; Higgins et al., 1985). More relevant is the finding by Wilson and Capitman (1982) that reading a "boy-meets-girl story" made male subjects subsequently more friendly toward a female confederate they met immediately after reading the story but had no effect when there was a 4-min delay before meeting the confederate.

It is not just the decay of goal activation over time that could result in an attenuation of the priming effect on the later trials, however, but also the power of the situation itself. It is clear from the neutral-priming results in the early trials that the power of the affiliation features of the situation (i.e., the confederate's withdrawal) was stronger than that of the achievement features in determining behavior. Since priming manipulations are meant to activate one or another goal relevant to the experimental situation but in an unrelated context prior to the subject entering that situation, it is not surprising that the features of the actual situation in which our subjects subsequently found themselves could activate a different goal later on.

An unanticipated aspect of our results was that, although the priming effect for the first two trials was reliable overall, the effect was much stronger for male than for female subjects. Since we replicated this sex difference in the next experiment, we save discussion of it until those results are presented.

INDIVIDUAL DIFFERENCES IN THE CHRONIC ACTIVATION OF ENDURING GOALS

As noted earlier, just like a social trait construct, a given goal can be activated both contextually and chronically. Thus far we have used temporary activation as a proxy for the effects assumed to occur in the case of one's chronic goals. That is, the priming manipulations have served temporarily to create increased activation of a competing goal. People are presumed to differ, however, in the level of chronic activation of these goals. In our third experiment, we replicate the achievement-versus-affiliation study procedure, but with the addition of measures of chronic achievement and affiliation motives.

On the basis of related work in social construct accessibility research, we predicted that the primed goal would determine behavior for the early trials of the word-search puzzle but that over time this temporary influence would recede and the subject's long-term chronic goal activation would again dominate. Higgins et al. (1985) and Lombardi et al. (1987) both found that the more recently primed trait construct determined impressions for a short time, but thereafter the more frequently primed construct won out. Bargh et al. (1988) obtained the same effect when chronically accessible trait constructs (assumed to be the most commonly used over time by the subject) were substituted for frequently primed constructs.

We measured subjects' achievement motive using a single picture from the Thematic Apperception Test (TAT; Murray, 1943)—a silhouette of a young man stepping up to and looking out an opened window (Picture 6 of the TAT)—to which subjects answered questions as to what they thought was going on in the picture. The TAT has served as the classic, standard measure of the strength of the achievement motive for many years (see Atkinson, 1958; Heckhausen, 1990) and can be considered a good measure of an enduring goal or motive (see Sorrentino & Higgins, 1986). In telling their stories about the picture, subjects responded to a structured series of questions, such as "What is happening?," "What led up to the situation?," "What is wanted?," and "What will happen?" Responses to these questions were coded by two independent judges using Heckhausen's (1990) scoring system, which consists of 13 categories relating to achievement and failure themes. Interjudge reliability on overall achievement motive scores was high.

The affiliation motive was measured by the affiliation subscale of the Personality Research Form (PRF, Jackson, 1984). All students in New York University's introductory psychology course had completed the TAT and PRF measures (among many others) as part of a mass testing session earlier in the semester. On the basis of their achievement and affiliation scores, two groups of subjects were selected for our third experiment—those with high achievement and low affiliation scores and those with low achievement and high affiliation scores. The experimental procedure was the same as for our Experiment 2 described above.

The results again showed a reliable priming effect for the early but not the later trials and only for male subjects. Achievement-primed male subjects outperformed affiliation-primed subjects by a wide margin—more than 1 SD. Most important, just as in the social construct accessibility studies, this priming effect was eventually overridden by a significant chronic goal effect. The primed goal determined performance early on but by the last trial was overtaken by a reliable chronic goal effect. That our priming manipulation interacted with chronic goals (demonstrating a shared underlying mechanism), just as primed trait constructs interact with chronic constructs over time in impression-formation studies, is additional evidence that we are successfully priming goals and not behavioral schemata or perceptual constructs.

Why did these effects occur precisely as predicted for males but not at all for females? It is important to note that females did not differ from males on the achievement motive, as measured by the TAT; the means and ranges for the male and female subjects in our experiments were nearly identical. Thus, one issue is why this achievement-motive measure did not predict achievement on the later trials for women as it did for men.

There are several possible explanations. First, the achievement-motivation literature has historically obtained effects only for males and not for females (see Horner, 1974)—to the point that data for females were not collected, and, when available, were not even analyzed (e.g., Reuman et al., 1984). In one sense then, the similar sex differences that we found in both the chronic and the primed effects—which were both reliable for men, but not for women—can be seen as additional evidence that our priming manipulation is activating goals. No such sex difference in trait-construct-priming effects has been reported in the impression-formation literature.

The reason for the sex difference would seem to have something to do with the different ways that men and women express their achievement goals—men do so more in competitive performance situations, and women more in social situations (Higgins, 1991). In retrospect, it may be that the achievement-goal-primed and chronic-achievement-goal female subjects expressed their achievement orientation by attending to the social demands of the situation (i.e., the confederate's unhappiness and withdrawal)—just as did the affiliation-goal-primed and chronic-affiliation-goal female subjects, resulting in the same effects on task performance but for different reasons.

Another explanation might be that automatic behavior effects occur only for men and not for women. There were no such sex differences in our first experiment (the "interruption study"), that primed being assertive or polite, however, so we do not believe this factor explains our results. In any event, we moved away from the achievement-versus-affiliation goal-conflict scenario in Experiment 4 partly to ensure that there were no sex differences in automatic goal activation effects in general, as well as to help differentiate between two competing explanations of our effects each of which could account for the results of all three experiments so far.

Activated Goals versus Activated Schemata

As mentioned earlier, Carver et al. (1983) proposed that priming effects on perceptual structures may spread to semantically related behavior production structures and thereby influence subsequent behavior. According to this account, trait priming has the simultaneous effect of activating a perceptual structure with which to interpret the behavior of others and a behavioral structure with which to engage in that behavior oneself. With some additional assumptions, their model (which we call the *behavioral schema model*) could account for the results of our first three experiments.

In this alternative interpretation, our priming actually activates and makes more accessible a behavior knowledge structure that is relevant to the subsequent situation: assertiveness or politeness, achievement or affiliation. When in that situation, the subject consciously chooses how to behave. This conscious choice is influenced by the relative accessibilities of the various behavior schemata available in memory; the priming thus has the effect of swaying the conscious choice of behavior to one type over another. As well as being able to account for our experimental evidence thus far, this model has the apparent advantage of parsimony: the same activated behavioral schema accounts for priming effects in both impression formation and behavior.

Our account, however, is different. We predict that enduring goals or motives are *directly* triggered by the environment without any intervening conscious choice among alternatives. Second, we predict that this direct activation of goals will result in a *motivational state*, with qualities that distinguish it from a purely cognitive phenomenon.

In the following experiment, we sought to distinguish between motivational and cognitive explanations for our automatic behavior effects. One approach to doing so would be to test for the presence of goal-striving behaviors as a result of our goal-priming manipulation. Goal pursuit has properties, such as persistence and energization, that are not predicted by the behavioral schema model (see Atkinson & Birch, 1970; Heckhausen, 1990; Kuhl, 1986; Lewin, 1951; Pervin, 1989; Wicklund & Gollwitzer, 1982). An individual will persist or strive for the desired goal in the face of obstacles, and return to the goal task after being interrupted, until a sense of completion is obtained; the mental goal representation will continue to be activated during this pursuit even when conscious thoughts have been taken up with other matters (Atkinson & Birch, 1970; see also Martin & Tesser, 1989). This phenomenon is also illustrated by the "incubation" effect (e.g., Norman & Bobrow, 1976), in which a sought-for answer to a question, or something one was trying hard to remember but could not, pops into the mind out of the blue, long after one has stopped (consciously) thinking about it and gone on to other matters.

THE PERSISTENCE STUDY

Our fourth experiment tested whether subjects will persist on a task longer as a function of goal priming, a quality associated with an active goal and one on which the behavioral schema model is silent. In other words, will subjects persevere longer on a task if the goal of achieving has been activated automatically through a priming manipulation? Moreover, we designed the study such that the primed goal, persistence on the task, would be in the opposite direction to the experimental instructions (the conscious goal), which was to stop as soon as the experimenter directed.

Subjects participated three at a time but were partitioned from each other's view. They were informed that the experiment had to do with language skills. In the first task (which constituted the priming manipulation), subjects either completed the achievement or the neutral word-search puzzle from our Experiment 2 (resulting in achievement-primed and neutral-primed conditions). Then, they were given a rack of eight Scrabble letter tiles (three vowels and five consonants) and instructed to find as many different words as they could using the letters in 2 min. The experimenter told the subjects that she had to go get another experiment ready down the hall and that, if she could not return in time, she would give the signal to stop over the intercom in the front of the room. She then told the subjects to begin and left the room.

Unknown to the subjects, a videocamera was hidden in a box at the front of the room, and their behavior was monitored. After 2 min the experimenter gave the stop command and then measured how long subjects continued to work on the task in her absence (and out of view of the other subjects). Again the results showed a powerful effect of the priming manipulation on the dependent variable of task persistence. Over 50% of the subjects in the achievement priming condition—more than twice as many as in the neutral priming condition—continued to work after the signal to stop. Whereas the effect was again stronger for males, it was nonetheless reliable and quite strong for females as well, indicating that automatic goal activation occurs for both sexes.[1]

Note also that the primed goal caused behavior in the direction opposite the instructions given to subjects by the experimenter (i.e., to stop when they heard the signal). This result is another demonstration of an automatic effect on behavior that is not an enhancement of behavior in line with an experimentally supplied task goal.

The results of this study demonstrate that our priming manipulation had a motivational and not only a cognitive effect on our subjects. We now turn to a different line of research that speaks to a heretofore untested assumption of our model—that there are chronic individual differences in automatic goal activation by situational features.

CHRONIC INDIVIDUAL DIFFERENCES IN AUTOMATIC GOAL ACTIVATION: THE CASE OF SEXUAL HARASSMENT

The auto-motive model specifically postulates that direct situation-to-goal-behavior links develop from consistent and frequent conscious choice of that goal in the situation. It follows that there should be individual differences in which goals are pursued by people in identical situations. For example, in a situation in which the person has authority or official power of some sort, some individuals may have the enduring or self-defining goal of responsibly using that power and scrupulously avoiding conflicts of interest. Others, however, may constantly use their official power in unauthorized ways, such as to pursue their own, individual goals (greater power, status, wealth, etc.). Thus the chronic goal that is automatically linked to a given set of situational features may vary from individual to individual, just as which social trait construct chronically activated by a given set of behavioral features varies among people (Higgins et al., 1982).

A research program into the cognitive bases of sexual harassment (Bargh et al., 1993b) has yielded evidence relevant to this issue. On the basis of Pryor's (1987) research into individual differences in quid pro quo sexual harassment tendencies, we first examined the hypothesis that men likely to become sexual harassers automatically associated the concepts of power and sex. In other words, when in a situation in which they had relative power over a woman (e.g., a boss-secretary relationship), those circumstantial features of power would automatically activate the goal of having sex.

Individual differences in the chronic power-sex association can be identified through Pryor's (1987) Likelihood to Sexually Harass (LSH) scale as well as Malamuth's (1988) Attractiveness of Sexual Aggression (ASA) scale. The LSH scale presents subjects with 10 scenarios in which they have some leverage or power over an attractive female and asks what the probability is that the subject would use that leverage to gain sexual favors. The ASA scale asks subjects to rate how arousing they find each of a number of sexual activities, including using force against a woman and having sex with her against her will.

In our experiment, we used a sequential priming procedure (e.g., Neely, 1977) to present a prime and a target word in rapid succession on a computer screen (250 ms apart). The subject's task was to pronounce the second of the two words on each trial as fast as he or she could; Balota and Lorch (1986), among others, have shown that pronunciation times are a sensitive and strategy-free measure of the automaticity of the association between the concepts related to the prime and target stimuli.

We had three types of stimuli: power-related words (e.g., "strong," "mighty"; from Pryor, 1987), ambiguous sex-related words (e.g., "bed," "hard," "motel"), and neutral words served as both primes and targets and in all possible combinations.[2] We calculated the degree to which power primed sex and sex primed power for each subject by subtracting the power-sex pronunciation latency mean from the neutral-sex latency mean, and the sex-power latency mean from the neutral-power latency mean. These scores thus represent the degree of facilitation in pronunciation times due to the presence of the power or sex prime, compared with a baseline prime condition.

Our prediction was that the power-sex facilitation effect would increase as a function of subjects' LSH and ASA (on just the forced-sex items) scores, thus demonstrating a chronic automatic association between the situational feature of power and the goal of sex. As predicted, the stronger the subject's tendencies toward sexual harassment, the stronger the association between the concepts of power and sex, as measured by the power-sex word facilitation on the pronunciation task. There did not appear to be merely a stronger semantic association between the concepts of power and sex for the high-LSH subjects, however, because there was no such increase in facilitation obtained for sex words priming power words.

These studies document chronic differences in automatic pathways between situational features and personal goals. We believe this automatic goal activation underlies the behavioral effects that Pryor (1987) has obtained in his studies validating the LSH scale. In those studies, subjects were assigned the role of golf instructor, for example, and how close they got to and how much they touched the female cosubject (actually a confederate)—such as by putting their arms around her from behind to show her how to putt—were measured. As predicted, there was more touching and closeness the higher the subject scored on the LSH measure.

Implementation Intentions: Setting up Contingencies between Situations and Behavior

We now turn to the second type of environmental control, the formation of implementation intentions, which is the strategic effort to prepare successful responses to certain situational contexts expected to occur in the future. More specifically, the individual forms the intention to respond to a certain situation X with a specific behavior Y. Implementation intentions are quite different from what present-day psychology refers to as intentions. Psychologists commonly talk of goal intentions (see, e.g., Bandura, 1991) that specify a desired end state (which may be an outcome or consequence of some behavior or the successful execution of this behavior) that the individual intends to achieve (Ajzen, 1988; Fishbein & Ajzen, 1975). Goal intentions create a link between a desired end state and the person who forms this intention so that he or she feels committed to achieve this end state. However, the link established by the formation of implementation intentions is different. Here, a specified anticipated situational context is mentally associated with a behavior to be performed, which results in a contingency of the sort that the individual commits himself or herself to initiate the critical behavior to be performed once the situational context is encountered.

Implementation intentions and goal intentions differ not only in terms of their structural features. They also serve a different function in people's attempts to achieve their wishes and desires. A closer look at the various problems people encounter when seeking the realization of their desires highlights the differences between goal intentions and implementation intentions. We will therefore analyze the role of goal intentions and implementation intentions through a comprehensive model of goal attainment recently introduced by Heckhausen and Gollwitzer (1987; Gollwitzer, 1990, 1991; Heckhausen, 1989). This model conceptualizes the course of realizing one's wishes and desires as the traversing of four subsequent action phases, and it is assumed that different tasks are to be solved in each phase.

In the first, the so-called *predecisional action phase*, the individual sets priorities between the many desires that are commonly entertained by deliberating on the desirability and feasibility of the wishes or desires at hand. A choice is made on the basis of these criteria so that highly attractive desires that are perceived as potentially achievable are given highest priority. In the subsequent *postdecisional, preactional phase* the individual faces the task of initiating behaviors that lead to the eventual fulfillment of the selected wishes and desires. The individual is expected to work out plans that specify *when*, *where*, and *how* this implementation is to be done, all to promote the timely initiation and effective execution of relevant behaviors and thus prevent any undue delays in achieving one's desires. Once behaviors are initiated, the individual has entered the so-called *action phase*, in which the focus is on coming up with a successful performance. In the final *evaluative phase*, the individual examines whether the outcomes obtained at last actually match what originally had been desired. If they do not, the whole sequence or parts of it may be traversed again to ensure a better agreement between actual and desired outcomes.

This sequence of action phases is a description of the conscious and reflective pursuit of one's wishes and desires. The fact that the model describes the conscious control of goal achievement makes it highly suitable for discussing the functions of intentions (Gollwitzer, 1993). After all, intentions are conscious mental acts formed in the service of wish fulfillment. Through the model of action phases it becomes evident that goal intentions and implementation intentions are formed for different purposes; in addition, they seem to serve these purposes in different ways.

Goal intentions play their role at the transition between the predecisional action phase and the postdecisional (preactional) phase. By forming goal intentions people end deliberation over their wishes and desires and set priorities by transforming some of them into binding goals. In this way conflict is ended and the individual becomes focused on the realization of his or her goals. Goal intentions further the realization of the implied end states in various ways. First, they put an end to deliberative thoughts about the pros and cons of their pursuit (see Gollwitzer, 1991; Jones & Gerard, 1967). Second, they turn people's thoughts toward issues of implementing the chosen wish or goal (Gollwitzer, 1991; Heckhausen & Gollwitzer, 1987), directing their attention toward goal achievement. Ruminative thoughts become focused on the desired goal state (Klinger, 1975; Martin & Tesser, 1989), and the experience of not having achieved the goal creates a sense of incompleteness that leads to negative affect (Bandura, 1991) and elicits goal-directed activity (Gollwitzer & Wicklund, 1985; Wicklund & Gollwitzer, 1982). If the goal endures so that the individual keeps pursuing it over time and if these efforts are consistently paired with the same kind of situational context, goal intentions may start to guide goal-directed behaviors by the auto-motive processes described above (see also Bargh, 1990).

In the model of action phases, *implementation intentions* play a different role from goal intentions. They are formed in the postdecisional, preactional phase, when the initiation of goal-directed behaviors becomes (or is anticipated to become) a problem. According to the model of action phases their role is to promote the initiation of goal-directed behaviors. Implementation intentions are thought to ease the transition from the postdecisional, but still preactional phase to the actual, behavioral pursuit of the goal in the actional phase. Accordingly, they are a vital part of planning the execution and in particular the initiation of goal-directed behaviors and are thus understood to be in the service of a respective goal intention.

In fact the initation of goal-directed behaviors easily becomes delayed. For instance, people become uncertain about acting here and now, as compared with acting later and somewhere else. Such conflict may also originate from the question of showing one or the other type of behavior or using one kind of means instead of another. In any case, goal achievement is halted until such conflicts are solved. But when no conflict is experienced goal pursuit also becomes delayed whenever the individual fails to recognize a given situation as suitable for goal pursuit (i.e., as a good opportunity). Moreover, even when the individual recognizes the present situation as a good opportunity to act, the individual may fail to respond fast enough and thus let the opportunity slip by.

Many situational contexts that are highly suitable for goal pursuit and thus qualify as good opportunities fail to be exploited because they are embedded in a more complex situational context that makes them hard to detect or because they present themselves for only a short time. Relevant examples are ubiquitous in the realm of social interaction. We know from experience that, even if one has decided to end an unpleasant conversation as soon as possible (i.e., has formed the respective goal intention), it is hard to discover a good time to break it off. Often, however, it is even harder to seize a good opportunity quickly when it appears. This example seems to suggest that good opportunities are only missed when they are hard to detect or present themselves very briefly, but this is just part of the reason people frequently fail to seize good opportunities. When people are highly absorbed in some ongoing activity, wrapped up in demanding ruminations, gripped by an emotional experience, or simply tired, they may even fail to make use of opportunities that are relatively easy to detect and present themselves for some time.

Would implementation intentions prevent people from letting opportunities slip by under such adverse circumstances? We believe they would. The underlying theory is that by forming implementation intentions people transfer control over goal-directed activities from the self to the environment (Gollwitzer, 1993). The intended behavior is subjected to external control through the environmental cues specified in one's implementation intention. When these cues are encountered they are expected to prompt the intended behavior directly, that is, without further conscious thoughts directed toward the initiation of goal-directed actions. Accordingly, it is hypothesized (Gollwitzer, 1993) that this heightened behavioral readiness rests on automatic processes. The specified opportunity sets directly in motion psychological processes that are instrumental to the execution of the intended behavior.

Before we turn to experimental studies testing this hypothesis, it seems appropriate first to demonstrate the postulated importance of implementation intentions. Thus, we asked the question of whether people actually furnish their goal intentions with implementation intentions and whether the formation of implementation intentions actually helps people to attain their goals.

Effects of Implementation Intentions on Goal Achievement

A CORRELATIONAL STUDY

Gollwitzer and Brandstätter (1990) asked female university students right before Christmas break to indicate a personal project (i.e., a goal intention) that they wanted to achieve during the break. Subjects named various projects: some were career related (e.g., writing a seminar paper), others were lifestyle related (e.g., finding a new apartment), or interpersonal (e.g., settling a fight with one's parents). To test our postulate that implementation intentions promote goal achievement, we asked subjects whether they had also formed an intention on *when* and *where* to get started. Subjects had to indicate by a simple "yes" or "no" answer whether they entertained such a supplementary intention. As it turned out, two-thirds of the subjects had formed implementation intentions.

A week after Christmas break, we wrote a follow-up letter to our subjects inquiring whether they had actually completed the critical project. They were asked to indicate on a simple questionnaire whether they had finished their project over Christmas break. Despite the heterogeneity of projects, subjects who had furnished their project with an implementation intention were significantly more successful in achieving their project during Christmas break than were subjects without an implementation intention. Actually, more than 60% of the subjects who had formed an implementation intention before Christmas did complete their project. Completion rate for subjects without an implementation intention was much lower; less than 25%.

This pattern of data suggests that the formation of implementation intentions is an efficient strategy to promote the achievement of one's goals. The college students who used it were twice as successful in achieving their goals as were those who did not employ it. Moreover, it appears that this strategy is rather popular. Two-thirds of our subjects had turned to it in an effort to ensure the completion of their projects before the end of Christmas break. Because of the correlational nature of this study, however, having formed an implementation intention may not have been the critical variable that produced this pattern of data. Some third variable might have affected both the formation of implementation intentions and the completion of subjects' projects. To rule out such alternative explanations, we conducted an experimental study in which implementation intentions were manipulated.

AN EXPERIMENTAL REPLICATION

In this study, we created the same goal intention in all of the subjects and then randomly instructed half of the sample to form a respective implementation intention. We ran the study with a large number of male and female university students, again before their Christmas break. In a cover story they were told that we were conducting a demographic study on how people spend Christmas Eve. They should therefore write a report on how they had experienced that evening and send this report to the institute. To ensure vivid reports, they should be written no later than 2 d after Christmas Eve (in Germany December 25 and 26 are holidays).

Half the subjects were then handed a questionnaire that instructed them to form an implementation intention specifying (in writing) *when* and *where* during these two holidays they intended to write their report. These subjects picked a specific time (e.g., right after church) and a certain place (e.g., in a quiet corner in the living room) for implementing this project. The other half of the subjects (control subjects) were not requested to form such intentions. When we analyzed the reports we received after Christmas in terms of the date when they were written, it turned out that more than two-thirds of the implementation-intention subjects wrote their reports within the requested time period as compared to less than one-third of the control subjects. We could confidently rule out the possibility that subjects deceived us by writing false dates on their reports by checking the postmarks on their return letters. Control subjects' letters carried significantly later postmarks than implementation-intention subjects.

Committing oneself to a specific time as well as to a specific place apparently helped implementation subjects to fulfill their goal, that is, to write a report about Christmas Eve within 2 d after this event. Since we had randomly assigned subjects to conditions, we can assume that both groups of subjects did not differ with respect to the degree to which they wanted to help us conduct our presumed demographic study on how people experience Christmas Eve. The only difference between groups was in whether subjects had formed an implementation intention, and this difference was an effective one. One may be tempted to interpret this effect of implementation intentions in terms of obedience to the authority of the experimenter. Being aware of this problem, the experimenter granted subjects absolute anonymity. Employing a sophisticated coding system made it possible to match the first questionnaire subjects had filled out with the reports they sent to the institute. It was impossible, however, to discover which subject handed in which questionnaire or report. Most important, the experimenter took great pains to explain to subjects this consequence of our coding system.

In summarizing the two studies presented, it appears that whenever a goal intention is furnished with implementation intentions its chances of becoming accomplished drastically increase. It seems worthwhile, therefore, to move on and raise the question of how implementation intentions work. Our hypothesis assumes a direct control of the intended behaviors through the situational contexts specified in implementation intentions. In a set of different experiments we tried to test various implications of this assumption (Gollwitzer, 1993). These will be elaborated in the section to follow.

How Do Implementation Intentions Work?

Automatic control of behavior implies that a situational context directly instigates psychological processes that favor the initiation of this behavior. Direct or automatic control of a process is commonly associated with one or more of the following features (see Bargh, 1992; 1994). First, the processes under automatic control should be instigated without any conscious intent once the critical situational context is encountered. As a consequence, high behavioral sensitivity is established with respect to critical situational contexts. Second, the psychological processes on which the initiation of the behavior is based should also be hard to control and rather inescapable, which means they are autonomous and involuntarily run to completion once they have been triggered. Finally, behavior that is under direct control of a certain situational context should be initiated rather efficiently, which implies that the critical situation elicits the behavior independent of the focus of conscious intention. This rather attentionless initiation allows us to place remaining attentional capacity on performing other tasks than the control of the behavior at hand.

In what follows we present experiments that were designed to test whether implementation intentions turn specified opportunities into direct elicitors of respective psychological processes and behaviors. More specifically, we test whether these processes are set in motion without conscious intent and whether these are controllable. In addition, the initiation of the intended behavior in the presence of the critical situational context is analyzed with respect to its efficiency.

SUBLIMINAL PRESENTATION OF THE CRITICAL SITUATIONAL CONTEXT

A recent dissertation study by Malzacher (1992) explored whether the opportunity specified in an implementation intention prompts cognitive processes that facilitate initiation of the intended action without conscious intent. The processes considered were the automatic activation of knowledge that is instrumental to the effective initiation of the intended action and the automatic inhibition of knowledge that potentially disturbs the initiation of this action. If, for instance, an intended action consisted of retaliating to an insult in the form of a verbal complaint, facilitory knowledge would entail attributes to be ascribed to an unfriendly person, whereas inhibitory knowledge would entail attributes one would ascribe to a friendly person. Malzacher (1992) actually used a retaliation paradigm (modeled after Zillmann & Cantor, 1976) to test this line of thought.

In her experiment, two of three groups were treated by the first experimenter in an unfriendly, provocative manner via a taped recording. The third group, who heard a neutral tape with the same voice, served as a control group. After the unfriendly episode had occurred, a second experimenter encouraged subjects in the goal-intention condition to confront the first experimenter at a later time. For subjects in the implementation-intention condition the second experimenter additionally made plans with the subjects as to when and how they would tell the unfriendly experimenter what they thought of her (in this case they were given some adequate adjectives). This resulted in the following implementation intention: "As soon as I see this person, I'll tell her what an unfriendly person she is!" Finally, all subjects were made familiar with the unfriendly experimenter (as well as other experimenters) by photographs.

In an allegedly independent second study (run by the second experimenter) subjects had to read a series of successively presented adjectives as quickly as possible from a screen. The adjective list consisted of positive and negative words, all suitable for describing people. Shortly before each adjective (average stimulus onset asynchrony [SOA]: about 100 ms), either the face of a neutral experimenter or that of the unfriendly experimenter was presented subliminally in random order. The faces were presented for an extremely short time (less than 10 ms on average) and were pattern masked. The chosen presentation time was below the individual perception threshold that had been determined at the outset of the experiment. This procedure ensures that subjects did not notice the faces presented prior to the adjectives, and, therefore, subjects' speed of reading the adjectives should not be affected by any conscious processes elicited by these faces. In addition, the narrow time gaps between the onset of the faces and the adjectives (SOAs) should also prevent conscious processes from taking control over subjects' reading responses (see Bargh et al., 1992; Neely, 1977; Warren, 1977).

In the implementation-intention condition, negative adjectives presented directly after the face of the unfriendly experimenter tended to be read faster than those presented directly after the face of a neutral experimenter. Moreover, positive adjectives were read much more slowly after presentation of the face of the unfriendly experimenter than after presentation of the neutral face. Most important, this pattern of data was observed neither in the control group nor in the goal-intention group. Apparently, when implementation intentions are formed, negative adjectives are more easily accessible in the presence of the critical stimulus, whereas access to positive attributes is hindered. This suggests that the stimulus specified in an implementation intention directly elicits processes (here it is the activation of relevant knowledge and the inhibition of irrelevant knowledge) that facilitate the initiation of the intended action. The present findings also tell us that the mere formation of a goal intention is not sufficient to produce this effect. Apparently, automatic facilitation of action initiation only occurs when goal intentions are supplemented with implementation intentions.

SPECIFIED SITUATIONAL CONTEXTS ATTRACT ATTENTION

Chances to promote goal achievement often fail to be utilized because good opportunities that present themselves in immediate social or nonsocial surroundings escape our attention. The reason for this is that attention is focused on other things that have nothing to do with the question of how to achieve the intended goal at hand. Implementation intentions would alleviate this problem if specified opportunities and means disrupt focused attention by attracting attention to themselves. It would be particularly helpful if this attention response is automatic in the sense of being inescapable.

How does one test whether opportunity-related stimuli manage to attract attention and thus disrupt focused attention in an uncontrollable manner? A typical focused attention paradigm is the so-called dichotic listening task, in which words are presented to both ears simultaneously and subjects are instructed to repeat (i.e., shadow) the words presented to one ear (i.e., the attended channel) and ignore the words presented to the other ear (i.e., the nonattended channel). Focusing attention to the shadowed ear becomes difficult when the words presented to the nonattended ear attract attention by themselves, whether these words relate to temporarily or chronically active categories or schemata (see Johnston & Dark,

1986, pp. 63–65). Examples are words related to a personal attribute (e.g., independence) with respect to which subjects are schematic (Bargh, 1982), sexually explicit words in a college student sample high on state anxiety (Nielsen & Sarason, 1981), and word passages with which subjects had been made highly familiar before performing the dichotic listening task (Johnston, 1978). Accordingly, we hypothesized that words related to intended opportunities and means should succeed in attracting attention to themselves despite subjects' attempts effectively to shadow irrelevant words presented to the attended ear.

Whether an item presented on the nonattended channel has the potential to attract attention and thus disrupt focused attention can be assessed in two different ways, by checking whether shadowing becomes faulty, that is, shadowing speed decreases and shadowing mistakes increase (see Dawson & Schell, 1982; Nielsen & Sarason, 1981), and, more sensitively, by testing whether subjects allocate more attention to the target channel in an attempt to hinder disruption and prevent faulty shadowing (Egeth, 1967; Kahneman, 1973; Logan, 1980). The amount of attention allocated to the shadowing task is commonly assessed by the probe reaction time technique (Bargh, 1982; Johnston, 1978; Johnston & Heinz, 1978), in which subjects are instructed to optimize shadowing while using remaining capacities to respond to a subsidiary probe stimulus (e.g., quickly turning off a light that goes on at irregular intervals). It is assumed (see also Kahneman, 1973; Logan, 1979) that the more attention is required by the shadowing task, the slower are subjects' responses to subsidiary visual probe stimuli.

Following these ideas, we (with Merit Mertin) recently performed two experiments in which words related to opportunities and means specified in implementation intentions were presented to the nonattended channel in a dichotic listening task. These critical words were solicited from subjects in the following manner. First they had to name a project (i.e., goal intention) that they intended to achieve in the near future and indicate the degree to which its implementation was given priority. Then they were asked to divide the implementation of this project into five major steps and commit themselves (in writing) to when, where, and how they wanted to implement each step. From these implementation intentions we took the critical words (i.e., the specified opportunities and means) for the dichotic listening task.

In the first study, subjects had to perform the dichotic listening task at a second visit to the institute (2 d later) where they first had to check whether their implementation intentions were still valid. Then they were asked (in an allegedly independent second study) to shadow four stimulus word blocks presented to the right ear after having worked on a sample block of words. All these words were irrelevant to subjects' implementation intentions, as were two of the four blocks of words presented simultaneously to the nonattended left ear. The other two word blocks were filled with critical words. A probing light was turned on at various points during the four stimulus word blocks, and subjects' probe reaction times were measured. Supporting our hypothesis that critical words related to specified opportunities and means attract attention, critical word lists reduced subjects' speed in turning off the probing light. Apparently, subjects had to pay more attention to the primary task (i.e., the shadowing task) and thus fell back on the subsidiary task. Moreover, with control subjects who had been yoked to experimental subjects (i.e., they studied the implementation intentions of one or the other experimental subject), we did not observe any effects of the critical word lists on probe reaction times.

In a replication study, we also assessed subjects' shadowing performance (in terms of both errors and speed), and we applied a recognition test that allowed us to determine whether subjects had switched attention to the critical words on the nonattended channel. Again, the critical words turned out to be highly disruptive to focused attention. Not only did they reduce subjects' speed in turning off the probing light as observed in the first study, they also worsened subjects' shadowing performance. As observed by Dawson and Schell (1982), shadowing errors are a clear indication that switches in attention to the nonattended channel have occurred. It is not surprising, therefore, that recognition performance was better for critical than for noncritical words.

Thus, it appears that, even when efforts to direct attention to the shadowing task are stepped up (as indicated by the reduced speed in turning off the probing light), subjects cannot escape the involuntary attention response to the critical words (as indicated by a weak shadowing and a high recognition performance). Further support for our hypothesis that opportunities and means specified in implementation intentions are disruptive to focused attention came from control subjects who had been yoked to experimental subjects as was done in the first study. For these subjects, critical words did not produce any of the effects observed in experimental subjects.

One has to keep in mind that, in this set of two experiments, intended opportunities and means were presented to subjects in terms of a verbal description only. When subjects in everyday life actually enter a situational context that entails these opportunities and means in reality, their potential to attract attention should be even stronger. This implies that they will not escape people's attention, even when attention is focused on other things than the respective goal pursuit.

EFFICIENT ACTION INITIATION

A central feature of the automatic initiation of an action is effectiveness. Automated actions are performed swiftly once the relevant situational context is encountered. If this were true for the initiation of the behaviors specified in implementation intentions, this would not only testify to the automatic, direct control of behavior through implementation intentions but also have the pragmatic consequence that people who have formed implementation intentions can successfully use good opportunities that only present themselves very briefly.

In the domain of social influence and persuasion good opportunities to make one's point do not last forever. They are particularly short-lived when it comes to making counterarguments to an opponent's determined expression of his or her point of view. Following this line of thought in her dissertation, Brandstätter (1992, Study 1) developed a new experimental paradigm that allowed her to study whether implementation intentions lead to the swift initiation of the intended behavior when the specified opportunity is encountered. Male university students were asked to take a convincing counterposition on racist remarks made by a confederate presented on videotape; all of the subjects readily complied to this request. After the subjects were made familiar with these remarks in a first viewing of the video, a second run was carried out so that subjects could mark those points on the tape that they considered to be suitable (i.e., a good opportunity) for a counterargument. One group of subjects was additionally asked to make a resolution to deliver certain counterarguments later at the marked places (implementation-intention condition). In a modified third run (eight new remarks of the confederate were added to the eight already presented), the subjects were finally allowed to stop the videotape at any point and deliver their opinion on audiotape.

Without subjects' being aware of it, a computer recorded the marks they had made on the videotape and also the time at which they started to speak. In this way it was possible to determine whether the subjects actually seized the opportunities they had marked on the tape for speaking up and to compute the relative frequency with which each subject spoke up within a narrowly defined critical time period surrounding the points previously marked. This relative frequency was significantly higher for the subjects in the implementation-intention condition than for control subjects, who had merely been requested to mark good opportunities without, however, forming any intentions that linked specific counterarguments to these opportunities. There was an additional control group to counter the alternative explanation that this effect was solely due to the implementation-intention subjects' concern with specific counterarguments. Subjects in this group expected to deliver specific counterarguments in writing at a later time. Still, they were comparatively less successful in using the marked opportunities to speak up than were the experimental subjects.

One might argue that subjects in the implementation-intention condition responded so readily to their "marks" because they wanted to appear consistent to the experimenter. This seems unlikely, however, because the experimenter's cover story focused subjects' concerns on choosing good opportunities to act and not on acting swiftly once these opportunities arise. Actually, subjects were not aware of the fact that the experimenter had recorded their "marks" and was thus in a position to determine how swiftly they responded to the opportunities marked. Also, at the outset of the experiment a number of personality dimensions had been measured through an adjective version (16 PA) of the 16 PF questionnaire (Brandstätter, 1988). If appearing consistent to the experimenter had been an issue for implementation-intention subjects, those high on the dimension of social dependency should have been particularly eager to achieve consistency and thus responded most readily. This was not the case, however.

The subjects in this study all intended to achieve the goal of taking a convincing counterposition to a racist view. Still, good opportunities elicited goal-directed behaviors (i.e., presenting counterarguments) with greater speed when subjects had linked critical situations (good opportunities) to behaviors (counterarguments) by forming implementation intentions. The mental act of forming such linkages obviously managed to increase the speed of action initiation. This "speeding" effect resembles one of the consequences of habits for the initiation of behavior. As we know from learning theory, habitualized behavior is elicited with comparatively higher speed (Guthrie, 1952, 1959; Hull, 1943, 1952; Thorndike, 1913). Thus, it appears that simple mental acts (i.e., implementation intentions) can mimic a central effect of habits. This is rather amazing in view of the fact that habits commonly result from time-consuming, laborious practice.

Encouraged by these findings, Brandstätter (1992, Study 2) explored whether the quick responding to opportunities specified in implementation intentions is efficient in the sense of requiring little attentional capacity. It was hypothesized that the demands of a dual task should not be reflected in the speed of responding to the critical stimulus, because an automatic or direct control of action initiation should not put much load on limited processing resources (Kahneman & Treisman, 1984; Norman & Shallice, 1986; Posner, 1978; Shiffrin & Schneider, 1977).

Along this line of thought, subjects were asked to work simultaneously on two tasks (dual-task technique), which were both presented on a computer monitor but in two adjacent windows. The primary task consisted of working on meaningless syllables that appeared one by one at a fixed time interval. This task was presented to each subject at low and high difficulty levels (i.e., freely associate to the meaningless syllables and memorize them, respectively), and it was designed in a way that demanded complete and steady attention. The secondary task was to press a button as quickly as possible when numbers appeared but not when letters were shown. Numbers and letters were presented at random intervals, and the numbers constituted the cues for the button-press response.

Half the subjects were instructed to form the intention to respond as quickly as possible to a specific number (i.e., critical number), whereas the other half (control group) were asked to familiarize themselves with the critical number by repeatedly writing it on a sheet of paper. Both groups of subjects were told to do this for the purpose of speeding up their responses to this number. Still, no difference in the speed of the pressing response for critical and noncritical numbers was observed for control subjects. In the implementation-intention group a marked acceleration of responding to the critical number was observed, which was undertaken without being detrimental to the speed of responding to noncritical numbers (the speed for noncritical numbers was similar to that of the control group). Also, this pattern of data was not affected by the level of difficulty of the primary task.

The results of both studies suggest that the initiation of behavior can be speeded up by forming implementation intentions. Most interesting, this effect seems to occur automatically in the sense of not requiring much processing capacity. Once the specified opportunity is encountered, action initiation is promoted very efficiently so that the individual's performance on dual tasks does not suffer.

Implications and Prospects

The research we have presented on how implementation intentions work suggests that the formation of an implementation intention is a conscious act that has automatic consequences. This discovery calls into question two currently popular views in research on automaticity. First, automatic control of behavior is commonly seen as a result of frequently performing this behavior in the same type of situation (e.g., Shiffrin & Schneider, 1977; for an exception see Logan, 1988). Contrary to this view, our experiments document that automatic processes instigated by implementation intentions are the result of a single mental act (i.e, the formation of an implementation intention). The type of automaticity observed in our experiments apparently plays by different rules. It seems possible that the commitment (or willpower) people attach to the situation-behavior contingencies they proclaim in their implementation intentions creates strong links, a strength that commonly can only be attained through frequent and consistent situation-response pairing. A second and related popular view in automaticity research is that only habitualized behaviors can be subject to automatic control, whereas the effective execution of willed or intended behaviors requires conscious control (see, e.g., Norman & Shallice, 1986). Again, our studies do not square with this view. The behaviors affected by implementation intentions are definitely intended and willed; still, they were subject to automatic processes.

Our findings are also relevant to recent theoretical work on planning as presented by cognitive psychologists (e.g., Bruce & Newman, 1978; Hayes-Roth & Hayes-Roth, 1979; Kreitler & Kreitler, 1987; Mannes & Kintsch 1991) and researchers in the field of artificial intelligence (Wilensky, 1983). Both of these research traditions construe planning in terms of the processes that lead to the viable sequencing of behaviors so that certain behavioral tasks or goals, such as fetching a book from the library, are performed smoothly and effectively. It seems plausible to assume that this kind of planning is subjected to conscious control as it demands the mental simulation of future events, activities, and hindrances (Miller et al., 1960; Taylor & Schneider, 1989).

In addition, the translation of such a plan into action should be primarily based on conscious control, because the execution of this plan is not overlearned and thus has not been habitualized. As a consequence, the plan needs to be retrieved from memory once the individual sets out to solve the task, and the various steps of the plan will be implemented in an intentional and controlled manner that should demand much attentional capacity.

Our research on implementation intentions suggests that people can (and do) complement the more complex and analytic form of planning by a comparatively simple and crude form of planning, that is, the formation of implementation intentions. Here, the individual commits himself or herself to initiating a certain behavior in the presence of a specified situational cue. This strategically formed contingency apparently leads to the direct control of the intended behavior through the situational cue. Possibly the strongest support for the proposition that these distinct aspects of planning are subject to different modes of control (i.e., conscious vs. automatic) comes from neuropsychology. Patients with lesions to the prefrontal region of the brain show major impairments when it comes to planning in the form of finding a viable route to the solution of a given behavioral problem (see Shallice, 1982). This effect is not surprising, because the frontal lobe is commonly considered to be the site of conscious control of thought and action (Luria, 1966; Walsh, 1978), and this type of planning requires conscious control. Most interesting, however, frontal lobe patients do not evidence any impairments when it comes to the aftereffects of planning in the sense of forming implementation intentions. In a recent dissertation experiment with frontal lobe patients, Lengfelder (1994) discovered that implementation intentions speed up the initiation of intended actions in the same way as was observed with university students (see Brandstätter, 1992, Study 2). Apparently this speed-up effect is based on automatic control processes; no conscious control is needed.

When do people form goal intentions? So far we have not conducted any research on when people form goal intentions, but we assume that they only form implementation intentions when they anticipate problems on the way to goal attainment; otherwise, their formation is unnecessary. This hypothesis corresponds with William James's (1890) distinction between ideo-motor action and willed action. According to James the application of will can only be expected when resistance to performing an action is anticipated or experienced by the individual. Most action, however, is mere ideo-motor action; thinking about the consequences of an action is quickly followed by its execution.

Indirect empirical support for our hypothesis that implementation intentions are formed when people anticipate barriers and hindrances comes from research on action identification theory (Vallacher & Wegner, 1985, 1987). This theory proposes that people may conceive of their goal pursuits at different levels of abstraction. High levels of identification define goals in terms of their ultimate purpose (e.g., getting exercise), whereas low levels of identification refer to the implementational steps (e.g., going to the gym after dinner). Although people generally prefer high levels of identification, they move toward low-level identifications whenever goal achievement becomes problematic (Vallacher et al., 1987). This tendency to think about the implementational intricacies once goal pursuit is hampered is a first step toward actually forming implementation intentions.

The hypothesis that people form implementation intentions only when problems in achieving the goal are anticipated implies that people may differ in their tendencies to form implementation intentions. It seems plausible that people who worry much about the successful implementation of their goals anticipate more hindrances than those who refuse to worry. As a consequence, the latter should be less willing to prepare themselves for these hindrances and therefore fail to form implementation intentions. Cantor (in this volume) has recently suggested individual differences that pertain to the strategies people prefer in achieving their life tasks. For instance, in the realm of achievement-related life tasks, such as being productive at work or getting tenure, Norem and Cantor (1986) discovered a strategy called "defensive pessimism" that is successfully used by people who suffer from fears in achievement settings. It implies a concern with the details of the upcoming achievement task, and preparing oneself ahead of time for performing this task. It seems likely that forming implementation intentions comprises part of this preparation. From this perspective it comes as no surprise that the strategy of defensive pessimism allows for efficient performance once the individual actually starts working on the achievement task (Showers, 1992).

The interplay of goal intentions and implementation intentions. The relation of the two types of intentions has been the starting point of an irreconcilable controversy in traditional German will psychology (see Ach, 1935, vs. Lewin, 1926, 1951). Two recent observations suggest that the effectiveness of implementation intentions is independent of the strength or importance of the respective goal intention. First, in an experimental study (Gollwitzer et al., 1990) subjects formed implementation intentions with respect to their wishes, that is, they had not yet formed goal intentions and were still undecided over pursuing the wish. Although these implementation intentions were not backed up by goal intentions, they proved to be effective. Subjects with implementation intentions evidenced an immediate and delayed (by 3 wk) increase in their readiness to form goal intentions, that is, in their willingness to turn their wishes into action. Second, research on action slips has identified a certain type of slip that further suggests that the effects of implementation intentions unfold independently of the respective goal intention. These action slips occur because the situation specified in an implementation intention still triggers the intended behavior although the respective goal intention had already been achieved by some other type of action (Heckhausen & Beckmann, 1990) or had become obsolete (Birenbaum, 1930).

As much as these observations speak for independence of implementation intentions and goal intentions, it is easy to find convincing arguments for the counterposition of dependence. After all, action slips of the kind noted above are the exception rather than the rule. This implies that implementation intentions possess the potential to be sensitive to the strength of the respective goal intention. Accordingly, one would expect that, in the retaliation study reported above (Malzacher, 1992), an apology should not only weaken subjects' goal intention to retaliate (see Ohbuchi et al., 1989); the observed effects on reading speed for positive and negative adjectives when primed subliminally by the face of the critical experimenter should also be attenuated. In other words, situations specified in implementation intentions should no longer trigger automatic processes that help the initiation of the intended behavior once the goal intention to retaliate has become obsolete.

In any case, there are good arguments for the dependence as well as the independence of implementation intentions and goal intentions. Given this state of affairs, empirical research on the interplay of goal intentions and implementation intentions should attempt to identify the conditions that make the effects of implementation intentions sensitive to the strength of the respective goal intention.

Impulse Control. So far we have studied the role of implementation intentions and the respective processes in the context of action initiation. But getting started may only be one of the conditions in which it pays to form implementation intentions; controlling one's impulses might be another. Imagine a person who has decided to stop drinking (i.e., formed the respective goal intention of staying away from alcohol) but is still tempted to take a sip of wine whenever he or she opens the refrigerator. One effective way of preparing for this temptation may be the formation of an implementation intention that favors the execution of an antagonistic behavior, such as eating instead of drinking (e.g., "I'll grab a bite to eat whenever I open the refrigerator").

It seems possible that this implementation intention will effectively suppress any competing responses related to drinking alcohol, at least in this situation. This possibility raises the question of whether urges related to harassment (as presented above) may also be curbed through the formation of implementation intentions. The problem, however, seems to be that people who are driven by such urges are not aware of the eliciting situational cues (i.e., the power-related stimuli in the interpersonal situation). Thus, even if harassers form the goal intention to prepare themselves against these urges, they would not know which situational cues to specify in their implementation intentions. In this case, some outside counseling on this matter would seem indispensable.

General Conclusion

The recent resurgence of research on goals (Bandura, 1991; Locke & Latham, 1990) has construed their operation by means of rather complex conscious processes rather than direct regulating action. For instance, studies by Bandura and Cervone (1983; see also Becker, 1978; Strang et al., 1978) point to the cognized discrepancies between actual performance and the to-be-achieved performance (standards) as specified in one's goals. It is assumed that experienced discrepancies create dissatisfaction (a negative incentive) that in turn instigates goal-directed action. The experience of a discrepancy is the result of explicit comparative thoughts, so this type of instigation of goal-directed activity must be considered conscious and deliberate.

There is a further conscious process related to the instigation of goal-directed action, one that works as a moderator of the instigation of goal-directed action through cognized discrepancies. It is the individual's thoughtful reflection on his or her capabilities to reduce the experienced discrepancy. People start to reduce the discrepancy only when they reach the conclusion that they possess the relevant capabilities (high respective self-efficacy beliefs; Cervone, 1989; Cervone & Peake, 1986; Peake & Cervone, 1989).

In the process of judging their capabilities, people may become involved with yet another conscious mental activity that is instrumental to goal achievement, that is, the preparation of the initiation and execution of goal-directed efforts aimed at discrepancy reduction by more or less thoughtful planning. There is evidence that goal setting per se manages to stimulate people to develop plans on how to attain their goals (Earley et al., 1987; Heckhausen & Gollwitzer, 1987; Smith et al., in press). No explicit experience of a discrepancy between actual performance and the performance one seeks to attain has to be induced to instigate planning.

Finally, there is a conscious mental strategy that positively affects goal-directed activities by focusing on the goal-related end states or standards. People can toy with raising or reducing these end states or standards. They are expected to employ this strategy, for instance, when they have just achieved a medium-level standard. By reactively raising the standard, they strategically induce a new discrepancy that in turn stimulates the initiation of further goal-directed activities (Bandura & Cervone, 1986).

None of these different but highly effective ways of consciously controlling goal-directed action have been discussed in this chapter. We do not doubt the powerful effects that conscious thought has on people's goal pursuits. Our concern is a different one: we want to point to the role of automatic processes in people's goal-directed activities. As the findings reported in this chapter suggest, individuals can capitalize on nonconscious processes. Actually, this direct control of goal-directed action is a vital aspect of people's attempts to achieve their goals, and therefore the resurgence of goal psychology should not diminish their importance. It remains to future research to analyze questions of how conscious and automatic control of goal-directed action interrelate, when and where each of these types of control is most effective, and what strengths and weaknesses are associated with conscious as compared with direct, environmental control of goal-directed action.

NOTES

1. There were more females than males in the experiment, so their data contributed more to the overall means.

2. The rationale for using the ambiguous sex words instead of more obviously sex-related words (e.g., "sex," "intercourse," "fondle") is that subjects may well have hesitated to say them in the pronunciation task, and even a slight hesitation would greatly distort those times (which averaged less than half a second per word in the experiment).

INTEGRATIVE VIEWS OF MOTIVATION, COGNITION, AND EMOTION

REFERENCES

Abelson, R. P. (1976). Script processing in attitude formation and decision making. In J. S. Carroll & J. W. Payne (Eds.), *Cognition and social behavior* (pp. 33–46). Hillsdale, NJ: Erlbaum.

Abelson, R. P. (1981). The psychological status of the script concept. *American Psychologist, 36,* 715–729.

Ach, N. (1935). Analyse des Willens. In E. Abderhalden (Ed.), *Handbuch der biologischen Arbeitsmethoden* (Vol. 6). Berlin: Urban & Schwarzenberg.

Ajzen, I. (1988). *Attitudes, personality, and behavior.* Chicago: Dorsey.

Anderson, J. R. (1983). *The architecture of cognition.* Cambridge, MA: Harvard University Press.

Anderson, J. R. (1987). Skill acquisition: Compilation of weak-method problem solutions. *Psychological Review, 94,* 192–210.

Anderson, J. R. (1992). Automaticity and the ACT* theory. *American Journal of Psychology, 105,* 165–180.

Anderson, J. R. & Bower, G. H. (1973). *Human associative memory.* New York: Winston.

Atkinson, J. W. (1958). *Motives in fantasy, action, and society.* Princeton, NJ: Van Nostrand.

Atkinson, J. W., & Birch, D. (1970). *A dynamic theory of action.* New York: Wiley.

Balota, D. A., & Lorch, R. F., Jr. (1986). Depth of automatic spreading activation: Mediated priming effects in pronunciation but not in lexical decision. *Journal of Experimental Psychology: Learning, Memory, and Cognition, 12,* 336–345.

Bandura, A. (1991). Self-regulation of motivation through anticipatory and self-reactive mechanisms. In R. Dienstbier (Ed.) *Nebraska Symposium on Motivation, 1991.* Lincoln: University of Nebraska Press.

Bandura, A., & Cervone, D. (1983). Self-evaluative and self-efficacy mechanisms governing the motivational effects of goal systems. *Journal of Personality and Social Psychology, 45,* 1017–1028.

Bandura, A., & Cervone, D. (1986). Differential engagement of self-reactive influences in cognitive motivation. *Organizational Behavior and Human Decision Processes, 31,* 92–113.

Bargh, J. A. (1982). Attention and automaticity in the processing of self-relevant information. *Journal of Personality and Social Psychology, 43,* 425–436.

Bargh, J. A. (1989). Conditional automaticity: Varieties of automatic influence in social perception and cognition. In J. S. Uleman & J. A. Bargh (Eds.), *Unintended thought.* New York: Guilford.

Bargh, J. A. (1990). Auto-motives: Preconscious determinants of social interaction. In E. T. Higgins & R. M. Sorrentino (Eds.), *Handbook of motivation and cognition.* New York: Guilford.

Bargh, J. A. (1992). The ecology of automaticity: Toward establishing the conditions needed to produce automatic processing effects. *American Journal of Psychology, 105,* 181–199.

Bargh, J. A. (1994). The four horsemen of automaticity: Awareness, intention, efficiency, and control in social cognition. In R. S. Wyer, Jr., & T. K. Srull (Eds.), *Handbook of social cognition* (2nd ed.). Hillsdale, NJ: Erlbaum.

Bargh, J. A., Barndollar, K., & Gollwitzer, P. M. (1993a). *Environmental control of behavior*. Unpublished manuscript, New York University, New York.

Bargh, J. A., Bond, R. N., Lombardi, W. J., & Tota, M. E. (1986). The additive nature of chronic and temporary sources of construct accessibility. *Journal of Personality and Social Psychology, 50*, 869–878.

Bargh, J. A., Chaiken, S., Govender, R., & Pratto, F. (1992). The generality of the automatic attitude activation effect. *Journal of Personality and Social Psychology, 62*, 893–910.

Bargh, J. A., Lombardi, W. J., & Higgins, E. T. (1988). Automaticity of person x situation effects on impression formation: It's just a matter of time. *Journal of Personality and Social Psychology, 55*, 599–605.

Bargh, J. A., & Pietromonaco, P. (1982). Automatic information processing and social perception: The influence of trait information presented outside of conscious awareness on impression formation. *Journal of Personality and Social Psychology, 43*, 437–449.

Bargh, J. A., & Pratto, F. (1986). Individual construct accessibility and perceptual selection. *Journal of Experimental Social Psychology, 22*, 293–311.

Bargh, J. A., Raymond, P., Pryor, J., & Strack, F. (1994). *The attractiveness of the underling: An automatic power → sex assocation in men likely to sexually harass and aggress*. Manuscript submitted for publication.

Bargh, J. A., & Thein, R. D. (1985). Individual construct accessibility, person memory, and the recall-judgment link: The case of information overload. *Journal of Personality and Social Psychology, 49*, 1129–1146.

Bargh, J. A., & Tota, M. E. (1988). Context-dependent automatic processing in depression: Accessibility of negative constructs with regard to self but not others. *Journal of Personality and Social Psychology, 54*, 925–939.

Bassili, J. N., & Smith, M. C. (1986). On the spontaneity of trait attribution: Converging evidence for the role of cognitive strategy. *Journal of Personality and Social Psychology, 50*, 239–245.

Becker, L. J. (1978). Joint effects of feedback and goal setting on performance: A field study of residential energy conservation. *Journal of Applied Psychology, 63*, 428–433.

Birenbaum, G. (1930). Untersuchungen zur Handlungs- und Affektpsychologie. *Psychologische Forschung, 13*, 218–284.

Brandstätter, H. (1988). Sechzehn Persönlichkeits-Adjektivskalen (16 PA) als Forschungsinstrument anstelle des 16 PF. *Zeitschrift für Experimentelle und Angewandte Psychologie, 25*, 370–391.

Brandstätter, V. (1992). *Der Einfluß von Vorsätzen auf die Handlungsinitiierung: Ein Beitrag zur willenspsychologischen Frage der Realisierung von Absichten*. Frankfurt: Lang.

Brewer, W. F., & Dupree, D. A. (1983). Use of plan schemata in the recall and recognition of goal-directed actions. *Journal of Experimental Psychology: Learning, Memory, and Cognition, 9*, 117–129.

Bruce, B., & Newman, D. (1978). Interacting plans. *Cognitive Science, 2*, 195–233.

Bruner, J. S. (1957). On perceptual readiness. *Psychological Review, 64*, 123–152.

Bruner, J. S. (1958). Social psychology and perception. In E. E. Maccoby, T. M. Newcomb, & E. L. Hartley (Eds.), *Readings in social psychology* (3rd ed.). New York: Holt, Rinehart, & Winston.

Cantor, N., & Kihlstrom, J. F. (1987). *Personality and social intelligence.* Englewood Cliffs, NJ: Prentice-Hall.

Cantor, N., & Mischel, W. (1977). Traits as prototypes: Effects on recognition memory. *Journal of Personality and Social Psychology, 35*, 38–48.

Cantor, N., & Mischel, W. (1979). Prototypes in person perception. In L. Berkowitz (Ed.), *Advances in experimental social psychology* (Vol. 12, pp. 3–52). New York: Academic Press.

Carver, C. S., Ganellen, R. J., Froming, W. J., & Chambers, W. (1983). Modeling: An analysis in terms of category accessibility. *Journal of Experimental Social Psychology, 19*, 403–421.

Cervone, D. (1989). Effects of envisioning future activities on self-efficacy judgments and motivation: An availability heuristic interpretation. *Cognitive Therapy and Research, 13*, 247–261.

Cervone, D., & Peake, P. K. (1986). Anchoring, efficacy, and action: The influence of judgmental heuristics on self-efficacy judgments and behavior. *Journal of Personality and Social Psychology, 50*, 492–501.

Dawson, M. E., & Schell, A. M. (1982). Electrodermal responses to attended and nonattended significant stimuli during dichotic listening. *Journal of Experimental Psychology: Human Perception and Performance, 8*, 315–324.

Devine, P. G. (1989). Stereotypes and prejudice: Their automatic and controlled components. *Journal of Personality and Social Psychology, 56*, 680–690.

Earley, P. C., Wojnaroski, P., & Prest, W. (1987). Task planning and energy expended: Explorations on how goals influence performance. *Journal of Applied Psychology, 72*, 107–114.

Egeth, H. (1967). Selective attention. *Psychological Bulletin, 67*, 41–57.

Emmons, R. A. (1989). The personal striving approach to personality. In L. A. Pervin (Ed.), *Goal concepts in personality and social psychology* (pp. 87–126). Hillsdale, NJ: Erlbaum.

Erber, R., & Fiske, S. T. (1984). Outcome dependency and attention to inconsistent information. *Journal of Personality and Social Psychology, 47*, 709–726.

Fazio, R. H., Chen, J., McDonel, E. C., & Sherman, S. J. (1982). Attitude accessibility, attitude-behavior consistency, and the strength of the object-evaluation association. *Journal of Experimental Social Psychology, 18*, 339–357.

Fazio, R. H., Sanbonmatsu, D. M., Powell, M. C., & Kardes, F. R. (1986). On the automatic activation of attitudes. *Journal of Personality and Social Psychology, 50*, 229–238.

Fishbein, M., & Ajzen, I. (1975). *Belief, attitude, intention and behavior: An introduction to theory and research.* Reading, MA: Addison-Wesley.

Fiske, S. T., & Neuberg, S. E. (1990). A continuum of impression formation, from category-based to individuating processes: Influences of information and motivation on attention and interpretation. *Advances in Experimental Social Psychology, 23,* 1–74.

Fitts, P. M., & Posner, M. I. (1967). *Human performance.* Monterey, CA: Brooks-Cole.

Gollwitzer, P. M. (1990). Action phases and mind-sets. In E. T. Higgins & R. M. Sorrentino (Eds.), *Handbook of motivation and cognition: Foundations of social behavior* (Vol. 2, pp. 53–92). New York: Guilford.

Gollwitzer, P. M. (1991). *Abwägen und Planen: Bewußtseinslagen in verschiedenen Handlungsphasen.* Göttingen: Hogrefe.

Gollwitzer, P. M. (1993). Goal achievement: The role of intentions. In W. Stroebe & M. Hewstone (Eds.), *European Review of Social Psychology* (Vol. 4, pp. 141–185). Chichester: Wiley.

Gollwitzer, P. M., & Brandstätter, V. (1990, June). *Do initiation intentions prevent procrastination?* Paper presented at the Eighth General Meeting of the European Association of Experimental Social Psychology, Budapest.

Gollwitzer, P. M., Heckhausen, H., & Ratajczak, H. (1990). From weighing to willing: Approaching a change decision through pre- or postdecisional mentation. *Organizational Behavior and Human Decision Processes, 45,* 41–65.

Gollwitzer, P. M., & Wicklund, R. A. (1985). The pursuit of self-defining goals. In J. Kuhl & J. Beckmann (Eds.), *Action control: From cognition to behavior.* Heidelberg: Springer.

Guthrie, E. R. (1952). *The psychology of learning* (rev. ed.). New York: Harper & Row.

Guthrie, E. R. (1959). Association by contiguity. In S. Koch (Ed.), *Psychology: A study of a science: General systematic formulations, learning, and special processes* (Vol. 2, pp. 158–195). New York: McGraw-Hill.

Hamilton, D. L. (Ed.) (1981). *Cognitive processes in stereotyping and intergroup behavior.* Hillsdale, NJ: Erlbaum.

Hayes-Roth, B. (1977). Evolution of cognitive structure and processes. *Psychological Review, 84,* 260–278.

Hayes-Roth, B., & Hayes-Roth, F. (1979). A cognitive model of planning. *Cognitive Science, 3,* 275–310.

Hebb, D. O. (1948). *Organization of behavior.* New York: Wiley.

Heckhausen, H. (1989). *Motivation und Handeln* (2nd ed.). Berlin: Springer.

Heckhausen, H. (1990). *Motivation and action.* New York: Springer.

Heckhausen, H., & Beckmann, J. (1990). Intentional action and action slips. *Psychological Review, 97,* 36–48.

Heckhausen, H., & Gollwitzer, P. M. (1987). Thought contents and cognitive functioning in motivational versus volitional states of mind. *Motivation and Emotion, 11,* 101–120.

Higgins, E. T. (1989). Knowledge accessibility and activation: Subjectivity and suffering from unconscious sources. In J. S. Uleman & J. A. Bargh (Eds.), *Unintended thought*. New York: Guilford.

Higgins, E. T. (1991). Development of self-regulatory and self-evaluative processes: Costs, benefits, and tradeoffs. In M. R. Gunnar & L. A. Sroufe (Eds.), *The Minnesota Symposia on Child Development: Self processes and development (Vol. 23)*. Hillsdale, NJ: Erlbaum.

Higgins, E. T., & Bargh, J. A. (1987). Social perception and social cognition. *Annual Review of Psychology, 38*, 369–425.

Higgins, E. T., Bargh, J. A., & Lombardi, W. (1985). The nature of priming effects on categorization. *Journal of Experimental Psychology: Learning, Memory, and Cognition, 11*, 59–69.

Higgins, E. T., King, G. A., & Mavin, G. H. (1982). Individual construct accessibility and subjective impressions and recall. *Journal of Personality and Social Psychology, 43*, 35–47.

Higgins, E. T., Rholes, W. S., & Jones, C. R. (1977). Category accessibility and impression formation. *Journal of Experimental Social Psychology, 13*, 141–154.

Horner, M. S. (1974). Fear of success in women. In J. W. Atkinson & J. O. Raynor (Eds.), *Motivation and achievement*. Washington, DC: Winston.

Hull, C. L. (1943). *Principles of behavior*. New York: Appleton-Century-Crofts.

Hull, C. L. (1952). *A behavior system*. New Haven, CT: Yale University Press.

James, W. (1890). *The principles of psychology*. New York: Holt.

Jackson, D. N. (1984). *Personality Research Form manual*. Port Huron, MI: Research Psychologists Press.

Johnston, W. A. (1978). The intrusiveness of familiar nontarget information. *Memory and Cognition, 6*, 38–42.

Johnston, W. A., & Dark, V. J. (1986). Selective attention. *Annual Review of Psychology, 37*, 43–75.

Johnston, W. A., & Heinz, S. P. (1978). Flexibility and capacity demands of attention. *Journal of Experimental Psychology: General, 107*, 420–435.

Jones, E. E., & Gerard, H. B. (1967). *Foundations of social psychology*. New York: Wiley.

Jussim, L. (1986). Self-fulfilling prophecies: A theoretical and integrative review. *Psychological Review, 93*, 429–445.

Kahneman, D. (1973). *Attention and effort*. Englewood Cliffs, NJ: Prentice-Hall.

Kahneman, D., & Treisman, A. M. (1984). Changing views of attention and automaticity. In R. Parasuraman, R. Davies, & J. Beatty (Eds.), *Varieties of attention*. New York: Academic Press.

Klinger, E. (1975). Consequences of commitment to and disengagement from incentives. *Psychological Review, 82*, 1–25.

Kreitler, S., & Kreitler, H. (1987). Conceptions and processes of planning. In S. L. Friedman, E. K. Scholnick, & R. R. Cocking (Eds.), *Blueprints for thinking: The role of planning in cognitive development*. Cambridge: Cambridge University Press.

Kuhl, J. (1986). Motivation and information processing: A new look at decision making, dynamic change, and action control. In R. M. Sorrentino & E. T. Higgins (Eds.), *Handbook of motivation and cognition* (Vol. 1, pp. 404–434). New York: Guilford.

Langer, E. J. (1978). Rethinking the role of thought in social interaction. In J. H. Harvey, W. I. Ickes, & R. F. Kidd (Eds.), *New directions in attribution research* (Vol. 2, pp. 35–58). Hillsdale, NJ: Erlbaum.

Langer, E. J., Blank, A., & Chanowitz, B. (1978). The mindlessness of ostensibly thoughtful action: The role of "placebic" information in interpersonal interaction. *Journal of Personality and Social Psychology, 36,* 635–642.

Lengfelder, A. (1994). *Action initiation with prefrontal lobe patients: The effects of implementation intentions.* Unpublished doctoral dissertation, Ludwig-Maximilians-Universität, Munich.

Lewin, K. (1926). Vorsatz, Wille und Bedürfnis. *Psychologische Forschung, 7,* 330–385.

Lewin, K. (1951). Intention, will, and need. In D. Rapaport (Ed.), *Organization and pathology of thought* (pp. 95–153). New York: Columbia University Press.

Locke, E. A., & Latham, G. P. (1990). *A theory of goal setting and task performance.* Englewood Cliffs, NJ: Prentice-Hall.

Logan, G. D. (1979). On the use of a concurrent memory load to measure attention and automaticity. *Journal of Experimental Psychology: Human Perception and Performance, 5,* 189–207.

Logan, G. D. (1980). Attention and automaticity in Stroop and priming tasks: Theory and data. *Cognitive Psychology, 12,* 523–553.

Logan, G. D. (1988). Toward an instance theory of automatization. *Psychological Review, 95,* 492–527.

Lombardi, W. J., Higgins, E. T., & Bargh, J. A. (1987). The role of consciousness in priming effects on categorization: Assimilation vs. contrast as a function of awareness of the priming task. *Personality and Social Psychology Belletin, 13,* 411–429.

Luria, A. R. (1966). *Higher cortical functions in man.* London: Tavistock.

Malamuth, N. (1988). Predictors of naturalistic sexual aggression. *Journal of Personality and Social Psychology, 50,* 953–962.

Malzacher, J. T. (1992). *Erleichtern Vorsätze die Handlungsinitiierung? Zur Aktivierung der Vornahmehandlung.* Unpublished doctoral dissertation, Ludwig-Maximilians-Universität, Munich.

Mannes, S. M., & Kintsch, W. (1991). Routine computing tasks: Planning as understanding. *Cognitive Science, 15,* 305–342.

Markus, H. (1977). Self-schemata and processing information about the self. *Journal of Personality and Social Psychology, 35,* 63–78.

Martin, L. L., & Tesser, A. (1989). Toward a motivational and structural theory of ruminative thought. In J. S. Uleman & J. A. Bargh (Eds.), *Unintended thought* (pp. 306–323). New York: Guilford.

McClelland, D. C. (1953). *The achievement motive.* New York: Appleton-Century-Crofts.

McClelland, D. C. (1985). *Human motivation.* Glenview, IL: Scott, Foresman.

Miller, G. A., Galanter, E., & Pribram, K. H. (1960). *Plans and the structure of behavior*. New York: Holt, Rinehart, & Winston.

Murray, H. A. (1943). *The Thematic Apperception Test manual*. Cambridge, MA: Harvard University Press.

Neely, J. H. (1977). Semantic priming and retrieval from lexical memory: Roles of inhibitionless spreading activation and limited-capacity attention. *Journal of Experimental Psychology: General, 106*, 225–254.

Neuberg, S. L. (1988). Behavioral implications of information presented outside of conscious awareness: The effect of subliminal presentation of trait information on behavior in the Prisoner's Dilemma game. *Social Cognition, 6*, 207–230.

Newell, A., & Rosenbloom, P. S. (1981). Mechanisms of skill acquisition and the law of practice. In J. R. Anderson (Ed.), *Cognitive skills and their acquisition* (pp. 1–55). Hillsdale, NJ: Erlbaum.

Nielsen, S. L., & Sarason, I. G. (1981). Emotion, personality, and selective attention. *Journal of Personality and Social Psychology, 41*, 945–960.

Nisbett, R. E., & Wilson, T. D. (1977). Telling more than we can know: Verbal reports on mental processes. *Psychological Review, 84*, 231–259.

Norem, J. K., & Cantor, N. (1986). Defensive pessimism: "Harnessing" anxiety as motivation. *Journal of Personality and Social Psychology, 51*, 1208–1217.

Norman, D. A., & Bobrow, D. G. (1976). On the role of active memory processes in perception and cognition. In C. N. Cofer (Ed.), *The structure of human memory* (pp. 114–132). San Francisco: Freeman.

Norman, D. A., & Shallice, T. (1986). Attention to action: Willed and automatic control of behavior. In R. J. Davidson, G. E. Schwartz, & D. Shapiro (Eds.), *Consciousness and self-regulation: Advances in research and theory* (Vol. 4, pp. 1–18). New York: Plenum.

Ohbuchi, K., Kameda, M., & Agarie, N. (1989). Apology as aggression control: Its role in mediating appraisal of and response to harm. *Journal of Personality and Social Psychology, 56*, 219–227.

Peake, P. K., & Cervone, D. (1989). Sequence anchoring and self-efficacy: Primacy effects in the consideration of possibilities. *Social Cognition, 7*, 31–50.

Pervin, L. A. (1989). Goal concepts in personality and social psychology: A historical perspective. In L. A. Pervin (Ed.), *Goal concepts in personality and social psychology* (pp. 1–18). Hillsdale, NJ: Erlbaum.

Posner, M. I. (1978). *Chronometric explorations of mind*. Hillsdale, NJ: Erlbaum.

Pratto, F., & Bargh, J. A. (1991). Stereotyping based on apparently individuating information: Trait and global components of sex stereotypes under attention overload. *Journal of Experimental Social Psychology, 27*, 26–47.

Pryor, J. (1987). Sexual harassment proclivities in men. *Sex Roles, 17*, 269–290.

Read, S. J., Jones, D. K., & Miller, L. C. (1990). Traits as goal-based categories: The importance of goals in the coherence of dispositional categories. *Journal of Personality and Social Psychology, 58*, 1048–1061.

Reuman, D. A., Alwin, D. F., & Veroff, J. (1984). Assessing the validity of the achievement motive in the presence of random measurement error. *Journal of Personality and Social Psychology, 47*, 1347–1362.

Rosenthal, R., & Jacobson, L. F. (1968). *Pygmalion in the classroom*. New York: Holt, Rinehart, & Winston.

Schneider, W., & Fisk, A. D. (1982). Degree of consistent training: Improvements in search performance and automatic process development. *Perception and Psychophysics, 31*, 160–168.

Shallice, T. (1982). Specific impairments of planning. *Philosophical Transactions of the Royal Society of London, 298* (Series B), 199–209.

Shiffrin, R. M., & Schneider, W. (1977). Controlled and automatic human information processing: II. Perceptual learning, automatic attending, and a general theory. *Psychological Review, 84*, 127–190.

Showers, C. (1992). The motivational and emotional consequences of considering positive or negative possibilities for an upcoming event. *Journal of Personality and Social Psychology, 63*, 474–484.

Skinner, B. F. (1953). *Science and human behavior*. New York: Macmillan.

Smith, K. G., Locke, E. A., & Barry, D. (in press). Goal setting, planning, and organizational performance: An experimental simulation. *Organizational Behavior and Human Decision Processes.*

Snyder, M., & Swann, W. B. (1978). Hypothesis-testing processes in social interaction. *Journal of Personality and Social Psychology, 36*, 1202–1212.

Sorrentino, R. M., & Higgins, E. T. (1986). Motivation and cognition: Warming up to synergism. In R. M. Sorrentino & E. T. Higgins (Eds.), *Handbook of motivation and cognition* (Vol. 1). New York: Guilford.

Spence, K. W. (1950). Cognitive versus stimulus-response theories of learning. *Psychological Review, 57*, 159–172.

Spiro, R. J. (1977). Remembering information from text: The "state of schema" approach. In R. C. Anderson, R. J. Spiro, & W. E. Montague (Eds.), *Schooling and the acquisition of knowledge*. Hillsdale, NJ: Erlbaum.

Srull, T. K., & Wyer, R. S., Jr. (1979). The role of category accessibility in the interpretation of information about persons: Some determinants and implications. *Journal of Personality and Social Psychology, 37*, 1660–1672.

Strang, H. R., Lawrence, E. C., & Fowler, P. C. (1978). Effects of assigned goal level and knowledge of results on arithmetic computation: Laboratory study. *Journal of Applied Psychology, 63*, 446–450.

Taylor, S. E., & Schneider, S. K. (1989). Coping and the simulation of events. *Social Cognition, 7*, 176–196.

Tetlock, P. E. (1985). Accountability: A social check on the fundamental attribution error. *Social Psychology Quarterly, 48*, 227–236.

Thorndike, E. L. (1913). *The psychology of learning*. New York: Teachers College Press.

Trzebinski, J. (1985). Action-oriented representations of implicit personality theories. *Journal of Personality and Social Psychology, 48*, 1266–1278.

Vallacher, R. R., & Wegner, D. M. (1985). *A theory of action identification*. Hillsdale, NJ: Erlbaum.

Vallacher, R. R., & Wegner, D. M. (1987). What do people think they're doing? Action identification and human behavior. *Psychological Review, 94,* 3–15.

Vallacher, R. R., Wegner, D. M., & Frederick, J. (1987). The presentation of self through action identification. *Social Cognition, 5,* 301–322.

Walsh, K. W. (1978). *Neuropsychology: A clinical approach.* Edinburgh: Churchill Livingstone.

Warren, R. E. (1977). Time and the spread of activation in memory. *Journal of Experimental Psychology: Human Learning and Memory, 3,* 458–466.

Wicklund, R. A., & Gollwitzer, P. M. (1982). *Symbolic self-completion.* Hillsdale, NJ: Erlbaum.

Wilensky, R. (1983). *Planning and understanding.* Reading, MA: Addison-Wesley.

Wilson, T. D., & Capitman, J. A. (1982). Effects of script availability on social behavior. *Personality and Social Psychology Bulletin, 8,* 11–19.

Wyer, R. S., Jr., & Srull, T. K. (1989). *Memory and cognition in its social context.* Hillsdale, NJ: Erlbaum.

Zillmann, D., & Cantor, J. R. (1976). Effect of timing of information about mitigating circumstances on emotional responses to provocation and retaliatory behavior. *Journal of Experimental Social Psychology, 12,* 38–55.

Social Intelligence and Intelligent Goal Pursuit: A Cognitive Slice of Motivation

Nancy Cantor
Princeton University
William Fleeson
Max Planck Institute

Introduction

As personality psychologists, we bring to this symposium volume a view of human social functioning that emphasizes the intertwining of cognition and motivation, the dynamics of person-by-situation interactions as individuals struggle to make sense of experience in the light of their preconceptions, goals, and needs, and the social "press" of their life environment. Such a perspective has a long and distinguished history in our field, represented both by cognitive-personality theorists following from George Kelly; by motivational-personologists in the tradition of Henry Murray, and by interpersonal-cultural theorists influenced by Adler, Harry Stack Sullivan, and Erik Erikson. Rather than try to do justice to the richness and variety of this tradition, it is our intention to look at one slice—a *cognitive* slice—of motivation and social adjustment.

The research described in this chapter was supported in large part by grants from the National Science Foundation (BNS 84–11778 and BNS 87–18467) and by grants to the second author from the Horace Rackham School of Graduate Studies. Much of the conceptual foundation for this perspective comes from collaborative work with John Kihlstrom and with Hazel Markus; we wish also to thank our many collaborators and students for their insights and continued efforts. Contributions to this line of work by Michele Acker, Hart Blanton, Aaron Brower, Carol Cook-Flannagan, Robert Harlow, Chris Langston, Paula Niedenthal, Julie Norem, Carolin Showers, and Sabrina Zirkel are especially appreciated, as are the many helpful comments of Paul Adami, Susan Jenkins, Steve Peck, Emily Reber, Catherine Sanderson, and Michael Tomberg. We also thank Vera Sohl and Michael Tomberg for their technical assistance and patience in producing this chapter.

We are interested in how individuals perceive their lives, their various selves, their struggles, the things they would like to accomplish, the ways they would like to be, and, ultimately, the way they use their minds to work on these tasks. We focus, therefore, on a form of self-regulatory motivation that can be distinguished from the implicit motives that make one way of pursuing a goal feel more pleasing to an individual than another (Fleeson, 1992a). These are goals that individuals know they have, goals that they frequently adopt deliberately, even though they use them spontaneously in the course of daily life. We are interested in the creative ways in which individuals think about themselves and find opportunities to address their goals in daily life and in the strategies used to reach these goals, however inadequate and frustrating they sometimes turn out to be.

We imagine a friend trying to "find a lifelong partner" and thus enact a "married person" possible self. We see this person picturing himself or herself with potential partners and reacting with disgust or glee or some uncomfortable mixture of emotions. We see our imagined friend gravitating spontaneously toward activities in which there are new people, even though he or she feels intimidated in those activities. We see this person sometimes behaving rather inappropriately, turning an ostensibly nonsocial event into a forum for the pursuit of intimacy, and ruminating endlessly about an awkward interaction rather than turning attention to more "productive" efforts. These are the thoughts, efforts, choices, interpretations, and experiences that comprise our slice of motivation. We have developed a model of personality that attempts systematically to capture and predict this often-neglected aspect of personality. And although much of this sort of goal pursuit is neither systematic and linear nor conscious, it is clearly thoughtful, and thus we call this "cognitive motivation."

Our focus is as much on intention and effort as on outcome and accomplishment—we do not see many people around us "reaching" their life-task goals or, for that matter, stopping their efforts on a task once they seem to have reached what at a distance looked like a "desired end state." In this regard, as Nuttin (1984) eloquently argued, a cognitive theory of motivation is more about process than product, about the movements toward goals rather than the regularities of tension reduction, about the ways in which the meanings of those goals change just as we get nearer to them (see also Pervin, 1983). Or, to borrow, as we have before, from Allport's description of the two sides of personality, our focus is more on people's efforts to create agency by "doing" than it is on what they can count on "having" already or accomplishing easily (Cantor, 1990). Our point is a simple one—that in the realm of personality and motivation, thinking is at least half the doing.

We take the liberty here of being both "ego centered" in our highly selective coverage of relevant work and biased in our emphasis on demonstrations of this active, creative side of personality and motivation. We do this for two purposes—first, the literature is so rich that we cannot hope to do justice to others' contributions and so we have chosen to provide instead an integrated tour through our own work and that of some of our former students. Second, we believe that the dominant emphasis currently in the literature often suggests a portrait of a rather passive, highly reflexive individual driven to confirm his or her "basic" dispositions in a stereotyped and obligatory fashion (e.g., Caspi & Moffitt, 1992; cf. McAdams, 1992; Cantor et al., 1992b), and we hope to balance this portrait with one of a more explicitly self-regulating (Cantor & Fleeson, 1991; Fleeson, 1992a) and intelligently evolving "social animal" (Cantor, 1990; Kihlstrom & Cantor, 1989).

The work we review is sometimes experimental but often correlational in design and almost always begins with individuals' appraisals and experiences in a specifically motivating life-task domain (Norem & Illingworth, 1992; Showers, 1992a, 1992b) or life-choice context (Niedenthal & Mordkoff, 1991). Frequently the analyses are within subject in nature, considering how a person (or groups of like-minded people) works on one task as compared with another engaging life tasks (e.g., Cantor et al., 1991). In almost all instances, the individual's conscious appraisals of his or her life tasks provide a basis for further analysis of personality processes in daily life (Cantor et al., 1992a; Fleeson, 1992a). As often as possible, these investigations make use of experience-sampling or daily diary reports to capture life-task pursuit as it unfolds over time and place (Cantor & Fleeson, 1991; Langston, 1990). In some cases, these life-task pursuits span significant changes in life stages (Vandewater et al., 1992; Zirkel, 1992). In all instances, the attempt is to provide, as Dan McAdams has stated: "an experience-near brand of personology," or, as Bergen and Dweck (1989) called it, the "actualized" part of personality.

These stylistic features of the work are not accidental; rather, they reflect the explicit objective of the work to capture with "middle-level" units the dynamics of personality processes in context (Buss & Cantor, 1989). The focus on middle-level units, such as self-prototypes or life tasks or strategies, permits an analysis of functional coherence in personality (e.g., the components of a strategy, unlike items in a trait factor, are objectively diverse but functionally coherent). This focus also leaves some "room for growth" (Kihlstrom & Cantor, 1989), in ways that a contrasting focus on broad trait factors rarely does. At this contextually embedded middle level, it is possible to see small changes within a domain in the ongoing efforts of daily life. In contrast, when attempting to show stability in "deep dispositional structure" (e.g., Caspi & Moffitt, 1992), it makes good sense to use units that are abstract enough to survive across life contexts and across the life course. If, on the other hand, one is interested, as we are, in the reflective, self-regulatory side of people, then it is imperative to study personality and motivation in ways that chart the day-to-day texture of people's strivings for mastery (Cantor et al., 1992b). Strivings for mastery are not only conditionally linked to contexts in their expression (e.g., Wright & Mischel, 1987), but are also important in terms of development and change (Thorne, 1989), and so it is critical to examine them closely.

Social Intelligence and Personality Processes

Over the past 12 yr we have constructed a perspective on personality that centers on the role played by social intelligence in serving individual motivations, enabling people to overcome personal uncertainties and to "take control" on key tasks, thereby increasing pleasure and satisfaction in daily living (Cantor, 1990; Cantor & Kihlstrom, 1982, 1987). Cantor and Kihlstrom (1987) used the term "social intelligence," with some hesitation, to characterize this cognitive basis of personality. Their hesitation centered on the associations of this term with an attributive and comparative meaning of intelligence as "social IQ." Instead, social intelligence was intended to cement personality processes in the creativity of the mind to address the ill-defined but pressing "problems" of daily life.

In considering this alternative meaning for social intelligence, Cantor and Kihlstrom (1987) tried to outline the kinds of knowledge—procedural and declarative—that are developed and cultivated in the service of addressing the everyday problems of living. In this sense, the social intelligence perspective is a problem-focused one, aimed at characterizing individuals in the light of the self-knowledge, personal goals, and problem-solving strategies that they characteristically develop and use to address *their* problems, as they define them (Cantor, 1990). In view of its emphasis on problem solving in daily life, the perspective also gives a central role to motivation in personality processes—individual behavior is given coherence and pattern by the goals that are pursued in daily life. In pursuing personal goals, individuals imagine alternative worlds and alternative selves—and that is a distinctly cognitive process (Bruner, 1986; Markus & Nurius, 1986). The *interpretive* process is at the very center of personality, in this perspective, and, in turn, personality is purposive: individuals' attempts to make sense of self, the social world, the life tasks that seem demanded or at least afforded in each new life period, and the successes and failures of past and present and possible efforts are in the service of goal pursuit in one form or another.

Figure 1 provides a simplified view of the components of social intelligence relevant to behavior in a daily life event. In principle, we can distinguish between declarative and procedural knowledge as we move down from age-graded tasks, self-knowledge, and life-task appraisals to the interpretation of what is going on in a particular situation to the strategies for problem solving in that context. In fact, it is difficult to distinguish the procedural from the declarative in these aspects of social intelligence—for example, self-knowledge includes both the "facts" of an individual's self-definition (e.g., McAdams, 1989) and the person's "rules" for interpreting new events in his or her life as variations on an old "theme" (Linville & Clark, 1989). The declarative structures of personality are, in this view, intertwined with procedural knowledge for interpreting the self, tasks, and situations and for mobilizing energy to pursue those goals in relevant contexts.

As the schematic diagram indicates, the interpretive process is characterized here as an effort to interpret an event in daily life as an opportunity for goal pursuit. (For the sake of simplicity, we refer to

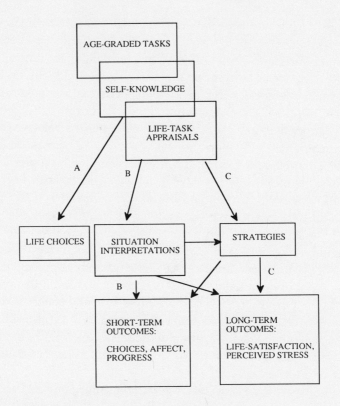

FIGURE 1. Social intelligence and the interpretive process.

the various connections in this diagram as *paths* in the interpretive process, although we do not intend these to represent formal paths in a causal model.) As shown at the top of Figure 1, we assume that an interpretive context is provided by the particular age-graded tasks that are emphasized within an individual's sociocultural environment (Cantor & Fleeson, 1991). People invoke their selves—past, present, and future—in these life-task arenas, often quite effortlessly and automatically (Bargh, 1982; Cantor et al., 1986). These accessible selves set the tone for interpreting this specific event through the more specific life tasks that become relevant for that person in that situation. In other words, the "self" becomes foregrounded in the interpretive process as the individual begins to think about how it typically feels to engage in an age-graded task in that situation. The individual's affective reaction in the event then follows from his or her appraisals of that life task (Norem & Cantor, 1991). In turn, faced with this task, the individual will invoke a strategy for working on the task in that situation, including ways of setting expectations, modulating effort, responding to "outcomes," and deciding when to "change" tasks.

Consider, for example, a relatively competitive person who often interprets a social event as both an arena for socializing and as a place to shine professionally. Even if this is the most relaxing social event of the week, the relevance of professional tasks will increase the stress level for this competitive person, to whom this life task is currently most taxing. In turn, the competitive person may vigilantly monitor the reactions of his or her superiors at the party while ignoring friends and making everyone tense with an unnecessarily combatative conversational style. As so often happens, this person's strategic efforts may work reasonably well to address the professional task while simultaneously exacting a price in another task, the pursuit of friendship. This self-defeating process is schematically illustrated in Figure 2.

These dynamic structures of social intelligence are best studied in light of outcome variables that emphasize how individuals function in daily life. A critical part of personality functioning is to make sense of a situation—that is, to decide who one is and wants to be in a situation, what task one is addressing, and how one feels about the task. Therefore, as part of this interpretive process, a connection is forged between self-knowledge and task appraisals on the one hand and different lifestyle *choices* of relevant activities, partners, or options, on the other hand (see Path A in Fig. 1). At the same time, as one works to make sense of a situation, relatively "short-term" or "on-line" reactions to the unfolding events take form as *affective reactions* and feelings of *progress* or of *frustration* associated with the tasks that have become relevant. As Path B in Figure 1 illustrates, an individual's affect and feelings of progress in a situation are linked in this model to what the person is "working on" in the situation and to how he or she feels about that task. As a person works repeatedly at a life task with certain characteristic strategies, then more long-term or cumulative outcomes become relevant, delineating a connection (Path C in Fig. 1) to *life satisfaction* and *psychological and/or physical stress*.

This analysis of personality processes is, therefore, predicated

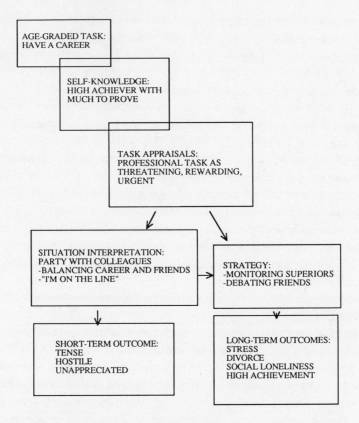

FIGURE 2. A self-defeating achievement scenario.

on a dynamic view of individual health and social functioning. It is the rare individual who does not have domains of self-confidence and domains of self-doubt, tasks that seem intimidating and tasks that seem manageable, and strategies that flow easily and those that somehow make matters worse. Even within a domain, a person can be managing well to overcome uncertainty and find short-term progress at a critical task, only to see with time the accumulated side effects of this strategy. However, this dynamic view does not preclude the assessment of individuals' selves, tasks, and strategies, nor does it prevent some prescriptive evaluation based on choices, affect, progress, and satisfaction. Social intelligence is supposed to enable people creatively to find opportunities for goal pursuit in daily life, to permit individuals to see the benefits and the costs in their characteristic strategies, and to encourage them to change their minds about themselves and their strategies.

How much flexibility people actually show and how often people actually change their strategies is an empirical question in this perspective. We expect discriminativeness in a person's reactions in different contexts precisely because the interpretive process will be guided by the domain-specific selves and task-specific appraisals invoked in those differing contexts. However, this kind of discriminativeness (Mischel, 1984) does not preclude generalized responding across contexts, instead, it makes consistency an open question—one that depends on the similarity in selves and task appraisals that a person brings to bear across contexts. There is plenty of room here for coherence—even specific consistency in behavior—as long as the coherence is appropriately understood as based in what a person is trying to do in each context. A person's strategies for addressing their different tasks may be quite consistent if he or she interprets different situations in similar ways as a function of accessing similar aspects of self and similar task appraisals. Personality consistency is possible, but variability is not alarming in light of the many different goals and varying opportunities for goal pursuit in daily life. In fact, viewed as discriminativeness (rather than inconsistency), this variability becomes a virtue, not a problem.

Alternativism, Functionalism, and Relativism: Sample Research

Our social intelligence perspective can be organized around the three premises of alternativism, functionalism, and relativism in human personality. These premises emphasize individuals' alternative construals of themselves and their social worlds (Cantor & Kihlstrom, 1982), what individuals are *trying* to do as compared with what they have at hand as attributes of personality (Cantor, 1990), and intelligence as a dynamic and contextualized process rather than as a stable and easily prescribed solution (Cantor & Kihlstrom, 1987). In the following text, we review work addressing these three premises, highlighting at each point the ways in which the analysis of social intelligence reveals the active, motivational core of personality functioning.

ALTERNATIVISM: DYNAMIC UNDERSTANDINGS OF SELF AND ONE'S WORLD

"Alternativism" has been a pervasive premise in personality psychology for some time. More specifically, in the cognitive-personality tradition, George Kelly's (1955) portrayal of the naive scientist actively trying to anticipate events and understand the self and the social world exemplifies this view. Kelly cements human experience in the interpretive process, as individuals give meaning to events in the light of their personal constructs. These construct systems, however, are rich, diverse, and dynamic, and the interpretive process is flexible such that not only are two individuals "experiencing" ostensibly the same event likely to "see" it differently, but the same individual can alternatively construct a familiar event differently on different occasions. A person's constructs, for example, could be differentially elaborated in different domains of life, reflecting the current interests and goals of the individual, and also malleable over time, so that, when those goals change, new domains of self may become salient (Kihlstrom & Cantor, 1984; Showers, 1992a). In deriving the essence of individuality from this malleable construct system and its creative application, Kelly argued that the structural basis of personality could indeed be dynamic—closer to doing than to having (Cantor, 1990; McAdams, 1992).

Unfortunately, emphasizing alternativism in the self-system can be dangerous—it is too easy to equate this complexity and malleability with variability and unpredictability. That is, it is too easy to assume that there is no pattern underlying these alternative selves, no consistency to the ways in which individuals interpret events and make choices. In our view, this is not the case. Instead, as we depicted in Figure 1, we see patterning to these alternative views of self and consistency in individuals' interpretations of experience, and we derive that patterning and consistency from individuals' goals. Individuals develop elaborate views of self, and access those constructs, in line with their currently salient life-task goals (Cantor et al., 1986). They focus attention on tasks that are currently important or especially rewarding, or, sometimes, they focus on tasks that provide a special challenge. Therefore, this complex and flexible self-system is given order by its connection to personal goals.

This regularity in the interpretive system will become clearer as we begin to consider in more detail life-task goals and the strategies that individuals use to reach them. For the moment, however, we want to provide a few examples of how individuals draw alternatively on their self-knowledge and highlight the importance of goals to regularity in this alternativism.

Self-ideals and alternative selves. A simple but important way in which the self-system is dynamic and provides alternative views of the self is in the age-graded focus on different aspects of self and experience across the life course. Zirkel's (1992) analysis of the changing meaning of personal independence for students as they make the transition out of college provides one striking example. As Zirkel suggested, independence is really a "metatask" for individuals—it involves doing the other specific tasks that are seen as age appropriate in any particular period. Therefore, she hypothesized that, as students made a transition out of college, those who were most absorbed by the "independence task" would show an especially strong shift in self-focus away from the achievement domain (the college task) to the social domain (the postcollege task). Her analyses, performed on the self-descriptions of a sample of honors students during and after college, showed a shifting content in the self-ideals of these students—during college these self-ideal descriptions were heavily focused in the achievement domain, and after college the domain of social intimacy became progressively more focal. Moreover, this shift in self-focus was much more apparent in the ideals of the independence-absorbed individuals than in those provided by the rest of the sample. In other words, their sustained concern with independence was reflected, alternatively, in different specific domains of self-focus as they moved on to a new life period.

Self-prototype evaluations in life choices. The next step, as outlined along Path A of Figure 1, is to ask how individuals then put these alternative views of self into action in their choices of activities in daily life. One way in which this seems to work is through a process in which people match themselves to prototypes of people suited for particular activities or lifestyle options. Most of us have ready access to an image of a "party person" or a "true librarian" (e.g., Cantor et al., 1982). At the same time, we also know where we stand now on those prototypic dimensions and where we would ideally like to be (Niedenthal & Mordkoff, 1991). Therefore, a natural decision heuristic would follow the congruence between self and prototype, encouraging people to construct a comfortable world through life choices that maximize fit (Buss, 1987; Emmons et al., 1986; Snyder, 1981). Indeed, evidence has accumulated in several domains, from college housing choices to choices of experimental partners or of "real" dating partners, to suggest that people's choice preferences maximize the similarity of self to a prototype (Cantor et al., 1984; Niedenthal et al., 1985; Snyder & Simpson, 1984).

In keeping with our emphasis on alternativism in the self-system, an interesting feature of this literature on self-prototype matching in lifestyle choices is the flexibility that individuals exhibit in the aspects of self on which they focus as they match their selves to prototypes. For example, Niedenthal and Mordkoff (1991) detailed prototype matching and the choices between different kinds of therapists. Their study revealed several examples of cognitive flexibility, but for our purposes the most relevant was the focus of these subjects on their *ideal* as compared with *actual* self-characteristics in the self-prototype comparison. As Niedenthal and Mordkoff (1991) observed, their data clearly showed how flexible people can be in the stance that they take on the self. In this case, perhaps people were focused on changing the self in making this therapist choice, and this focus may have made ideals of self the more relevant comparison standard.

Personal goals also seem to predict how vigilantly individuals attend to self-prototype fit in making lifestyle choices. This was evident in a study of college housing choices in which the students' self-descriptions on a variety of traits were matched to the trait profiles for prototypes of the type of person best suited to live in each of seven common housing choices (e.g., the prototypic co-op member). In that study, Niedenthal et al. (1985) found that students' actual housing preferences maximized self-prototype match most clearly for those who had indicated that interpersonal goals were important to them in this choice. Those for whom financial or other pragmatic goals were most important did not exhibit this pattern nearly as strongly. In other words, interpersonal goals in this choice may have made the personal characteristics of people well suited to live in the different housing options an important issue. Similarly, those students in the sample who viewed themselves in particularly narrow or restrictive terms (i.e., for whom only a few traits were very self-descriptive) also seemed to make choices that most took account of self-prototype fit. Again, for those students, the fit between their self-concepts and how they viewed the prototype for each housing option may have loomed large as an important requirement for satisfaction with their housing choice in view of their relatively restrictive self-images.

These studies highlight several aspects of the dynamic system of self. They support the view that, as Kelly and many others have suggested, individuals are quite capable of and inclined to consider alternative selves, to adopt stances on the self that alternatively emphasize actual and ideal characteristics, and to focus alternatively on different domains of self in line with the demands inherent in a current life context. In these ways, these self-*structures* of personality— the "having" side of personality—are, by virtue of their variety and malleability, almost indistinguishable from personality *processes*— the "doing" side (Allport, 1937; Cantor, 1990; McAdams, 1992). In fact, in the present perspective, the bridge that links these self-structures to the adaptive processes of personality are the goals of individuals—the life tasks that give concrete form and direction to the translation of a dynamic self into strategic action in daily life. Therefore, we turn now to consideration of these bridging units of personality, the life tasks that organize purposive behavior in an ongoing daily life context.

FUNCTIONALISM: SETTING THE COURSE FOR MOTIVATED BEHAVIOR

As we move from the "having" to the "doing" in personality, the role of personal goals in organizing behavior in a daily life context becomes critical (Cantor & Zirkel, 1990). What a person is trying to do in that domain of life at that time in life is the core organizing principle of personality coherence in this approach (see also Emmons, 1989; Little, 1989). Goals give coherence and concrete form to the choices people make of what to pursue day to day, to the immediate experiences of these events, and to the strategies that contribute to life satisfaction and life stress.

In taking this functionalist perspective, we are describing a certain kind of motivation—motivation that involves trying to take control of one's life, seeing the way one wants to be, and making choices conducive to being that way. This can involve choosing to do what is fun and inherently pleasing, or it can involve choosing to pursue a difficult and taxing challenge. In this kind of motivation, people are not always spectators to internal forces pushing them toward the easiest or most enjoyable activities but rather directors, choosing when to work on enjoyable tasks and when to forgo some pleasure to take on a difficult but valued project (Nuttin, 1984).

Certainly other forms of motivation guide behavior: for example, implicit motives (McClelland, 1985) define for an individual those qualities of action that are enjoyable for that person, as when a person with a strong motive for power finds more enjoyment in a dominance relationship with friends, as compared with a relationship built on cooperative interplay (Fleeson, 1992a). Nevertheless, we believe that more deliberately adopted goals play a fundamental role too in purposive behavior, particularly as individuals try to tackle tasks that they (and their culture) value at particular points in the life course (see Cantor & Malley, 1991, for an analysis of how conscious life tasks can address implicit needs).

MOVING FROM CULTURE AND SELF TO TASK PURSUIT

In its broadest form, this kind of motivation is reflected in culturally shared knowledge about the kinds of life-task projects that an individual "ought" to be doing at a certain point in his or her life (e.g., Havighurst, 1953). These age-graded and culturally defined life tasks are conveyed in various ways in the social organizations in which we all take part (e.g., Higgins & Parsons, 1983; Erikson, 1950). As such, American high school and college students know that they are to "find an identity"—and quickly—before they go on to the broader world of work and marriage. However, these are very abstract and loosely defined prescriptive tasks, and it is only as they become actualized for an individual in his or her current life context that they assume a regulatory role in that daily life.

Cultures provide individuals with forceful nudges in the direction of life-task adoption by marking critical transitions in the life course and critical events when new tasks are supposed to be assumed. Stewart's (1982; Stewart & Healy, 1985) model of emotional stances in a life transition from receptivity to self-determination provides one very useful metaphor for this "actualization" process—individuals begin a life period experimenting with the various age-typical tasks modeled in their social group and ultimately come to adopt one or more of these tasks as their own. Cantor and Fleeson (1991) documented just such a shift in attention to age-typical life tasks in their analyses of the life tasks of students in a longitudinal study of the transition through college—as first-year students, these subjects' life tasks were spread across various age-typical categories (e.g., academics, social life, independence, intimacy); by senior year, students tended to have focused in on one or two of these tasks as *their* tasks (although as a group their tasks were still spread across the full set of age-typical tasks).

As Erikson (1950) noted, this actualization (or personalization) process is greatly eased by the rituals of daily life in different life periods that guide individuals to focus attention on certain life tasks (e.g., Higgins & Parsons, 1983). As one example of this developmental task shift, Vandewater et al. (1992) observed a shift in attention from career tasks at age 31 to lifestyle tasks by age 43 on the part of a sample of women followed longitudinally from postcollege through middle adulthood. In that study, the developmental task shift was evident both for women in the sample who chose careers early in adulthood and for those who early on focused on the family domain (after Helson et al., 1984). Therefore, even within these different models of life-choice trajectories, the shifting in life task commitments shows some developmental regularity.

This shift of focus to new life tasks in a new life period can also be seen in the kinds of possible selves that individuals elaborate at different points in the life course (Ryff, 1991; Cross & Markus, 1991). As described earlier, Zirkel (1992) observed such a shift of self-focus in her analysis of changes in the meaning of the independence life task in the transition from college. She noted that individuals concerned with "developing independence" imbued that task with whatever the salient age-graded task was that they were currently facing. This change in meaning was reflected in their self-ideals. As individuals come to personally take on age-graded life tasks, their self-knowledge comes to reflect the newly relevant concerns (Cantor et al., 1986).

Both the age-graded task and the possible selves that it evokes become forces in daily life through the individual's personal appraisals of what it is like to do this task. This step to appraisals of particular life tasks is a critical one in our view. As Figure 1 suggests, we believe that individuals' answers to these appraisal questions (of the value or difficulty or rewardingness of the task pursuit *for them*) influence what they do, their affect when they do it, and their strategies for reaching their goals. In particular, this step moves the individual from a focus on end states—for example, "I need to become independent"—to a *task* focus on the process of pursuing these goals in daily life—for example, "doing my laundry is one, albeit small, way in which I can feel more independent here." Many, if not all, life-task goals persist for long periods of time, and, therefore, it is critical to focus on the task more than on the desired end state. The task appraisals are critical precisely because individuals will find some tasks easy and others hard, and yet they may still "choose" to try them. Task appraisals move a person who is intimidated by the distance between his or her current and ideal self one step closer to a strategy for taking control.

In support of this guiding role of life-task appraisals, we have analyzed the daily life pursuits of several samples of college students as they addressed their pressing tasks. Before describing some examples of the appraisal connections in Figure 1, we will pause here to describe some of our assessment procedures that follow most closely from this view of cognitive motivation.

Consensual life tasks. First, as noted above, we believe that most of people's personal goals are really personal versions of age-graded life tasks (Cantor & Fleeson, 1991). Certainly some goals that each person pursues are completely spontaneous and idiosyncratic, arising either in the particular nexus of that person's contexts, in their constellation of personal attributes, or in a particularly creative construal of their environment. Still, many also come from a fairly regular set of tasks that a particular age-graded cultural context sets for individuals. We emphasize the very personal meanings that individuals create of these consensual age-graded tasks.

Therefore, we begin our investigations by asking individuals to describe their personal tasks and to match those tasks with a set of age-graded tasks typical for their group (e.g., for college students, "doing well academically," "getting along with others; making friends," "finding intimacy," "being on my own, away from family"). We then move to open-ended descriptions of each consensual task: the situations and activities in which the person believes the task will be relevant, plans for working on the task, and descriptions of what success at the task means to the individual. Much of our work focuses on close-ended appraisals of how working on the task typically feels for that person (Cantor et al., 1987, 1991b). It is at this point, in the appraisals and open-ended descriptions of these consensual tasks, that we begin to see how different people can create vastly different meanings of the same consensual task. Zirkel and Cantor (1990), for example, did just this, comparing the experiences of college students who think about the "independence" task in grandiose and philosophical terms with those of other students who think about independence in more practical terms.

Appraisals of consensual tasks. A particularly informative part of our analyses of these personal versions of life tasks is the appraisal profiles that subjects provide for each consensual task. In the manner of the pioneering work of Brian Little (1983, 1989) on personal projects, we have chosen several appraisals of meaning that are central to a cognitive theory of motivation. We wish to capture agency in striving, that is, individuals' efforts to take control of their lives, both difficult and not-so-difficult aspects, to achieve particularly valued experiences. Thus, Cantor et al. (1987) start with an appraisal of the importance of the task to the individual and then move to the difficulty, stress, conflict, and challenge of the task. We assess individuals' beliefs about their own ability to control and initiate the task and about how rewarding the task is to them (e.g., progress on and enjoyment from the task). Recently, Cantor et al. (1991b) have also asked explicitly about individuals' motivational stance toward the task—for example, about their concern with avoiding unhappiness on the task or with achieving satisfaction at the task.

Table 1 shows the appraisals that have been used in each of our three main life-task assessment studies. These studies cover a cross-section of students living in different college environments—an honors college sample, a sorority sample, and a nonselected sample of undergraduates. Table 1 indicates the results of factor analyses on the appraisal ratings, showing which factor each dimension loaded highly on in each study. There are several points of note here. First, there is a high degree of convergence across the three studies. When appraisals were used in more than one study, they tended to load on the same factor, despite the divergence in samples. When new appraisals were introduced, they loaded with other appraisals that were conceptually related. Second, the factors represent themes that we emphasize generally in this perspective, including a factor representing the challenge of the task, another factor representing the rewardingness of the task, and occasionally a factor representing control over the task. Despite this high level of convergence, a third point of note is that there are some interesting divergences across samples. For instance, the control dimensions formed their own factor in the honors project, whereas they fell in the rewardingness factor in the other two studies. Thus, for many people, a feeling of control on a task is associated with enjoying the task, whereas for others, control is a separable component of task meaning and is as likely to be combined with challenge as with rewardingness. Another example is provided by the clustering of the importance appraisal: in the honors project, importance was associated with challenge; in the sorority project, importance was associated with rewardingness; in the undergraduate project, importance loaded highly on *both* challenge and rewardingness. Finally, although we do try to include in each study a core set of appraisals that capture these themes of agency in goal strivings, it is also important to note that different samples may focus on different components of the alternative meanings of these consensual tasks and so it may be necessary to vary more of the content of the appraisals to fit the specifics of a sociocultural life context (Norem & Cantor, 1991).

When to be idiographic and when to aggregate? In moving to appraisals and open-ended descriptions of *consensual* life tasks, a concern might arise that we sacrifice the idiographic nature of goal striving with such an assessment procedure. In a contrasting procedure,

Table 1

Appraisals and Factors from Three Studies

Appraisal	Honors project	Sorority project	Undergraduate project
Challenge	Challenge	Challenge	Challenge
Difficulty	Challenge	Challenge	Challenge
Stress	Challenge	Challenge	NA
Time spent	Challenge	Challenge	NA
Absorption	Challenge	NA	NA
Other's view	Challenge	None	Challenge
Conflict	NA	Challenge	NA
Failure unpleasant	NA	NA	Challenge
Sacrifice for	NA	NA	Challenge
Interference	NA	NA	Challenge
Success pleasant	NA	NA	Challenge
Importance	Challenge	Reward	Challenge, Reward
Enjoyment	Reward	Reward	Reward
Progress	Reward	Reward	Reward
Intrinsic value	NA	NA	Reward
Control	Control	Reward	Reward
Initiative	Control	Reward	Reward
Extrinsic value	NA	Outcome	NA
Avoid unhappiness	NA	Outcome	NA
Achieve satisfaction	NA	Outcome	NA
Ambivalence	NA	None	NA

Note. Appraisal dimensions are rated in each of three of the major studies in four factors they loaded; NA, appraisal was not rated in the study; *none* indicates that the appraisal was rated but did not load highly on any of the factors.

Little (1983) has subjects freely generate their own personal projects and then appraise those *personal* projects, not a consensual list (see Emmons, 1989, for a similar procedure). This methodology preserves the idiographic nature of the goals, although it also makes it somewhat harder to contrast personal meanings of the same task, as we often wish to do (e.g., Zirkel & Cantor, 1990). (In fact, to perform such comparisons, investigators using the idiographic goals procedures often code their subjects' goals into consensual categories, such as those of achievement, affiliation, and intimacy goals; see Emmons & McAdams, 1991; Little et al., 1992.)

In our view, there are three points to be made about the sacrifice of idiographic goal content in our procedure. First, we have consistently found that the great bulk of idiographic goals can be rather easily matched with consensual categories. In our assessment procedure, we first ask subjects to generate their own life-task lists before they see any examples of consensual tasks; we find that subjects can rather easily then match most of their idiographic tasks to these consensual tasks (e.g., across the three college student samples in our main studies, the percentage of tasks matched to consensual tasks was first-year honors students, 74%; sorority students, 69%; and nonselected undergraduates, 71%). Moreover, we have observed the same relationships between appraisals and outcomes using consensual tasks as others find using appraisals of idiographic goals (cf. Cantor et al., 1992a, with Emmons & King, 1989). This convergence most likely occurs because the individuals in our samples are as "engaged" by these consensual life tasks as by their idiographic strivings.

Second, and more to the point, there is a distinct advantage in having subjects appraise the same task categories. One benefit of working with consensual tasks is that it is then easier to see the specificity in how people approach different tasks. We have found, for example, in analyses with various student samples from the honors college, sorority group, and nonselected college students, that interpersonal and achievement tasks function very differently. First, there are rather general differences in appraisal profiles for academic and social life tasks (e.g., Cantor et al., 1987, 1991b; Fleeson, 1992a). Even subjects with considerable social anxiety in these samples still appraise their academic tasks as more taxing than their social tasks and experience their academic daily life events as more "unpleasant" than they do social events (Langston & Cantor, 1989). In analyses of the relationship between appraisals and subjects' commitment to tasks, Fleeson (1992b) found that students take on academic tasks more frequently to the extent that they see them as difficult and challenging as well as important, whereas social tasks are adopted more frequently on the basis of intrinsic rewardingness in addition to importance. Finally, the strategies used to work on achievement and interpersonal tasks are typically either different or have different effects in these two domains (see Norem, 1989, for a discussion of social vs. academic defensive pessimism). In other words, the content of the task has implications that run the gamut from task adoption to appraisal to strategies, and therefore it is important to preserve some comparative information across different tasks or goals.

There is a third, and perhaps more critical, reason that we prefer a method of aggregation in which individuals' tasks are matched to consensual categories, as compared with one in which the individual tasks are preserved but the appraisals are then *summed* across a person's whole task system. From our perspective, the summed-appraisal index provides good insight into a general style of pursuing goals (e.g., see Little et al., 1992), but it sacrifices understanding of the idiographic pattern of meanings across tasks *within* individuals. Little (1989) and Emmons (1989) have shown that appraisals averaged over a person's goal system are temporally stable and thus represent stable ways of pursuing one's goals. Fleeson and Cantor (1992a), in contrast, have shown that the appraisal *distinctions* individuals make between the different tasks in a consensual set show temporal stability as well. In an analysis of appraisal ratings from our honors project, we separated, for each appraisal of each task, the unique component of the appraisal by residualizing the appraisal of one task on the same appraisal of the other five tasks. For example, the unique appraisal of the difficulty of making friends was obtained by residualizing it on the difficulty of the other five tasks, thereby showing the distinction each individual makes between the difficulty of making friends and the difficulty of his or her tasks in general. This procedure was repeated at two points 18 mo apart, and the unique components were correlated over time. Table 2 shows these correlations. As can be seen, 40 of the 60 correlations were significant at the .05 level, showing a large degree of stability in these distinctions. In sum, this analysis demonstrated that these highly specific ways of thinking about tasks also constitute stable patterns of meaning. In other words, while our approach may sacrifice the idiographic nature of the goals themselves, it gains the idiographic nature of the meanings of goals. And we think that this is precisely where the idiographic nature of motivation comes into play, reflecting people's alternative selves and alternative goals for self (Kihlstrom & Cantor, 1984).

These appraisal distinctions are in turn also reflected in the patterning of life satisfaction across domains within persons. For example, in our sorority study the within-person rank ordering of tasks on the appraisal cluster of "rewardingness" was significantly associ-

Table 2

Stability Coefficients of the Unique Component of Life-Task Appraisals in the Honors Project

Appraisals	Grades	Goals	Friends	On own	Identity	Time
Importance	.45***	.24*	.37***	.32**	.31**	.16
Enjoyment	.18*	.49***	.54***	.34**	.24*	.33**
Difficulty	.23*	.02	.26**	.31**	.24*	.02
Control	.30**	.13	.21*	.14	.21*	.01
Initiative	−.12	.02	.30**	.13	.06	.07
Stress	.37***	.19*	.41***	.30**	.14	.12
Progress	.40***	.37***	.07	.11	.29**	.14
Challenge	.30**	.14	.33**	.26**	.31**	.35***
Absorption	.27**	.23*	.36***	.12	.23*	.16
Time	.34***	.31**	.38***	.25**	.30**	.48***

Note. Table entries represent the correlation between the unique component of an appraisal of a task at time 1 with the unique component of the same appraisal of the same task at time 2 (18 mo later); N's varied from 90 to 95.
*$p < .05$. **$p < .01$. ***$p < .001$.

ated with within-person ratings of life satisfaction in relevant domains, as measured 4 wk later, even when we controled for the daily life affect experienced in intervening events (Cantor et al., 1991b). This pattern was replicated with the nonselected college student sample (Fleeson, 1992a). In that study, appraisals of the "rewardingness" of the grades, friends, and intimacy tasks were associated with satisfaction with the corresponding task 2 wk later. Moreover, as expected, appraisals of one task, such as the rewardingness of grades, were not associated with life satisfaction in the other task domains, such as friends or intimacy. Comparable analyses in the honors project (Cantor et al., 1987) also revealed discrimination in the appraisal to life satisfaction relationships in the academic and social life task domains.

These aspects of specificity are lost when we aggregate over tasks and present profiles of individuals high or low in overall task-system conflict or the like. These aggregate indices, like the implicit motives or big-five traits with which they correlate (e.g., Emmons & McAdams, 1991; Little et al., 1992), are very useful in describing habitual responses to all kinds of pursuits and habitual levels of personality adjustment. They are also useful in describing the ways in which traits become part of daily life through the medium of goal pursuits. What they cannot do, however, is help us to demonstrate how individuals discriminate in their task appraisals between tasks or to show how an individual's particular strategy for task pursuit follows from his or her specific appraisals of that task. For that purpose, we are better served by within-person comparisons across specific tasks or by comparisons between groups of people who differentially appraise a common life task. The following samples of our life task research provide some view, we hope, of the benefits of this assessment approach.

Task appraisals and investment. As Figure 1 suggested, we believe that life-task appraisals organize behavior largely through the individual's investment in opportunities to pursue valued tasks in daily life. This investment is reflected in the choice of task-relevant situations or activities, the interpretation of events as opportunities for task pursuit, emotional arousal in task-relevant events, and a focus of interest away from other, less immediately relevant events. Various appraisals can signal such investment, although the most straightforward appraisal measure in this case is simply the self-report of a task as especially important (relative to either one's other, current tasks or other peers' appraisals of the importance of that task). However, in keeping with the view of this motivation as directed at taking control in important but not necessarily easy domains, individuals also often invest in activities in which they can pursue their important but difficult and anxiety-provoking tasks.

We have repeatedly observed an appraisal-investment relationship in each of our three main life-task studies. Our approach in these studies has been to measure the appraisal of the importance of a life task at the outset of the study (typically at the beginning of a term) and then later to measure investment in task-relevant activities with experience-sampling methods. As part of the experience-sampling phase in these studies, subjects carried "beeper watches" programmed to go off on a random schedule during the day, typically producing five beeps per day for anywhere from 10 d to 3 wk. During each beep, the subject filled out a quick event report, describing the activity and interpersonal context of the event, the day of the week and time it took place, and a brief record of his or her affective experience in the event. Measures of the relevance of the event to each life task were obtained, separately, as part of diaries filled out each night of the experience-sampling phase. Finally, mea-

148

sures of satisfaction and performance in task-relevant life domains, such as academic, romantic, and family life, were gathered at the end of each study.

These studies have produced many examples of an association between life-task importance and task relevance in daily life. For example, in the sorority study, Cantor et al. (1991b) assessed the within-person rank-order relationship between the appraised importance of each of seven consensual life tasks and the relevance of each task to daily life events. They observed a consistent and significant fit between task importance and the subject's interpretation of specific daily events as task relevant. In subsequent analyses, we have explored the parameters of this basic task importance to investment relationship. That is, we have focused on the effects of the event context and on how importance of one task siphons off attention from another. For example, we have shown how importance increases the relevance of a task in contexts that are atypical for that kind of task pursuit (e.g., Cantor et al., 1991a). In the sorority study, importance of the task of "finding intimacy" was positively correlated with relevance of the task across many event contexts, such as academic situations, in events when the person was alone, and during weekday events—all relatively unusual event contexts for pursuit of the intimacy task.

Investment can also be signaled by a shift of focus away from interest in events or activities relevant to one task toward those relevant to another. In our data, this intensification via narrowing of interests often follows from anxiety or concerns associated with the target task. For example, in their analysis of life-task conflict associated specifically with the task of finding intimacy, Cantor et al. (1992a) found that those women in the sorority sample who were in a serious relationship and who appraised their intimacy task as engendering conflict for them exhibited a narrowing of motivational focus (relative to their less anxious peers). For the women in this sample currently involved in a relationship, intimacy-task conflict was associated with less interest and more negative affect in academic events, even though their academic task was not particularly conflictual or difficult for them. We interpreted this finding as reflective of their intensified investment in intimacy—an investment also revealed in a strong focus on sharing and communion in the relationship and a lessened interest (relative to their less conflicted peers) in other close, confidant relationships. Of course, we should also note that these women experienced their relationships not only as absorbing but also as highly satisfying and not requiring change. For them, this life-task investment was apparently worthwhile, despite their reports of task conflict.

This motivational narrowing on the part of these intimacy-focused women raises an important point about life-task pursuit— that is, life tasks represent a system, and so investment in one task may well imply consequences for work on other tasks (Little, 1989). We have just begun to examine more broadly these cross-task consequences of investment, looking, for example, at the extent to which the importance of one task may be associated not only with increased relevance of *that* task in daily life events but with decreased relevance of *other* tasks in those same events. In the sorority study, such a pattern of narrowed relevance emerged in analyses of the "grades" task. For example, appraisal of the grades task as important is both positively correlated with grades task relevance and negatively correlated with intimacy task relevance across diverse daily life event contexts. It seems likely, in fact, that a challenging and time-consuming task will generally draw attention away from other tasks when it is particularly important to the person to master the challenge. Similarly, for some individuals, such as the women described above, tasks that are typically viewed as nonproblematic may be difficult, thus seeming to require a narrowed focus of investment at the cost of lessened commitment to other tasks. Experience-sampling data provide a nice window on these dynamics of the task system.

These experience-sampling studies are consistent with the presumed influence of task appraisals on the interpretation of events in daily life. In each case it is difficult to explicitly prove a causal chain of influence (as in Fig. 1), since we trade here the precision of an experimental manipulation for in vivo realism and correlational analyses. However, in addition to these converging patterns of appraisal-investment relationships, these studies also show considerable task specificity that is consistent with our perspective. The sorority women who are in conflict over intimacy are no more likely than their peers to be in conflict over academics—enabling a clearer interpretation of the motivation behind their diluted interest in academic-relevant events. The honors students who are absorbed by independence and who invest this task with academic meaning do not also show heightened emotional arousal or affective negativity in everyday *social* events. Further, when subjects in these studies discriminate between their age-graded life tasks as to personal importance, these relatively small distinctions are reflected too in the patterning of their investment in daily events.

Life tasks and changing the experience of events. Another fundamental piece of this functionalist perspective is that individuals can *change* or redirect their experience of events through the tasks with which they frame the event. This point harkens back to Kelly's *constructive alternativism*—events are experienced alternatively in the light of relevant constructs. In this case, we add a functionalist twist to Kelly's point; that is, the proposition that the content of the experience is predictable specifically from the life task(s) being currently pursued (Fleeson & Cantor, 1992b). Further, we add a self-regulatory element to this proposal by claiming that people can, therefore, structure their life experiences in part by the life tasks that they set and pursue with regularity (Vandewater et al., 1992) and by their appraisals of those tasks.

Fleeson and Cantor (1992b) recently undertook an analysis of experience-sampling data directed at demonstrating this basic alternativism point. Using the experience-sampling and daily diary data from the sorority sample described earlier (Cantor et al., 1991b), we showed how the affective experience of an event shifted predictably when it was perceived as relevant to a life task that was unusual or atypical for that event. We focused on the two life tasks of "doing well academically" and "getting along with others" that were most frequently rated by the sorority women as relevant in the 15 d sampling period and on three different kinds of event contexts—defined by activity, day of the week, or interpersonal context. In general, for these sorority women (and, in fact, for all of the college student samples with whom we have worked), events seen as relevant to academic tasks were also experienced with more negative affect than those seen to be relevant to social tasks. Therefore, we predicted that the women would experience typically positive events, such as time with others or weekend days or parties and other social events, in less positive terms had they construed those events as also relevant to their "depressing" grades task. Conversely, they should experience events that are typically experienced in relatively more negative ways, such as those occurring on "blue Monday," or time alone, or in class, as considerably more affectively uplifting if they were construed, atypically, as relevant to their friends task. Within-person comparisons in all these cases followed our predictions, and in some cases, as in the day of the week (and time alone vs. time with others) comparisons, the affective experience was completely reversed by the construal in the light of an atypical life task. In other words, the well-documented "blue Monday" effect on mood was completely negated by their construal of weekday events as relevant to an uplifting social life task; similarly, time alone in which a friends task was relevant (e.g., thinking about a new friend) was often every bit as pleasant as time with others.

Of course, these reversals in affect in the light of atypical tasks also worked to individuals' short-term disadvantage in the case of the more negatively experienced grades task—for example, the uplift typically experienced by these women on weekends as compared with weekdays was also reversed completely when weekend events were relevant to the grades task. In fact, this affective cost was experienced as much by women who had appraised the academic task as especially important (but still relatively difficult) as by those for whom it was somewhat less important. Fleeson (1992a) has also recently replicated this result in his experience-sampling study with the nonselected college student population. In that study, he also found that the experience of (un)pleasantness when working on the difficult grades task was unrelated to the experience of progress on the academic task in the event. To be sure, accumulated progress on a goal is associated with uplifts, but there are still short-term costs to working on tasks that are appraised as difficult. In other words, we would argue that interpreting an event as task relevant contributes substantially, sometimes positively but other times quite negatively, to the "on-line" affective experience of the event, above and beyond whatever differences in longer-term rewards accrue to those for whom the task is especially valued.

In our view, as illustrated in Figure 1, the key to these task relevance–affective experience relationships resides in the individual's task appraisals. For example, the depressing impact of the grades task for the sorority women is consistent with our findings that appraisals of a task (such as the grades task) as difficult or as nonrewarding are associated with lessened positive affect on a daily basis (Cantor et al., 1991b). Therefore, one potent avenue for change in this model is the feedback that individuals derive from accumulated progress at a task. For example, it is quite possible that, with sufficient experience with progress on a hard task, satisfaction may build up enough to prompt a revision in the appraisals of the task that, in turn, would be reflected down the line in the affective experience of task-relevant events. This kind of dynamic interplay between task appraisals and experiences is at the base of Bandura's (1986) self-efficacy treatment programs.

Capturing this dynamic interplay between experience and appraisals is a central objective in our model and research strategy. Fleeson (1992a), for example, has begun to describe some of the ways in which satisfaction with a task can change appraisals, which in turn change satisfaction. In his undergraduate project, he used three data collection points over the course of a month to address this dynamic. In the first data phase (T1), the subjects reported their satisfaction with three life tasks; in the second phase (T2), they appraised the rewardingness of these three tasks; and in the third phase (T3), 2 wk later, they again reported on their satisfaction with these tasks. Figure 3 shows the results, with path strengths represented by standardized regression coefficients. We wish to highlight three aspects of this figure. First, there is stability in satisfaction. Second, there is a clear dynamic interplay: appraisals in part reflect previous experience, but then influence later satisfaction independently of previous satisfaction. Finally, these results suggest that appraisals are not simply reflections of an independent and stable level of satisfaction—they have their own impact on satisfaction. Or, in other words, appraisals are not simply "news reports" of ongoing activities; they can also shape daily life experience. Together, this pattern suggests the possibility for interventions that shift the experience of events by changing the appraisals of relevant tasks.

LIFE TASKS AND THE INTERPRETIVE PROCESS

In addressing a theme of *functionalism*, the research described above has focused on ways in which appraisals of important life tasks are reflected in the interpretations individuals make in everyday events

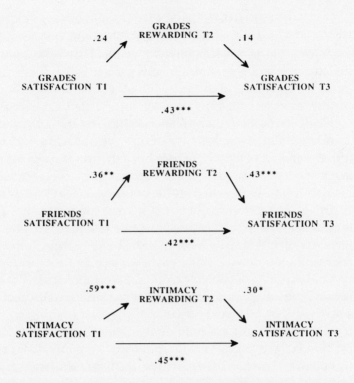

FIGURE 3. Dynamic relations between satisfaction and appraisals. Hierarchical regressions were performed for each task. The first regression predicted T3 satisfaction from both T1 satisfaction and T2 appraisals. The second regression predicted T2 appraisals from T1 satisfaction. Coefficients are standardized regression coefficients; $*p < .05$, $**p < .01$, $***p < .001$.

and in their affective experiences in those events. Life tasks thus serve an orienting function in daily life, operating, as Simon (in this volume) argued in describing the role of goals, to "fix attention" on relevant events and information and to "block out" distractions. As Figure 1 suggests, we believe that many important life tasks are personalized forms of age-graded tasks and that task appraisals contribute significantly to the experience of daily life events. Our research demonstrates that people have no trouble classifying their personal tasks into the consensual categories we provide and that there is regularity to the ways in which they adopt these tasks over time (Cantor & Fleeson, 1991). The distinctions that individuals make between the meanings of various consensual tasks are not only temporally stable but have specific reflections in the interpretive process (Path B of Fig. 1). The more important the task, the more an individual will work on it; this is true sometimes in unusual contexts or when it is a difficult task and sometimes involves other tasks receiving less attention. Appraisals of tasks are hypothesized to have their effects mainly through the interpretation of events: as several studies showed, alternative interpretations of events in terms of tasks are associated with systematic variation in the affective experience of those events. As Fleeson (1992a) showed, there is room for structuring those experiences, because appraisals themselves make independent contributions to daily life experience (see also Cantor et al., 1991b). Moreover, although not explicitly represented in Figure 1, it is clear that the experiences of daily life will return to alter the appraisals that individuals have of life tasks. One hope for personality change thus resides in this dynamic interplay between experience and appraisals, which leads us to question more directly what the precipitants of appraisal shifts might be. What experiences encourage a new look on an old life task?

Of course, these are only some of the questions of future interest, and the interpretive process outlined in Figure 1 does not stop at this point of situation interpretation or affect in situations or task satisfaction. Gollwitzer (1992), for example, distinguished between two mind-sets implicated in goal pursuit: a deliberative mind-set for defining goals and an implemental mind-set for enacting goals. Similarly, Cantor & Kihlstrom (1987) pointed to the frequency with which people form strategies to guide their performances before, during, and after these task-relevant events. These strategies reflect what individuals see as possible for themselves in those task contexts—that is, the current relevant selves and task appraisals. Yet they can also serve a proactive self-regulatory function, as when a person's strategy facilitates task performance on an otherwise intimidating, even overwhelming task (Norem, 1989). The accumulated impact of a strategy may be reflected in changes in self-knowledge and task appraisals; although sometimes those changes make matters worse (Baumeister & Scher, 1988). Therefore, we turn now to a consideration of this slice of social intelligence—strategic self-regulation.

RELATIVISM: THE CULTIVATION OF
INTELLIGENCE IN DAILY LIFE

In accord with the dynamic view of self-knowledge and the self-regulatory view of life tasks, Cantor and Kihlstrom (1989) used a gar-
dening-cultivation metaphor to describe social intelligence. As they
said: "Intelligence . . . is the essential ingredient of the active, creative, evolving side of personality. Just as the most interesting thing
about self-esteem is not whether you have it or not, but how you use
and maintain and enhance it (whatever *it* is); intelligence is a resource to be cultivated and we are all gardeners first and foremost"
(p. 198). However, by using this gardening metaphor, they did not
intend to imply that all one has to do is water native intelligence and
it flourishes and grows; rather, they meant that the individual had to
work and plan and envision his or her garden, continuously replant-
ing and rearranging in an attempt to make it beautiful and to keep it
healthy.

Thus, in considering how the self and task "structures" of personality become translated in daily life as characteristic ways of solving particular problems, we focus on individuals' active attempts to
take control—to create agency and make progress on personally relevant life tasks. In other words, we are interested not only in those
people who seem to feel already in control in a task context but also,
or perhaps more so, in those people for whom the task is an important challenge that requires marshaling their resources, cultivating
their intelligence, and overcoming their uncertainties.

Our view is that everyone has expertise for addressing life's
tasks, although each of us feels more or less facile at different tasks
(e.g., resolving an interpersonal conflict vs. meeting new people)
(Showers & Cantor, 1985). By analogy to the literature on expert
problem solving, our strategies for handling work and play and family and health, for example, vary in quantity and quality, just as the
flexibility and insight that a chess master brings to the game probably will not characterize his or her strategies for solving physics
problems. This expertise is highly contextualized, rooted in particular ways of seeing the self and the task that do not always generalize
to other domains—the facility one feels with colleagues, for example, may vanish as one struggles toward a strategy for calming a
frustrated 3-yr-old (Cantor & Harlow, 1992b). As Linville and Clark

(1989) note, these daily life strategies, like production systems, are built from bottom up, though one certainly never tires of attempting to fit one "problem" into the structure of a more familiar one (doesn't a frustrated 3-yr-old feel as we do when an experiment has failed?).

Like most expert systems, there are always multiple "good" solutions to the problems of daily living, and, at the same time, there are almost no perfect solutions achieved without some cost now or in the future (Kihlstrom & Cantor, 1989). When we look at strategies of problem solving in a daily life context, it is immensely difficult to be prescriptive about better or worse ways of coping independent of the particular goals and current concerns of the individual, the weighing of short-term gains against long-term costs, and the sacrifices for other goals of adopting any given strategy (cf. Baron, 1989). To illustrate this need for "relativism" in evaluating the "intelligence" of these problem-solving strategies we turn now to three examples of goal pursuit in college students' academic and social life.

The unit of analysis for these demonstrations of the complexity of social intelligence in action is the problem-solving *strategy* (Norem, 1989). We conceive of a strategy as a coherent pattern of thought, feeling, effort, and action in the service of progress on a personally meaningful but not necessarily easily accomplished life task. Strategies organize action and energy and are guided by or gain force from individuals' *self-knowledge* and *life task appraisals* (see Path C in Fig. 1). They are both contextualized and dynamic in that they unfold in time and situational context in characteristic ways—for example, one strategy may make use of effort in anticipation of a task, another may be more intensive in its ruminations after the performance; one achievement strategy may characteristically take place in private while studying, another may rely on social support and leisure-time activities. In other words, strategies describe coherences in how, when, and where an individual characteristically pursues a particular life task (Cantor & Fleeson, 1991). Strategies are strategic not in the sense of always requiring conscious manipulation but rather in the highly specific ways that they unfold to handle particular problems in particular contexts (Cantor, 1990). In fact, as Gollwitzer's (in this volume) demonstrations of the consequences of implementation intentions suggest, strategies, once in place, may come to organize action effortlessly in relevant settings. Unfortunately, it is the

rare strategy that works to address one problem (or "goal intention") without creating others.

Defensive pessimism and harnessing anxiety. Defensive pessimism (Norem, 1989; Norem & Cantor, 1986a, 1986b; Showers, 1992b) is
an anticipatory strategy in which a person who acknowledges having done well at a task in the past "harnesses" current anxieties by
setting (unrealistically) low expectations and reflecting in some detail on negative possibilities for a forthcoming performance. These
anticipatory cognitive maneuvers of expectation setting and reflection serve both to protect the self should an unusually poor performance occur (Norem & Cantor, 1986a) and to motivate special efforts
to avoid such a negative outcome (Norem & Cantor, 1986b; Showers,
1992b).

Individuals use defensive pessimism specifically in task domains in which they experience *both* substantial success and substantial uncertainties about their efficacy at controlling performance
and repeating these good outcomes. For defensive pessimists, their
self-uncertainties are specifically connected to appraisals of a target
task domain (e.g., achievement or social tasks) and their strategy involves a motivated effort to reduce the discrepancy between self and
ideals for this task (Cantor et al., 1987). This is a strategy for taking
control of a task in which one has reason to be hopeful based on past
experience, but at the same time one does not already feel in control.

The hallmark of the defensively pessimistic strategy is that the
cognitive-motivational work occurs in advance of the performance,
thus prompting the person to mobilize effort for the task. Norem
and her colleagues (see Norem, 1989; Norem & Illingworth, 1992)
have demonstrated the performance-facilitating effects of this anticipatory work for defensive pessimists as compared with optimists,
both in laboratory tasks and in a naturalistic field setting as part of a
daily experience-sampling study. This characteristic temporal course
of the strategy is critically associated with its effectiveness, as compared, for example, with the post-hoc negative attributions and
endless ruminations of depressive and helpless individuals —that
is, of "real" pessimists (Showers & Ruben, 1990). Moreover, for individuals who characteristically use this strategy in a particular task
domain, the preparatory work seems to preclude the necessity of
post-hoc attributional tricks, such as the denial of control over poor

performance that "optimists" characteristically show (Norem & Cantor, 1986a).

The contrast between what works for defensive pessimists and what is performance facilitating for optimists is striking. Figure 4 illustrates this contrast for the pessimists and optimists in our longitudinal honors project study (Cantor et al., 1987; see also Cantor & Norem, 1989). The figure presents contrasting regression models predicting academic performance (at the end of the first term at college) from various measures of self and task appraisal in the academic domain (obtained at the outset of the first year). As shown, the defensive pessimist is not debilitated, as most people would be, by seeing a large discrepancy between his or her actual and ideal academic self or by reflecting in detail on how to handle academic tasks, as long as he or she also sees the academic task as basically rewarding. In contrast, the optimist is debilitated by such discrepancy and reflectivity, as Norem and Illingworth (1992) also demonstrated in their laboratory and field studies (see also Higgins, 1987; 1990).

However, as well as this preparatory work serves the defensive pessimist, it is also central to the costs of the strategy. Because the protective and motivating work of the strategy occurs before the task, it is difficult to regulate this preparatory effort, and, after the fact, it is easy to feel drained by what now seems to be unnecessary worrying. Cantor and Norem (1989) argued, in the context of their longitudinal study of honors students who used this strategy in the achievement domain, that the accumulation of this wear and tear can ultimately diminish intrinsic motivation for the task. Similarly, Showers (1992b) elegantly demonstrated the emotional letdown after a defensively protected performance in the social context of an experimental conversation task—the defensively pessimistic subjects who were asked to engage in "negative-focused" thought listing before the conversation performed especially well in the task but experienced emotional fatigue and letdown after the conversation.

In this way, defensive pessimism stands as a clear example of the complexities involved in evaluating the intelligence of strategies for anxiety-provoking tasks. On one hand, this strategy must be evaluated against the standard of immobilization and performance decrements that we know to occur for individuals with this kind of anxiety who do not use some protective and energizing strategy (see Fowles, in this volume, for a broader discussion of anxiety and be-

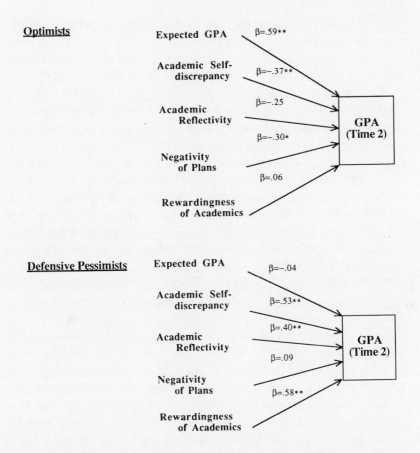

FIGURE 4. Components of optimist and defensive pessimist strategies and grade-point average. Coefficient significance as follows: $*p < .10$, $**p < .05$. (From Cantor et al., 1987.) Copyright 1987 by the American Psychological Association. Reprinted by permission.

havioral inhibition). Achievement anxiety and social anxiety are typically associated with negative outcomes that simply do not befall those using this strategy (Norem, 1989). Nonetheless, the accumulated wear and tear of this effort may, in the long run, have diminishing returns—it may get harder and harder to convince oneself that negative outcomes are likely and thus to energize oneself, or it may get harder and harder to see, in retrospect, the preparatory energy as necessary (once the task went well) and, thus, the effort as well spent. In the end, the defensive pessimist's balance sheet is likely to be very idiosyncratic, highly dependent on personal values and priorities at any particular time in life.

Social constraint and exacerbating social anxiety. As Showers (1992b) has shown, defensive pessimism is a relatively effective strategy for overcoming social anxiety and encouraging active participation in social conversations (e.g., the defensive pessimists who were given time to "focus negatively" before the conversation engaged in more talking and were rated as putting more effort and being more sociable in the conversation). Although it is by no means without costs, especially in light of the emotional letdown that defensive pessimists feel after such social activities, it does enable forceful performance in the face of anxiety (as compared with withdrawal) and, perhaps most critically, it does not appear to involve substantial rumination and self-deprecation after the interaction (Showers & Ruben, 1990). In other words, defensive pessimists cut their loses even if they do not savor their gains. Of course, not all active and strategic efforts to overcome social anxiety work as well as defensive pessimism, as Langston's analysis of the social constraint strategy shows (Langston, 1990; Langston & Cantor, 1989).

On the basis of videotaped interviews with students in the honors project, Langston and Cantor (1989) identified a social constraint strategy that was associated both with active participation in social life and with a downward cycle of self-deprecation in this domain. As schematically illustrated in Figure 5, individuals using a social constraint strategy overcome their intense self-focused anxiety and feelings of immobilization before social interactions by being other-directed, that is, by taking the lead of others and looking for others' cues in the interaction. Whereas other-directedness, in combination with the other components of the strategy, is actually positively associated with satisfaction and confidence, the strategy as a whole may foster harmful ruminations after the fact (e.g., "I'm *really* no good at socializing—I always have to follow others' leads"). After several years in this particular study, those students who characteristically used the social constraint strategy were feeling even less satisfaction and confidence in the social life arena than would be expected on the basis of their initial levels of social anxiety. Unlike those using social defensive pessimism, the social constraint students showed a significant proclivity for retrospective self-analysis.

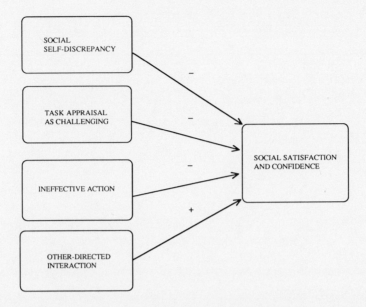

FIGURE 5. Components of the social constraint strategy. The signed arrows represent the associations, for individuals using a social constraint strategy, between each component and social satisfaction. (After Langston & Cantor, 1989.)

For example, a year after college, these students reported feeling significantly more responsible for the outcomes of social events than did their peers—an ironic twist of self-blame in light of their other-directed strategy.

The social constraint strategy provides a clear example of how tricky it is for people to overcome self-doubt and engage in vigorous goal pursuit without incurring side effects over time. In this strategy, as the temporal dynamics unfold, the very tendency that facilitates the positive thrust to take part socially (and to avoid self-focused immobilization) serves, over the long run, as evidence for the self-deprecating retrospections that lead to more self-doubts. As time goes on, individuals using this strategy presumably not only have to answer to their "basic" anxieties about their social life tasks but also to the ancillary evidence produced by their passivity in social interactions.

Langston and Cantor (1989) illustrated that this cost is specifically associated with the social constraint strategy by comparing the path from appraisals of anxiety on the friends task through the strat-

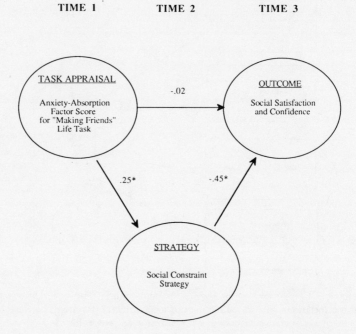

FIGURE 6. Path model predicting social satisfaction and confidence. Path coefficients are standardized bs; $N = 53$; *$p < .05$, **$p < .01$, $R^2 = .23$. Time 1, first year in college; time 2, sophomore year; time 3, junior year. (From Langston & Cantor, 1989.) Copyright 1989 by the American Psychological Association. Reprinted by permission.

egy to social (dis)satisfaction with the direct path from the anxiety appraisals to social (dis)satisfaction. As shown in Figure 6, anxiety appraisals of the social task did not by themselves necessarily doom a student in this sample to social dissatisfaction several years later; nevertheless, traveling along the social constraint path did significantly predict such dissatisfaction. As such, the side effects of this strategy seem to exact a greater cost than may be necessary for the benefit of overcoming social anxiety.

Outcome focus and overcoming uncertainty. Both the defensive-pessimist strategy and the social constraint strategy exact a price for overcoming anxiety in the target domain itself—defensive pessimism is associated with an emotional letdown after the task and some diminution in intrinsic motivation for the task over the long run; social constraint exacts an even steeper price as it is associated with an exacerbation of self-doubt in the target domain over time. In contrast, some strategies are quite effective in the target domain but exact costs in other important life-task domains.

Harlow (Cantor & Harlow, 1992a; Harlow & Cantor, 1994) has investigated one such strategy in which *outcome focus* in the academic task is associated with a stepped-up pursuit of academics in social situations—a pursuit that serves to tarnish the individuals' enjoyment of social life, even as it seems effective in terms of academic performance and satisfaction. Using the appraisal rating and self-concept data from the sorority project (Cantor et al., 1991b), Harlow and Cantor (1994) identified a group of women in the sample who appraised the academic task as difficult but rewarding and especially important in the eyes of others. These women described their academic self-concept in positive terms but also stated significant uncertainty about their abilities. Analyses of experience-sampling reports then revealed a connection (unique to this subgroup in the sample) between the occurrence of negative events in their academic life and increased pursuit of academics in *social* situations.

This social pursuit strategy involved two critical components, as illustrated in Figure 7. First, these women reacted to negative events in their academic life by stepping up their pursuit of academic interests in social situations, such as at parties and in leisure time with friends. Harlow referred to this aspect of their strategy as a "hangover" of attention, as illustrated in the top portion of Figure 7. This hangover, however, was very specific in its occurrence in social situations; these women did not react to negative academic events by spending more time on academics while alone or when running errands or the like. They most likely looked to social events to provide a forum for gaining clarity about their academic tasks by obtaining others' views. In this sense, their strategy was patterned in a way consistent with the emphasis on others' views in their academic task appraisals.

As reasonable then as this social pursuit of academics may have been, it also forged a costly connection for these women between social satisfaction and academics. As illustrated in the bottom part of Figure 7, their social satisfaction and enjoyment of social life came to depend, in large part, on how happy they were feeling in their *academic* activities. For example, their reports of happiness in class (ob-

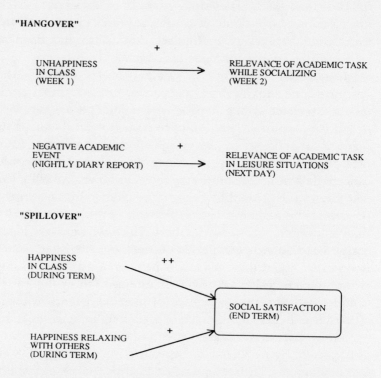

FIGURE 7. The social pursuit of academics by outcome-focused individuals. (After Harlow & Cantor, 1994.)

tained from experience-sampling reports during the term) were more strongly correlated with social satisfaction at the end of the term than were their reports of happiness while relaxing with others. (This association between happiness in class and social satisfaction was not observed for the nonoutcome-focused women in the sample.) This "spillover" may have been costly for the women in the outcome-focused subgroup because it linked social satisfaction to the on-line experience of academics, an experience that we know to have been typically less than pleasant for this sample.

The women in the outcome-focused group who had uncertainty in the academic and not in the social arena reported relatively low satisfaction at the end of the term in their social but not in their academic lives, as compared with the non-outcome-focused women. Their strategy may have precipitated this sacrifice in social satisfaction in two ways—first by linking social satisfaction to the often unpleasant happenings in academic events and second and more directly by diluting their enjoyment of "down time" with friends in the service of struggling over academics in otherwise relaxing social and leisure events.

The strategy of the women in the outcome-focused subgroup is, in some respects, a wise one—these women persevered with considerable success at their academic tasks even in the face of uncertainty and self-doubts. As the achievement and motivation literatures have suggested (e.g., Darley & Goethals, 1980; Thoits, 1986), reflected appraisals and social support can be very useful in alleviating uncertainty. However, their admirable persistence and satisfaction in academics may have been bought at the price of sacrifices in their social life, an initially far less problematic domain. Moreover, these women would probably not associate their dissatisfaction with social life with the tendency to bring academics to bear in these social arenas. Therefore, to make matters worse, not only does this strategy entail costs in another key domain, it also leaves the participant unlikely to recognize these costs.

DYNAMICS OF SOCIAL INTELLIGENCE

Strategies such as defensive pessimism, social constraint, and the social pursuit of academics demonstrate the ingenuity with which people approach their uncertain and challenging tasks, although they also reveal (often unanticipated) side effects and sacrifices associated with these mundane daily life victories. In considering such strategies, one is almost forced to take the view that social adjustment is a dynamic, highly unstable attribute of individuals. How, for example, are we to evaluate the "health" or, for that matter, the "intelligence" of people who anticipate worst-case outcomes for tasks on which they have succeeded many times, people who overcome immobilizing social anxiety by looking to others, only to bemoan their social passivity later, and people who sacrifice the quality of social life to gain reassurance about their academic ability? In retrospect, these strategic proclivities appear at a distance rather shortsighted, sometimes unnecessary, and other times simply too costly. However, if there is one lesson to be learned in this context it is the hazards of retrospective evaluations that, almost by necessity, fail to correct for the initial problem to which the strategy was addressed (cf. Baron, 1989).

Strategies arise to address particular needs, goals, and perceived deficits—real or otherwise—in specific tasks. They are linked to specific self-views and task appraisals that are salient at particular times in a person's life and in particular task contexts. In keeping with this impetus, they unfold in highly regularized but often quite specific temporal sequences and situational contexts; these characteristic dynamics of strategies are critical to their effectiveness precisely because they address the root problem for that individual. Norem (e.g., Norem & Illingworth, 1993), for example, has repeatedly shown both in laboratory and experience-sampling field studies how the cognitive-preparatory work that is highly effective (perhaps even necessary) for defensive pessimists serves only to disrupt performance and diminish satisfaction for optimists; conversely, a defensive pessimist cannot successfully protect the self and ensure future good performance after the task but an optimist can. What is effective (i.e., strategic) for one is highly counterproductive (i.e., nonstrategic) for the other in light of their different personal goals in the task context (i.e., the pessimist needs to overcome initial anxiety, whereas the optimist needs to reestablish control after the fact).

To the extent that such strategies make sense relative to these specific initiating conditions, it follows that most strategies should not be used (or overused) across the board or in too casual or routine ways. Discrimination in strategy use is critical first because the strategies probably will not be effective in too many diverse contexts. For example, the social pursuit of Harlow's subjects in the outcome-focused condition probably would not work to ease their academic uncertainties if it spilled over into nonsocial situations, such as time alone or on errands, in which reflected appraisals and social support were unavailable. Reassurance seeking in those situations could quickly turn into depressing rumination that might backfire and interfere further with their sense of control in academics (Nolen-Hoeksema, 1987).

Second, such restraint in strategy use is also necessary to minimize negative side effects and sacrifices in other task domains. As such, the women in the outcome-focused group need to be attuned in the long run to their social sacrifices, keeping constant check on exactly how much they are willing to sacrifice to gain clarity in the academic domain. In a similar vein, when a defensive pessimist starts to prepare for all trivial negative possibilities, then he or she will in all probability significantly exacerbate the strategy's side effects in emotional wear and tear and diminished motivation (Norem, 1989). The dynamics of social intelligence support the constant effort to take control, while also guarding against routinization or overuse of familiar strategies in either unnecessary or inappropriate contexts (Kihlstrom & Cantor, 1989; Linville & Clark, 1989). "Intelligent" defensive pessimism maximizes the constructive harnessing of anxiety for task performance while also minimizing the retrospective impression of "wasted" effort.

Is there room, then, in this relativism about social intelligence for any prescriptive standards for effective social functioning (Baron, 1989)? The answer is, of course, yes and no. The "no" refers to the strong dynamic presumption in this perspective—there is no room for complacency about problem solving in daily life because a solution to one problem may create others. The self-satisfied optimist can easily be made to pay for engaging in distraction rather than preparation in the face of an unexpectedly difficult, even dangerous task. Further, there is no room for complacency because it is inevitably true that, as soon as a life task becomes manageable, life changes and the task takes on new meaning that makes old solutions inadequate or inappropriate. When Zirkel (1992) studied the evolution of the task of being independent, she observed rather poignantly the dynamics of life-task pursuit: just when the college students began to feel in control in establishing an independent academic identity, they left school only to find concerns of social independence suddenly looming large in their new life. As Stewart and her colleagues (Stewart & Healy, 1985, 1989) have forcefully argued, personality functioning is a very delicate process in need of constant recalibration to newly arising social demands, opportunities, and pressures. There is too much change in most social environments to be complacent for too long; wisdom demands openness to such changes (Baltes et al., 1992; Brandstaedter & Renner, 1990).

Nevertheless, there is some room for prescriptive standards, however unstable and inexact they must be. The main prescription is to encourage individuals to take and invent opportunities for goal pursuit, even in unusual settings or when the task seems daunting

(Cantor & Harlow, 1992b). This prescription, as Pollyannaish as it may seem, derives from our view of the dynamics of self-esteem and satisfaction—that is, from our belief that even the happiest of individuals needs actively to take control rather than sit passively in control (Dweck, 1992).

We are persuaded that there is an active or proactive opportunism associated with self-esteem that may sometimes be unappreciated (see Gollwitzer & Wicklund, 1985; Steele, 1988, for examples of active opportunism). To be sure, the literature on self-esteem contains many persuasive demonstrations of how individuals can be buffered rather automatically from the full impact of negative life events by their self-illusions or by organizing self-knowledge in self-protective ways (Linville, 1982; Showers, 1992a). Nonetheless, other work suggests that high-self-esteem individuals may go to great lengths to self-affirm after negative events or in finding symbolic ways to complete a self-goal (Gollwitzer & Wicklund, 1985; Steele, 1988). These studies warn us not to underestimate the amount of "care and feeding" required both to maintain self-esteem and to cope with daily life events.

Langston (1990) used an accounting metaphor to capture this care-and-feeding aspect of self-esteem: he suggested that individuals actively mark their positive daily life events, both privately and socially, in the service of building up a "bank account" in the event of future "recessions." In other words, he emphasized the need for people to actively manage their coping resources rather than rely passively on their ability to bounce back. In an experience-sampling and daily diary study, he found that when people took active note of positive daily events, such as by telling friends or taking time out to reflect on the event rather than simply continue their routines, their positive affect and emotional arousal increased during the rest of the day. In the case of negative events, high-self-esteem subjects, but not those low in self-esteem, also benefited from "marking" those events—possibly gaining this relief by actively seeking social support and counsel.

Blanton and Cantor (1992) suggest that individuals who are secure in a task domain can draw actively on this bank account by working on these tasks in times of stress in less secure domains, thus creating an environment of security and positive affect to buffer the impact of stress in this other target domain. For example, they have recently collected daily diaries covering a 3-wk period from students who either feel secure in their friends task or not; they have concentrated on how the students secure in the friends task can alleviate stress in the academic arena by systematically increasing their social activities, creating a base of positive affect, and then turning more energetically to their academic work. This active juggling of different life-task pursuits can facilitate task persistence by balancing the stress of a challenging task against the reserve of rewards built up from less taxing activity in another central life-task domain.

These examples of opportunistic coping often emerge in domains in which people already feel at least somewhat in control in the relevant tasks. Nevertheless, in light of a dynamic system of self (Markus & Wurf, 1987), the prescriptive content here should also be generalizable to contexts in which a person is in need of strategies to take control. It should be possible to build efficacy by enhancing opportunities for active goal pursuit while simultaneously drawing on a reserve of control in other less threatening domains (e.g., Bandura, 1986).

To return, then, to Kihlstrom and Cantor's gardening metaphor, individuals need to work with and on their social intelligence. We need to cultivate opportunities to grow new plants and also to be attuned to the weeds that accumulate—the side effects and sacrifices entailed by those efforts. Further, we cannot afford to give in to despair when on reflection (and with the hindsight of knowledge of the weather!) it seems clear that a different planting would have been easier.

Cognitive Motivation and Creating Agency

We have reviewed a diverse body of work that is directed, in one way or another, to making a simple point—the essence of cognitive motivation is in individuals' efforts to create agency in the mundane reality of their daily lives. Of course, not all purposive behavior is thoughtful—that is, "willful" in the usual sense of the word; similarly, not all that we "intend" gets accomplished or even expressed. Still, we present this view as a contrast to those who would portray a cognitive theory of motivation as mute with respect to questions of will or choice or intention, or the affect associated with purposive behavior (cf. Pervin, 1983). We agree with those, such as Markus (1983) or Bandura (1986), for whom the "expanded self" and "self-reflection" create the motivation for individuals to be willful and to keep trying.

Like Markus and Bandura, we have something very specific in mind when we use the words "willful" or "intentional" and when we refer to a cognitive slice of motivation. We are referring to motivation and behavior that arises from what individuals think and say about themselves and their current goals. We refer to the ways in which individuals' own age-graded tasks, their current and ideal selves, and, most specifically, their life-task appraisals guide their choices and interpretations of daily life events. These tasks, selves, and appraisals represent knowledge that people *can* access deliberately, knowledge that people *can* use in an effortful and controlled way.

Whereas people *can* use this knowledge with some effort to direct their experience, it is important to note that frequently such knowledge is accessed automatically in the midst of an event (Bargh, 1989; this volume). In fact, we expect that in the context of familiar and/or nonthreatening daily life events, selves and tasks become relevant and guide the interpretation of events quite spontaneously, as in Bargh's (in this volume) explication of environmental features that activate individuals' goals and intentions without their awareness. For example, we are certain that much of the time our college student subjects were not explicitly thinking of their appraisals of a task as especially important when they interpreted a familiar event as task relevant (e.g., seeing a party as a forum for intimacy). On the other hand, we also believe that people use their knowledge in more deliberate, less spontaneous ways in contexts that are unfamiliar or challenging or when the demands of an event conflict with personal values or intentions. As such, we expect that these subjects were relatively more aware of their task appraisals when pursuing intimacy with a stranger or grades during an exam or when deciding to study rather than to party on the weekend.

This characterization of spontaneous but controllable thought is one that Uleman (1989) proposed to explain the impact of processing goals or instructional sets on individuals' (otherwise) spontaneous trait inferences. Similarly, we suggest that, when individuals need deliberately to access their knowledge of self and tasks to cope with challenge in daily life, they do so. This deliberation is a large piece of what distinguishes cognitive or self-regulatory motives from implicit motives (Fleeson, 1992a). It is also why we believe that behavior can change—people *can* control and change the ways in which they think about themselves and their tasks; those "thoughts" in turn have an impact on experience. Sometimes that effect is actually self-defeating, as we illustrated in the case of the social constraint strategy. Nonetheless, with explicit attention people can use their experience to change their appraisals, and those appraisals can then make an independent contribution to subsequent experience, as Fleeson (1992a) demonstrated. It may be effortful and slow, but it is possible.

Our cognitive slice of motivation, therefore, encompasses both the spontaneous and the deliberative thought with which events are interpreted in the light of personal goals. We believe that, whether spontaneous or deliberative, these thought processes determine a significant part of our experience of daily life events. That is, we do not see such processes as an afterthought to experience. Just as Bandura (1986) argues that self-efficacy beliefs are more important than ability in shaping performance, we believe that life-task appraisals constitute a critical determinant of the experience of an event, and just as Bandura (1986) shapes interventions to increase individuals' feelings of efficacy at a task, we point to individuals' own strategic efforts to harness anxiety by thinking differently about the task. These strategic efforts can be deliberate, as when a defensive pessimist prepares for a task, or they can be quite spontaneous, as in the case of the social pursuit of outcome-focused individuals. In either case, the individual's interpretation of events in terms of goals makes a critical contribution to experience.

In this chapter, we have reviewed work that highlights several different contexts in which there are "thoughtful" contributions to daily life experience. As we sketched in Figure 1, we believe that the interpretive process is guided by the implicit knowledge of the age-graded tasks that a person "ought" to care about at that time in life, somewhat more focal images of selves made salient by a new life context or life period, and these actual and possible selves that, in turn, become concrete as a person thinks about actually doing a task (as reflected, e.g., in life-task appraisals) and about his or her strategies for how, where, and when to do it and for what to think after it is done. Our focus on alternativism has explicated the left side of Figure 1, showing how self-knowledge is adaptively recruited in making important life choices. Our focus on functionalism has explicated the middle of Figure 1, showing how individuals' life tasks and their personalized meanings are reflected in the experience of daily life, and our focus on relativism has explicated the right side of Figure 1, showing how specific self-knowledge, task appraisals, and interpretive experience all come together in the form of strategies for goal pursuit. In this way, we suggest that social intelligence provides input to experience at many points before, during, and for long after an event.

There is a contribution to the choices of what to do in daily life, to the interpretation of what is going on in an event and the affect one feels as this happens, and to the satisfaction or stress one feels in general. In making life choices, people compare themselves to prototypes of the person best suited to each choice option; these self-prototype comparisons demonstrate the many alternative views of self that inform our experience. Most likely, these comparisons occur spontaneously, as do the choices of partners or activities that follow from them. Once in a situation, people interpret events as relevant to their pressing and highly valued life tasks, even if pursuing those tasks in that situation may present a challenge. These interpretive choices may sometimes unfold deliberately, as when a person shifts his or her focus of attention from one life task to another. Regardless of how effortful these task-relevance interpretations are, they are always associated with particular affective experiences. In fact, our experience-sampling data with various college student samples suggest that the affective experience of everyday life events, such as a night in the library or time spent alone, can be shifted substantially from its typical baseline when an unusual task is seen as relevant. Moreover, people take advantage of opportunities for such task pursuit, even when the on-line experience is not a terribly uplifting one.

This opportunism in task pursuit is complemented by the strategies that individuals form to take control of tasks that require extra effort. Rather than succumb to uncertainty or anxiety about a task, people sometimes think through their fears, observe others' behavior, or pursue the task in unusual places, all in the service of facing, rather than withdrawing from, the task. These strategies contribute directly to satisfaction at the task, although they also often have indirect side effects in terms of emotional wear and tear or even in terms of sacrifices in other domains. We believe that there are a large number of such strategies that individuals try out for a while and either abandon or keep. Focusing on self-knowledge, important tasks, appraisals of those tasks, and patterns of choice and affect in daily life should continue to reveal these creative attempts at taking control of life.

Strategies can enable individuals to overcome themselves, as they do things that seem in the abstract too difficult or anxiety provoking, but they rarely provide a stable or cost-free solution to the problems of living. In the end, as people get nearer to "the" goal, the goal changes, as when a seemingly good solution in one task domain ends up creating dissatisfaction in another domain. This has to be viewed as a dynamic system: people must be willing continuously to reflect on their current state—who they are, what they want now, and how they can get it without paying too steep a price. This continual reassessment is probably too much to ask too often, but we look to the pressure from age-graded life tasks to keep reminding us of the need for self-reflection. The process of taking on a normative life task rather automatically turns us all back on our selves, and the cycle starts over.

REFERENCES

Allport, G. W. (1937). *Personality: A psychological interpretation*. New York: Holt.

Baltes, P. B., Smith, J., & Staudinger, U. M. (1992). Wisdom and successful aging. In T. Sonderegger (Ed.), *Nebraska Symposium on Motivation 1991* (pp. 123–167). Lincoln: University of Nebraska Press.

Bandura, A. (1986). *Social foundations of thought and action: A social cognitive theory*. Englewood Cliffs, NJ: Prentice-Hall.

Bargh, J. A. (1982). Attention and automaticity in the processing of self-relevant information. *Journal of Personality and Social Psychology, 43*, 425–436.

Bargh, J. A. (1989). Conditional automaticity: Varieties of automatic influence in social perception and cognition. In J. S. Uleman & J. A. Bargh (Eds.), *Unintended thought* (pp. 3–51.) New York: Guilford.

Baron, J. (1989). Why a theory of social intelligence needs a theory of character. In R. Wyer & T. Srull (Eds.), *Advances in social cognition* (Vol. 2, pp. 61–70). Hillsdale, NJ: Erlbaum.

Baumeister, R. F., & Scher, S. J. (1988). Self-defeating behavior patterns among normal individuals: Review and analysis of common self-destructive tendencies. *Psychological Bulletin, 104,* 3–22.

Bergen, R. S., & Dweck, C. S. (1989). The functions of personality theories. In R. S. Wyer & T. K. Srull (Eds.), *Advances in social cognition* (Vol. 2, pp. 81–92). Hillsdale, NJ: Erlbaum.

Blanton, H., & Cantor, N. (1992). *Implicit theories of stress and coping.* Unpublished manuscript, Princeton University, Princeton, NJ.

Brandstaedter, J., & Renner, G. (1990). Tenacious goal pursuit and flexible goal adjustment: Explication and age-related analysis of assimilative and accommodative strategies of coping. *Psychology and Aging, 5,* 58–67.

Bruner, J. (1986). *Actual minds, possible words.* Cambridge, MA: Harvard University Press.

Buss, D. M. (1987). Selection, evocation, and manipulation. *Journal of Personality and Social Psychology, 53,* 1214–1221.

Buss, D. M., & Cantor, N. (Eds.), (1989). *Personality psychology: Recent trends and emerging directions.* New York: Springer.

Cantor, N. (1990). From thought to behavior: "Having" and "doing" in the study of personality and cognition. *American Psychologist, 45,* 735–750.

Cantor, N., Acker, M., & Cook-Flannagan, C. (1992a). Conflict and preoccupation in the intimacy life task. *Journal of Personality and Social Psychology, 63,* 644–655.

Cantor, N., Fleeson, W., & Cook-Flannagan, C. (1991a, May). *The flexible pursuit of life tasks in daily events.* Paper presented at the Society of Personality and Social Psychology at the meetings of the American Psychological Society, Washington, DC.

Cantor, N., & Fleeson, W. (1991). Life tasks and self-regulatory processes. In M. Maehr & P. Pintrich (Eds.), *Advances in motivation and achievement* (Vol. 7, pp. 327–369). Greenwich, CT: JAI.

Cantor, N., & Harlow, R. (1992a, April). *Keeping "friends" and "grades" separate: The role of self-assurance in life task pursuit.* Invited paper presented at the First Annual Conference on Agency, Self-Efficacy, and Self-Esteem, Athens, GA.

Cantor, N., & Harlow, R. (1992b, in press). Social intelligence and personality: Flexible life task pursuit. In R. Sternberg & P. Ruzgis (Eds.), *Intelligence and personality.* Cambridge: Cambridge University Press.

Cantor, N., & Kihlstrom, J. F. (1982). Cognitive and social processes in personality. In G. T. Wilson & C. M. Franks (Eds.), *Contemporary behavior therapy: Conceptual and empirical foundations* (pp. 142–201). New York: Guilford.

Cantor, N., & Kihlstrom, J. F. (1987). *Personality and social intelligence.* Englewood Cliffs, NJ: Prentice-Hall.

Cantor, N., & Kihlstrom, J. F. (1989). Social intelligence and cognitive assessments of personality. In R. S. Wyer & T. K. Srull (Eds.), *Advances in social cognition* (Vol. 2, pp. 1–59). Hillsdale, NJ: Erlbaum.

Cantor, N., Mackie, D., & Lord, C. (1984). Choosing partners and activities: The social perceiver decides to mix it up. *Social Cognition, 2,* 256–272.

Cantor, N., & Malley, J. (1991). Life tasks, personal needs, and close relationships. In G. J. O. Fletecher & F. D. Fincham (Eds.), *Cognition in close relationships* (pp. 101–125). Hillsdale, NJ: Erlbaum.

Cantor, N., Markus, H., Niedenthal, P., & Nurius, P. (1986). On motivation and the self-concept. In R. M. Sorrentino & E. T. Higgins (Eds.), *Motivation and cognition: Foundations of social behavior* (pp. 96–121). New York: Guilford.

Cantor, N., Mischel, W., & Schwartz, J. (1982). Social knowledge: Structure, content, use and abuse. In A. H. Hastorf & A. M. Isen (Eds.), *Cognitive social psychology* (pp. 33–72). New York: Elsevier North Holland.

Cantor, N., Norem, J. K., Niedenthal, P. M., Langston, C. A., & Brower, A. M. (1987). Life tasks, self-concept ideals, and cognitive strategies in a life transition. *Journal of Personality and Social Psychology, 53*, 1178–1191.

Cantor, N., & Norem, J. K. (1989). Defensive pessimism and stress coping. *Social Cognition, 7*, 92–112.

Cantor, N., Norem, J. K., Langston, C., Zirkel, S., Fleeson, W., & Cook-Flannagan, C. (1991b). Life tasks and daily life experience. *Journal of Personality, 59*, 425–452.

Cantor, N., & Zirkel, S. (1990). Personality, cognition, and purposive behavior. In L. Pervin (Ed.), *Handbook of personality: Theory and research* (pp. 135–164). New York: Guilford.

Cantor, N., Zirkel, S., & Norem, J. K. (1993). Human personality: Asocial and reflexive? Commentary prepared for: *Psychological Inquiry, 4*, 273–277.

Caspi, A., & Moffitt, T. (1993). Continuity amidst change: A paradoxical theory of personality coherence. *Psychological Inquiry, 4*, 247–271.

Cross, S., & Markus, H. (1991). Possible selves across the life span. *Human Development, 34*, 230–255.

Darley, J., & Goethals, G. R. (1980). People's analyses of the causes of ability-linked performances. In L. Berkowitz (Ed.), *Advances in experimental social psychology* (Vol. 13). New York: Academic Press.

Dweck, C. (1992). The study of goals in psychology. *Psychological Science, 3*, 165–167.

Emmons, R. A. (1989). The personal striving approach to personality. In L. A. Pervin (Ed.), *Goal concepts in personality and social psychology* (pp. 87–126). Hillsdale, NJ: Erlbaum.

Emmons, R. A., Diener, E., & Larsen, R. J. (1986). Choice and avoidance of everyday situations and affect congruence: Two models of reciprocal interationism. *Journal of Personality and Social Psychology, 51*, 815–826.

Emmons, R. A., & King, L. A. (1989). Personal striving differentiation and affective reactivity. *Journal of Personality and Social Psychology, 56*, 478–484.

Emmons, R. A., & McAdams, D. P. (1991). Personal strivings and motive dispositions: Exploring the links. *Personality and Social Psychology Bulletin, 17*, 648–654.

Erikson, E. H. (1950). *Childhood and society.* New York: Norton.

Fleeson, W. (1992a). *Life tasks, implicit motives, and self-regulation in daily life.* Unpublished doctoral dissertation, University of Michigan, Ann Arbor, MI.

Fleeson, W. (1992b). *Broad motives and life task adoption, commitment, and satisfaction.* Unpublished manuscript. University of Michigan, Ann Arbor, MI.

Fleeson, W., & Cantor, N. (1992a, August). *Temporal stability of discriminations in life-task appraisals.* Paper presented at the meetings of the American Psychological Association, Washington, DC.

Fleeson, W., & Cantor, N. (1992b). *Life tasks and affective experience: Ruling out situational explanations.* Unpublished manuscript. Max Planck Institut, Berlin.

Gollwitzer, P. (1992, in press). Goal achievement: The role of intentions. In: M. Hewstone & W. Stroebe (Eds.), *European Review of Social Psychology* (Vol. 4). Chichester: Wiley.

Gollwitzer, P., & Wicklund, R. (1985). The pursuit of self-defining goals. In J. Kuhl & J. Beckman (Eds.), *Action control: From cognition to behavior* (pp. 61–85). New York: Springer.

Harlow, R., & Cantor, N. (1994). The social pursuit of academics: Side-effects and "spillover" of strategic reassurance seeking. *Journal of Personality and Social Psychology, 66,* 386–397.

Havighurst, R. J. (1953). *Human development and education.* New York: Longmans, Green.

Helson, R., Mitchell, V., & Moane, G. (1984). Personality and patterns of adherence and nonadherence to the social clock. *Journal of Personality and Social Psychology, 46,* 1079–1096.

Higgins, E. T. (1987). Self-discrepancy: A theory relating self and affect. *Psychological Review, 94,* 319–340.

Higgins, E. T. (1990). Personality, social psychology, and person-situation relations: Standards and knowledge activation as a common language. In L. A. Pervin (Ed.), *Handbook of Personality: Theory and Research* (pp. 301–338). New York: Guilford.

Higgins, E. T., & Parsons, J. E. (1983). Social cognition and the social life of the child: Stages as subcultures. In E. T. Higgins, D. N. Ruble, & W. W. Hartup (Eds.), *Social cognition and social development: A sociocultural perspective* (pp. 15–62). New York: Cambridge University Press.

Kelly, G. A. (1955). *A theory of personality: The psychology of personal constructs.* New York: Norton.

Kihlstrom, J. F., & Cantor, N. (1984). Mental representations of the self. In L. Berkowitz (Ed.), *Advances in experimental social psychology* (Vol. 17). New York: Academic Press.

Kihlstrom, J. F., & Cantor, N. (1989). Social intelligence and personality: There's room for growth. In R. S. Wyer & T. K. Srull (Eds.), *Advances in social cognition* (Vol. 2, pp. 197–214). Hillsdale, NJ: Erlbaum.

Langston, C. A. (1990). *The dynamics of daily life: Responses to positive and negative events, life-task activity, mood and well-being.* Unpublished doctoral dissertation, University of Michigan, Ann Arbor, MI.

Langston, C., & Cantor, N. (1989). Social anxiety and social constraint: When "making friends" is hard. *Journal of Personality and Social Psychology, 56*, 649–661.

Linville, P. W. (1982). Affective consequences of complexity regarding the self and others. In M. Clark & S. Fiske (Eds.), *Affect and cognition: The 17th annual Carnegie Symposium on Cognition* (pp. 79–109). Hillsdale, NJ: Erlbaum.

Linville, P. W., & Clark, L. F. (1989). Production systems and social problem solving: Specificity, flexibility, and expertise. In R. S. Wyer & T. K. Srull (Eds.), *Advances in social cognition* (Vol. 2, pp. 131–152). Hillsdale, NJ: Erlbaum.

Little, B. (1983). Personal projects: A rationale and methods for investigation. *Environment and Behavior, 15*, 273–309.

Little, B. (1989). Personal projects analysis: Trivial pursuits, magnificent obsessions and the search for coherence. In D. M. Buss & N. Cantor (Eds.), *Personality psychology: Recent trends and emerging directions* (pp. 15–31). New York: Springer.

Little, B. R., Lecci, L., & Watkinson, B. (1992). Personality and personal projects: Linking big five and PAC units of analysis. *Journal of Personality, 60*, 502–525.

Markus, H. (1983). Self-knowledge: An expanded view. *Journal of Personality, 51*, 543–565.

Markus, H., & Nurius, P. (1986). Possible selves. *American Psychologist, 41*, 954–969.

Markus, H., & Wurf, E. (1987). The dynamic self-concept: A social psychological perspective. *Annual Review of Psychology, 38*, 299–337.

McAdams, D. P. (1989). The development of a narrative identity. In D. M. Buss & N. Cantor (Eds.), *Personality psychology: Recent trends and emerging directions* (pp. 160—174). New York: Springer.

McAdams, D. P. (1992). The five-factor model in personality: A critical appraisal. *Journal of Personality, 60*, 329–361.

McClelland, D. C. (1985). *Human motivation*. Glenview, IL: Scott, Foresman.

Mischel, W. (1984). Convergences and challenges in the search for consistency. *American Psychologist, 39*, 351–364.

Niedenthal, P., Cantor, N., & Kihlstrom, J. (1985). Prototype-matching: A strategy for social decision-making. *Journal of Personality and Social Psychology, 48*, 575–584.

Niedenthal, P. M., & Mordkoff, J. T. (1991). Prototype distancing: A strategy for choosing among threatening situations. *Personality and Social Psychology Bulletin, 17*, 483–493.

Nolen-Hoeksema, S. (1987). Sex differences in unipolar depression: Evidence and theory. *Psychological Bulletin, 101*, 259–282.

Norem, J. K. (1989). Cognitive strategies as personality: Effectiveness, specificity, flexibility, and change. In D. M. Buss & N. Cantor (Eds.), *Personality psychology: Recent trends and emerging directions* (pp. 45–60). New York: Springer.

Norem, J. K., & Cantor, N. (1986a). Anticipatory and post hoc cushioning strategies: Optimism and defensive pessimism in "risky" situations. *Cognitive Therapy and Research, 10*, 347–362.

Norem, J. K., & Cantor, N. (1986b). Defensive pessimism: "Harnessing" anxiety as motivation. *Journal of Personality and Social Psychology, 51*, 1208–1217.

Norem, J. K., & Cantor, N. (1990a). Capturing the "flavor" of behavior: Cognition, affect, and interpretation. In B. S. Moore & A. M. Isen (Eds.), *Affect and social behavior* (pp. 39–63). New York: Cambridge University Press.

Norem, J. K., & Cantor, N. (1990b). Cognitive strategies, coping and perceptions of competence. In R. J. Sternberg & J. Kolligian, Jr. (Eds.), *Competence considered* (pp. 190–204). New Haven, CT: Yale University Press.

Norem, J. K., & Cantor, N. (1991). *Life task analysis.* Workshop at the Henry Murray Center, Radcliffe College, Cambridge, MA.

Norem, J. K., & Illingworth, K. S. S. (1993). Strategy-dependent effects of reflecting on self and tasks: Some implications of optimism and defensive pessimism. *Journal of Personality and Social Psychology, 65*, 822–835.

Nuttin, J. (1984). *Motivation, planning, and action: A relational theory of behavior dynamics.* Hillsdale, NJ: Erlbaum.

Pervin, L. A. (1983). The stasis and flow of behavior: Toward a theory of goals. In M. M. Page (Ed.), *Nebraska Symposium on Motivation 1982* (pp. 1–53). Lincoln: University of Nebraska Press.

Ryff, C. D. (1991). Possible selves in adulthood and old age: A tale of shifting horizons. *Psychology and Aging, 6*, 286–295.

Showers, C. (1992a). Compartmentalization of positive and negative self-knowledge: Keeping bad apples out of the bunch. *Journal of Personality and Social Psychology, 62*, 1036–1049.

Showers, C. (1992b). The motivational and emotional consequences of considering positive or negative possibilities for an upcoming event. *Journal of Personality and Social Psychology, 63*, 474–484.

Showers, C., & Cantor, N. (1985). Social cognition: A look at motivated strategies. In M. Rosenzweig & L. W. Porter (Eds.), *Annual review of psychology* (Vol. 36, pp. 375–305). Palo Alto, CA: Annual Reviews.

Showers, C., & Ruben, C. (1990). Distinguishing defensive pessimism from depression: Negative expectations and positive coping mechanisms. *Cognitive Therapy and Research, 14*, 385–399.

Snyder, M. (1981). On the influence of individuals on situations. In N. Cantor & J. Kihlstrom (Eds.), *Personality, cognition, and social interaction* (pp. 309–329). Hillsdale, NJ: Erlbaum.

Snyder, M., & Simpson, J. A. (1984). Self-monitoring and dating relationships. *Journal of Personality and Social Psychology 47*, 281–291.

Steele, C. (1988). The psychology of self-affirmation: Sustaining the integrity of the self. In L. Berkowitz (Ed.), *Advances in experimental social psychology* (Vol. 21, pp. 261–302). New York: Academic Press.

Stewart, A. J. (1982). The course of individual adaptation to life changes. *Journal of Personality and Social Psychology, 42*, 1100–1113.

Stewart, A. J., & Healy, J. (1985). Personality and adaptation to change. In R. Hogan & W. Jones (Eds.), *Perspectives on personality: Theory, measurements, and interpersonal dynamics* (pp. 117–144). Greenwich, CT: JAI.

Thoits, P. A. (1986). Social support as coping assistance. *Journal of Consulting and Clinical Psychology, 54,* 416–423.

Thorne, A. (1989). Conditional patterns, transference, and the coherence of personality across time. In D. M. Buss and N. Cantor (Eds.), *Personality psychology: Recent trends and emerging directions* (pp. 149–159). New York: Springer.

Uleman, J. S. (1989). A framework for thinking intentionally about unintended thought. In J. S. Uleman & J. A. Bargh (Eds.), *Unintended thought* (pp. 425–449). New York: Guilford.

Vandewater, E. A., Stewart, A. J., & Cantor, N. (August 1992). *Understanding women's lives through time: Life tasks and personality development.* Paper presented at the meetings of the American Psychological Association, Washington, DC.

Wright, J. C., & Mischel, W. (1987). A conditional approach to dispositional constructs: The local predictability of social behavior. *Journal of Personality and Social Psychology, 53,* 1159–1177.

Zirkel, S. A. (1992). Developing independence in a life transition: Investing the self in the concerns of the day. *Journal of Personality and Social Psychology, 62,* 506–521.

Zirkel, S. A., & Cantor, N. (1990). Personal construal of life tasks: Those who struggle for independence. *Journal of Personality and Social Psychology, 58,* 172–185.

A Motivational Theory of Psychopathology

Don C. Fowles
University of Iowa

Introduction

A motivational approach to psychopathology has numerous advantages. First, psychiatric disorders have traditionally been recognized as emotional disorders, and the overlap between concepts of motivation and emotion suggests the relevance of motivation to psychopathology. Second, it builds on the rich history of research in the area of animal learning and motivation that was once the mainstay of experimental psychology. Although this area no longer occupies center stage in psychology, it makes more sense to exploit its contributions than to abandon them. Third, the experimental base in animal research has made possible at least initial steps in the direction of integrating the black-box motivational constructs with underlying neurobehavioral processes, and behavioral neurochemistry is currently a vigorous and rapidly developing area of research. Fourth, this integration of motivation and behavioral neurochemistry provides points of articulation to important areas of biological research in psychopathology: genetic contributions to etiology, pharmacological approaches to treatment, and the mechanisms by which abused drugs exert their influence on behavior. It is reasonable to propose that genetic and pharmacological influences operate, at least in part, by way of effects on neurochemical systems influencing behavior. Further, to the extent that motivation is relevant to psychopathology, it is also reasonable to expect that the neurochemistry of motivation will be implicated. Fifth, since the behavioral and motivational theories are drawn from the study of *learning,* effects of the environment are inherently important. Thus, such theories are particularly well suited to bring together biological and environmental contributions in psychopathology. Sixth, motivational constructs from animal work can be compatible with the currently popular cognitive approaches to motivation, making it unnecessary to adopt an either/or perspective. Specifically, the motivational theory to be employed here includes expectancy constructs, especially concerning the efficacy of one's behavior in producing desirable outcomes or in avoiding undesirable outcomes. Thus, these expectancy constructs are entirely compatible with the importance of perceptions of lack of control, hopelessness, or helplessness that constitute cognitive contributions to psychopathology. A final attraction of this approach is that similar constructs are already in use as explanations for psychopathology. Much of the review that follows consists simply of pointing out similarities between the motivational concepts in question and current etiological theories seen across a wide range of psychopathology. In many cases, a central feature of psychopathology appears to be too much or too little activity in a motivational system. By taking such an overview, one can see the usefulness of a motivational approach to psychopathology.

To the extent that these arguments are valid, they suggest a further, perhaps more grandiose perspective: a motivational approach may provide a general theoretical framework for an integrated theory of psychopathology. As noted previously (Fowles, 1988), the following are the *minimum* elements for a theory of psychopathology:

Genes
Enzymes
Neural substrates for behavior (neurotransmitter systems)
Environment
Behavior and psychological processes
Psychopathology

In the current enthusiasm for biological (especially genetic) hypotheses, what often seems to go unnoticed is that the repeated demonstration that Darwin was correct and that genes do make a difference does not tell us *what* is inherited and *how* such inheritance leads to psychopathology. Since psychiatric disorders are defined in terms of disturbances of behavior, emotions, cognitive and other psychological processes, and so on, an adequate theory requires a causal pathway involving behavior and psychological functioning, as well as the contribution of environmental influences. The absence of such a theory constitutes a theoretical gulf between hypothesized genetic influences and the phenotypic characteristics of psychiatric disorders.

Furthermore, physiology and biochemistry are essential to an understanding of physical medical diseases. These disciplines provide a theoretical structure of normal functioning, against which can be understood deviations from normality. In the same way, an integration of concepts from psychology and neuroscience should provide such a theoretical framework for understanding psychopathology. This chapter suggests that a motivational theory may provide a start in this direction (see also Fowles, 1993a).

A Motivational Theory

APPETITIVE AND AVERSIVE MOTIVATION

An important theoretical tradition in the animal literature on motivation makes a fundamental distinction between appetitive and aversive motivational systems that are mutually antagonistic. The essential features of this approach are described by Mackintosh (1974, p. 348):

> The argument . . . has rested on assumptions about the reciprocal nature of appetitive and aversive reinforcers. Response facilitation or reinforcement was regarded as a consequence of an anticipated increase in appetitive, or decrease in aversive stimulation; conversely, response suppression or punishment was regarded as a consequence of an anticipated increase in aversive, or decrease in appetitive stimulation. This symmetry, in turn, relies on a set of presuppositions about mutual antagonism or inhibition between appetitive and aversive systems, a point of view most clearly enunciated by Konorski (1967).

In considering applications to psychopathology, it is convenient to employ Jeffrey Gray's explication of this approach to motivation. Gray (e.g., 1976, 1977, 1982, 1987b) has used this theory to conceptualize the effects of anxiolytic drugs and to examine the consequences of individual differences in proneness to anxiety. In addition, much of his work has been concerned with the neurobiological substrate for the motivational system associated with anxiety. These features of his work facilitate the application to psychopathology.

Before turning to Gray's theory, however, it should be noted that these appetitive and aversive constructs have a counterpart in recent studies of emotional states in humans. Factor analyses by Tellegen, Watson, and Clark (Tellegen, 1985; Watson & Clark, 1984; Watson & Tellegen, 1985) of self-reports of current mood have repeatedly found two large factors of positive and negative affect (although extracted as orthogonal, these factors usually actually are slightly negatively correlated). Additionally, in work on the startle response, Lang and his colleagues (Lang et al., 1990, 1993) found that positively and negatively valenced emotional stimuli showed reciprocally antagonistic effects on the startle response.

GRAY'S THEORY

Gray's work has focused on the aversive motivational system or, as he calls it, the *behavioral inhibition system* (BIS). The aversive motivational system *inhibits* behavior in response to *conditioned* stimuli (CSs) for punishment and frustrative nonreward and to novel stimuli and innate fear stimuli (Gray, 1982, p. 12). In addition to inhibiting behavior, BIS activity increases nonspecific arousal, allocates attention to "the maximum possible analysis of current environmental stimuli, especially novel ones" (Gray, 1982, p. 13), and prepares for vigorous action (Gray, 1987b, p. 263). Gray (e.g., 1987b, pp. 263–264) sometimes calls the BIS the "stop, look, and listen" system to emphasize the redirection of attention to the environment. The nonspecific arousal increases the vigor of those responses that occur despite the threats of punishment or nonreward.

In inhibitory effects on behavior, the prototypical paradigms are passive avoidance and extinction. Passive avoidance is attributed to inhibition of behavior by the BIS in response to cues for punishment, whereas extinction is attributed to inhibition of behavior by the BIS in response to cues for frustrative nonreward. Note that there is an *anticipatory* quality to BIS activity: it is activated by CSs for threats and even by novel uncertain threats, and it promotes a vigilant scanning of the environment for potential threats. Similarly, it is centrally involved in appraising the threat value of the environment. As will be seen below, these features are prominent in generalized anxiety disorder. As further noted below, Gray argues that the anxiolytic drugs have in common the property of diminishing the efficacy of the BIS. In view of this specificity and the nature of the stimuli to which the BIS responds (threats of punishment and frustration), he has argued that activity in the BIS is associated with anxiety—that is, for Gray it constitutes the neurophysiological substrate for anxiety.

The appetitive motivational system *activates* behavior in response to CSs for reward and relieving nonpunishment. The prototypical paradigms are approach and active avoidance, although Gray (1982, p. 12) also includes skilled escape and predatory aggression. Whereas Gray originally called the appetitive system the approach system, I (Fowles, 1980) have named it the *behavioral activation system* (BAS) to emphasize the parallelism with the BIS. There is a positive, hedonic tone to activation of the BAS: the emotional labels applied to this positive affect are "hope" in the case of approach for rewards and "relief" in the case of active avoidance. Like the BIS, the BAS has inputs into a nonspecific arousal system.

Gray (1982, p. 13) describes a third system, called the *fight/flight system*, which responds to *un*conditioned punishment and nonreward with greatly increased activity—for example, running, jumping, hissing, and attacking a suitable target (Gray, 1987b, p. 244). These behaviors are characterized (Gray, 1982, pp. 11–12) as centering around defensive aggression (fight) or attempts at unconditioned escape (flight). Gray's use of fight/flight terminology refers to Cannon's well-known work on the emergency reaction: animals exposed to immediately stressful stimuli (e.g., a cat exposed to a barking dog) showed a massive reaction of the sympathetic branch of the autonomic nervous system in preparation for vigorous activity. To anticipate material presented below, one would expect strong cardiovascular activity in connection with activity in this third system (Gray, 1987b, pp. 55–56).

Gray sees a fundamental distinction between the BIS and the fight/flight system, because the behavioral effects of unconditioned and conditioned aversive stimuli are often diametrically opposed:

that is, vigorous behavior (fight/flight) versus "tense, silent immobility" (1987b, p. 254). Because the antianxiety drugs attenuate responses mediated by the BIS yet have little effect on escape and defensive aggression, Gray (1987b, p. 256) argues that fear and anxiety are related to the BIS and not to the fight/flight system, which he identifies with a central state of pain (e.g., Grey, 1987b, p. 19). His argument might be strengthened by considering that pathological anxiety is, by definition, not associated with unconditioned punishment and frustration—that is, pathological anxiety is irrational, being experienced in the absence of real threats or frustrations. For these reasons, then, Gray and others using his theory have not incorporated the fight/flight system into a theory of anxiety. In strong contrast, Barlow (1988) has made the fight/flight system an important component of his theory of panic, as will be detailed below.

Gray (1987a, 1987b) has summarized his current understanding of the neural basis for these systems. The BIS includes the septo-hippocampal system and the closely related Papez loop, ascending adrenergic (from the locus ceruleus) and serotonergic (from the raphe nuclei) pathways that innervate the septo-hippocampal system, and neocortical structures (entorhinal, prefrontal, and cingulate cortex) with two-way communication with the septo-hippocampal system (Gray 1987b, pp. 291–306; see also Depue & Spoont, 1986, for an extensive review of the critical role of serotonin in the BIS). The substrate for the fight/flight system includes the amygdala, the ventromedial nucleus of the hypothalamus, and the central gray of the midbrain or mesencephalon (Gray 1987b, pp. 320–324). In Gray's view, the ventromedial nucleus maintains tonic inhibition of the midbrain central gray, which in turn is the ultimate executive organ for fight/flight. Output from the amygdala inhibits the ventromedial nucleus, with a resulting release of the fight/flight response. While he has not been as concerned with the neural basis of the BAS, he does suggest that dopaminergic pathways are involved (Gray, 1987b, pp. 308–309, 330). Specifically, as detailed below, there is consistent evidence that the mesolimbic dopaminergic pathway that ascends from the A10 nucleus in the ventral tegmental area to the nucleus accumbens and other regions of the ventral striatum plays a key role in incentive motivation—that is, discharging the functions attributed to the BAS—and mediates the rewarding effects of addictive drugs such as heroin and cocaine. Consequently, it is likely that this pathway plays a central role in the BAS. Finally, the nonspecific arousal mechanism is identified with the ascending reticular activating system, especially with the noradrenergic fibers originating within the locus coeruleus that project to much of the neocortex and most of the limbic system (Gray, 1987b, pp. 272–276).

It is perhaps useful at this point to note that, whereas Gray begins with constructs from animal learning theory, Panksepp (1992) begins with the perspective of neuroscience and finds strong evidence for four emotional systems, three of which appear to correspond to Gray's systems. These systems are fear (cf. BIS), expectancy (cf. BAS), panic (cf. fight/flight), and rage. Panksepp suggests further that panic includes separation distress and that this emotional system evolved from an older system that mediated the affective distress of pain—a suggestion consistent with the role of the fight/flight system in responding to unconditioned punishment stimuli. Rage is viewed as related to frustration and as having evolved initially as a response to physical constraint. Thus, panic and rage were initially tied to responses to unconditioned stimuli (pain, physical restraint), but they appear to have evolved into more flexible emotional systems that are not restricted to responding to unconditioned stimuli. At least with respect to panic, this view supports Barlow's suggestions concerning an alarm reaction that is implicated in panic (see below).

I propose that the BAS, the BIS, and the fight/flight system, or variations on these themes as we learn more about them, play an important role in both emotional responding and the regulation of behavior and, further, that it should be possible to identify their contribution to many major forms of psychopathology. These systems may be seen as contributing to psychopathology in three ways:

- They may mediate the effects of environmental influences, such as aversive environments or exposure to addicting drugs.
- Quantitative individual differences in their reactivity (i.e., a temperament hypothesis) may make a person overly reactive (e.g., to aversive stimuli in anxiety-prone individuals) or insufficiently reactive (e.g., to threats of punishment in impulsive individuals) to environmental input, contributing to vulnerability to psychopathology.

- They may malfunction qualitatively and cease to respond to environmental input as may be the case for particularly severe psychopathology (e.g., unrestrained reward-seeking and behavioral activation in mania or severe anhedonia in bipolar depression).

With this background, we can now turn to a review of motivational constructs in psychopathology, beginning with the anxiety disorders. To a significant extent, I will emphasize prominent theories of psychopathology that already employ motivational constructs. However, in places my own work will be cited and speculations offered concerning the implications of a motivational perspective for specific forms of psychopathology. In view of the scope of this present review, only broad outlines of the issues will usually be presented, with references to original sources providing direction for more detailed discussions.

Anxiety Disorders

Since Gray (e.g., 1975, 1976, 1977, 1978, 1979) presented his work on the BIS as a "neuropsychological theory of anxiety," the BIS has obvious implications for anxiety disorders (i.e., that a particularly strong BIS will cause too much anxiety). These ostensible implications are further strengthened by the consideration that Gray's early work was especially concerned with understanding, from the perspective of the constructs of animal learning theory, the effects of alcohol, barbiturates, and minor tranquilizers—all of which appear clinically to reduce anxiety. On the basis of an extensive review of the literature, Gray (1977, 1982, chap. 2; see also Gray, 1979, for a summary) concluded that these anxiolytic drugs specifically disinhibit behavior in paradigms believed to elicit activity in the BIS (e.g., passive avoidance, extinction), providing a theoretical link between a concept of motivation and the effects of widely used psychotropic drugs. That is, the antianxiety drugs disinhibit behavior in passive-avoidance paradigms, and they increase resistance to extinction in the case of extinction after continuous reinforcement. Rates of responding are also reliably increased under fixed-interval, fixed-ratio, and differential reinforcement of low-rate (DRL) schedules. These paradigms all involve a non-REW-CS, an event signaling that the animal's responses will not be rewarded for a period of time. In contrast, the antianxiety drugs do not affect behavior in paradigms primarily involving the BAS (e.g., simple reward learning and one-way active avoidance). Gray's assertion that the BIS represents an anxiety system is, therefore, supported by this specific effect of anti-anxiety drugs on the BIS and by the aversive quality of the stimuli to which the BIS responds. Consistent with Gray's view, Quay (1988b) commented that the internalizing disorders in children, characterized by anxiety and withdrawal, reflect an excess of BIS activity.

BARLOW'S THEORY

An enriched understanding of the appropriate application of Gray's theory to anxiety disorders can be achieved by an examination of Barlow's (1988) theory of the nature and etiology of panic disorder and generalized anxiety disorder. Only a brief summary of Barlow's theory is possible here, but I have treated this topic in more detail elsewhere (Fowles, 1992a). The starting point in this theory is Barlow's distinction between two types of anxiety (1988, pp. 158–159), which he calls *anxiety* and *fear*. The nature of anxiety is better indicated by the term *anxious apprehension,* while fear refers to an *alarm reaction*. Anxiety or anxious apprehension prepares the organism to cope with the challenges and stresses of everyday life, and it is comprised of negative affect, high arousal, perceptions of helplessness or inability to control future events, and "worry" (the allocation of attention to negatively valenced self-evaluative concerns and/or the autonomic correlates of the arousal itself).

If, in the interest of parsimony, we map Barlow's systems onto Gray's, anxious apprehension resembles Gray's BIS. Both involve anticipation of aversive outcomes (punishment, failure) and produce arousal that invigorates behavior. Although Gray's emphasis on behavioral inhibition is not prominent in Barlow's account of preparatory anxiety, the role of the BIS in conflict situations (approach-avoidance conflict) and in situations of uncertain reward (potential frustration) is consistent with Barlow's emphasis on preparation for stresses and challenges, as is Gray's (1987b, p. 263) comment that the BIS prepares for vigorous (future) action (p. 263) and that the septo-hippocampal system, which is a core structure in the BIS, looks out for and detects anxiogenic stimuli and activates appropriate behavioral routines (p. 293). Gray's (1982, p. 13) comment that the BIS allocates attention to "the maximum possible analysis of current environmental stimuli, especially novel ones" and his (1987b, p. 263) description of the BIS as the "stop, look, and listen" system are, to some extent, consistent with Barlow's emphasis on "worry." Given that the BIS is responding to potential threats (including uncertain novel threats), it is reasonable to see this vigilant anticipation and appraisal of threats as involving worry. With respect to differences, Gray's emphasis on behavioral inhibition as a consequence of BIS activity is not found in Barlow's treatment of anxious apprehension. Anxious apprehension is seen as impeding performance in many instances, but Barlow invokes the Yerkes-Dodson law to account for these performance decrements. Thus, while Barlow argues that anxious apprehension interferes with successful performance, he does not attribute this directly to inhibition of behavior. Overall, then, the two theoretical constructs share about as many features as one might expect from constructs focused on animal learning theory, on the one hand, and patients with anxiety disorders, on the other hand.

The most frequent alarm reaction involves strong behavioral and cardiovascular activation. (The alarm reaction can also involve "freezing" or "tonic immobility" with decreased cardiovascular activity, but this is an infrequent response.) Barlow calls this strong behavioral response the ancient alarm reaction of *fear* (1988, p. 209), which he equates with Cannon's (1929) "fight or flight" response (Barlow, 1988, pp. 3–4, 158). Since he invokes Cannon, there is necessarily considerable overlap with Gray's fight/flight system (see also Barlow, 1988, p. 258). The major difference between the two is that Gray sees unconditioned punishment and nonreward stimuli as eliciting the fight/flight response, whereas Barlow believes the reaction occurs without such cues (false alarms, as described below).

Generalized anxiety disorder involves unrealistic or excessive chronic anxiety or worry (apprehensive expectation) about life circumstances. Barlow views anxious apprehension as the process underlying generalized anxiety disorder. Anxious apprehension is a complex phenomenon involving several features. First, Barlow assumes a continuity between pathological anxiety and the trait of mild generalized anxiety. This trait is variously called nervousness or emotionality and is reflected in the factor of anxiety or neuroticism on self-report measures of personality (Barlow, 1988, pp. 167, 172–173). This anxious apprehension often will have become associated with so many different situational contexts that effective avoidance is precluded (Barlow, 1988, p. 249)—that is, there will be no clear stimulus and the anxiety will appear to be free-floating. With respect to the etiology of anxious apprehension (or generalized anxiety disorder), Barlow (1988, p. 233) identifies four risk factors: a high level of biologically based stress reactivity of genetic origin, perceptions that the alarms and/or negative events are neither predictable nor controllable (discussed further below), an absence of good coping skills, and inadequate social support.

Panic attacks involve a rapid onset of intense but uncued anxiety, accompanied by somatic symptoms and by a fear of dying and/or losing control; they are viewed as alarm reactions (see also Gray, 1987b, p. 366, for a similar view that the fight/flight system mediates panic attacks). Alarm reactions in response to life-threatening events are "true alarms," whereas uncued panic attacks are "false alarms," which are common both among patients with anxiety disorders (Barlow, 1988, p. 97 and Table 3.5) and in the general population (Barlow, 1988, p. 104). These false alarms are almost identical to true alarms phenomenologically, except that the person cannot identify an antecedent triggering event (Barlow, 1988, p. 210). False alarms are further said to constitute an intense unconditioned stimulus (UCS) intense enough to bring about one-trial conditioning (see Gray, 1987b, p. 365, for a similar proposal that panic attacks may serve as a UCS). These dual assumptions—that uncued panic is common in the population and that it constitutes a powerful UCS for further conditioning—allow Barlow to suggest that false alarms (the initial uncued panic attacks) *may* serve as the UCS for classical conditioning of panic attacks to a variety of CSS. In the traditional learning-theory approach to the conditioning of panic attacks to CSS, there must be an initial traumatic event or UCS, such as being bitten by a dog. In Barlow's theory, no *external* traumatic event is necessary to account for learned fear. The initial traumatic event may be an unlearned, uncued panic attack, which constitutes the UCS for conditioning, leading to conditioned panic attacks or, as Barlow calls them, *learned alarms.*

In simple phobias, a true or false alarm may serve as the initial event. If the alarm is true, the traditional conditioning model adequately explains the conditioned anxiety. If the alarm is false, the response may nevertheless be conditioned to whatever external stimuli are present and salient (e.g., Barlow, 1988, pp. 228, 481). This conditioning is more likely to happen with stimuli for which an alarm response is biologically "prepared," such as small animals (Barlow, 1988, p. 228). In vicarious or observational conditioning, the intensity of the model's fear elicits similarly strong alarm in the observer. The strength of the observer's alarm reaction predicts future phobic behavior (Barlow, 1988, pp. 228–229).

In panic disorder, there is no obvious external cue for the panic attacks. Citing the literature on interoceptive conditioning (Martin, 1983; Razran, 1961), in which internal physiological cues become css for anxiety, Barlow (1988, p. 229) suggests that uncued panic attacks derive from learning an association between an initial false alarm and internal cues. A similar proposal was offered by Mineka (1985). Thus, "uncued panic" attacks are actually just as cued as phobic panic attacks, but the cues are less obvious. In support of this hypothesis, a large literature documents the sensitivity of panic patients to internal physiological cues (e.g., Barlow, 1988, pp. 108, 232). This conditioning to internal cues is most likely occur in the absence of salient external stimuli, such as prepared stimuli or stimuli that prevent escape. Consequently, interoceptive conditioning is more likely to occur when the initial false alarm is experienced at home, where the absence of external cues allows attention to be directed to the internal cues associated with the panic attack (Barlow, 1988, p. 231). An intermediate case occurs where the initial false alarm occurs outside the home but in the absence of obvious phobic stimuli, which is associated with the development of panic with agoraphobia (Barlow, 1988, p. 232).

The conditioning model presented above accounts for the occurrence of learned alarms in the population, but Barlow (1988, p. 233–234) suggests that something more is needed to account for the development of a panic *disorder*. Many individuals experience learned and/or unlearned alarm reactions, yet they are not disabled by them and do not seek treatment. The difference between these nonclinical panickers and those who seek treatment, he proposes, is that the latter become anxiously apprehensive about possible future panic attacks. That is, panic disorder develops in individuals who experience learned and/or unlearned alarms and who also have a temperament involving a high degree of preparatory anxiety (anxious apprehension). In panic disorder, it is obvious that patients fear the recurrence of the uncued panic attack (Barlow, 1988, p. 232). Even with simple animal phobias, however, interviews with patients revealed that it was not attack by the feared animal that concerned them. Rather, they feared another panic attack and its consequences, should they be unable to avoid the phobic stimulus (Barlow, 1988, p. 227). Thus, in both panic disorder and simple phobias, patients are primarily anxious about future panics or false alarms. In simple phobias, this fear leads to passive avoidance of the external cs. In panic with agoraphobia, they avoid situations in which they would feel trapped in the event of a panic attack or in which it would be embarrassing to have a panic attack and seek places in which, and people with whom, it is safe to experience a panic attack (Barlow, 1988, pp. 232–233). These observations suggest that, among those individuals who experience alarm reactions (cued or uncued), only those with high levels of the trait of anxious apprehension will develop a panic disorder.

From this brief treatment of Barlow's review, it can be seen that Gray's construct of a behavioral inhibition system cannot account for all major phenomena of anxiety disorders, although it does play a central role. Specifically, the bis does not account for the phenomenon of panic—Barlow's alarm reaction. On the other hand, the addition of Gray's fight/flight system as the equivalent of Barlow's alarm reaction does provide the necessary concept for panic. As noted earlier, this system has been ignored in applications of Gray's theory to psychopathology, but that neglect now appears to have been a mistake. With the addition of Gray's fight/flight system, then, a motivational model can be seen to provide a theoretical framework for anxiety disorders.

It may be useful to note a probable contribution of anxious apprehension to the alarm reaction. Barlow (1988) cites considerable evidence that panic attacks are related to high levels of anxious apprehension. First, marked generalized anxiety is characteristic of almost all panic disorder patients (Barlow, 1988, pp. 171, 174)—that is, most of these patients are severely anxious even when not experiencing panic attacks. Second, across a wide range of techniques for inducing panic attacks in panic disorder patients in the laboratory,

INTEGRATIVE VIEWS OF MOTIVATION, COGNITION, AND EMOTION

the best predictor of which patients develop an attack is a combination of high self-reported anxiety and a high heart rate (Barlow, 1988, p. 155; see also pp. 126, 220). Barlow argues that this combination of subjective apprehension and high autonomic arousal serves as a *necessary* "platform" for panic attacks (1988, p. 155) and that panic may "spike off" such a baseline of high anxiety (Barlow, pp. 177, 220). Third, as just noted, panic disorder patients are apprehensively anxious about future alarm reactions (Barlow, 1988, pp. 233–234). Thus, the anticipatory, worrying anxiety of the BIS appears to contribute in some measure to the development of the acute, here-and-now, action-oriented anxiety of the fight/flight system.

THE PERCEPTION OF CONTROL

It was stated at the outset that a motivational theory would provide a means of incorporating environmental influences in the understanding of the etiology of psychopathology. An important point of articulation is Barlow's conclusion that a risk factor for anxious apprehension is the perception that alarm reactions and/or negative events are neither predictable nor controllable. This perception can be seen as related to the expectancies of response-contingent reward or relieving nonpunishment associated with activation of the BAS. Positive expectancies reduce the perceived threats of frustrative nonreward (failure) and punishment and, thereby, reduce input to the BIS, while activation of the BAS has a direct inhibitory effect on the BIS. In contrast, negative expectations have the opposite effects.

The development of a sense of mastery and control has been widely thought to depend on success during early development in controlling the environment, especially the social environment (Mineka, 1985; Mineka & Kelly, 1989). Even though highly suggestive, the evidence for this proposal has been entirely correlational in nature. For that reason, Mineka's (Mineka et al., 1986) experimental manipulation of control in a study with young rhesus monkeys is critically important. The monkeys were raised with peers in groups of four. Between 6 and 11 mo, the master groups could operate manipulanda at specific times to deliver a variety of reinforcers. The yoked control groups received the reinforcers at the same time, but had no control over them. During tests between 6.5 and 11 mo, the master-group monkeys showed less fear of a toy monster, more exploratory behavior in a novel environment, and better adaptation to an intruder test (as an intruder, they explored the environment more and ate and drank more; as hosts, they showed fewer fearful and submissive behaviors to the intruder). The fact that these results were obtained with control over appetitive events and with inanimate aspects of the environment provides particularly strong support for the hypothesis that a history of control exerts a general effect of diminishing the impact of threatening situations and suggests that an early history of control may reduce vulnerability to developing anxiety disorders in adulthood (Mineka et al., 1986; Mineka & Kelly, 1989). It also suggests that even the BAS is important in the anxiety disorders.

Substance Abuse

POSITIVE AND NEGATIVE REINFORCEMENT

The literature on substance abuse has shown a substantial move toward the view that "abuse of reinforcers" conveys the essence of drug abuse (e.g., Falk et al., 1982; Jaffe, 1990). In keeping with this orientation, Stewart et al., (1984) emphasize a positive-reinforcement mechanism, and Wise (1988) sees reinforcement as occurring either through the termination of distress or dysphoria, returning the subject to a normal mood state (negative reinforcement), or through the induction of pleasure or euphoria in a subject who is already in a normal mood state (positive reinforcement). Negative reinforcement is invoked especially to argue that withdrawal distress associated with the development of physical dependence provides a new source of reinforcement once the drug is consumed in large amounts (Jaffe, 1980; Solomon, 1980), but it can also account for reinforcement by way of reducing preexisting states of psychological pain (e.g., Wise, 1988, p. 124). The present discussion will focus especially on positive reinforcement—the direct, rewarding effects of drugs of abuse. Such a mechanism suggests an involvement of Gray's behavioral activation system. It will be recalled that the BAS responds to cues for rewards, activates behavior, and generates a positive emotional state—features seen in discussions of substance abuse.

In the case of stimulant drugs (e.g., cocaine, amphetamines) and opioids (e.g., heroin, morphine), abuse is maintained "by the generation of positively affective motivational states" (Stewart et al., 1984, p. 252). Stewart et al. (1984) argue that conditioned incentive stimuli (environmental stimuli previously associated with the consumption of these drugs) generate appetitive motivational states and energize drug-seeking behavior, thereby contributing to relapse. Former addicts often relapse in the presence of cues previously associated with drug consumption. Animal studies demonstrate that previously extinguished drug-taking responses could be reinstated by priming doses of the drug in question. By extension, conditioned incentive stimuli (previously associated with drug consumption) should similarly reinstate drug-taking responses, that is, promote relapse.

PSYCHOMOTOR ACTIVATION

Wise (1988) adopts a very similar position but emphasizes the importance of behavioral activation. He finds that the common element of positively reinforcing drugs—including amphetamine, cocaine, opiates, barbiturates, benzodiazepines, alcohol, nicotine, caffeine, cannabis, and phencyclidine—is forward locomotion (approach behavior), or "psychomotor activation." This theory holds that a common brain mechanism of psychomotor activation is stimulated by all positive reinforcers and that the same mechanism mediates both the positive reinforcing effects and the psychomotor stimulant effects of these agents. Thus, the common mechanism in Wise's theory of drug abuse responds to rewards, activates behavior, and induces positive affect—a description identical to Gray's BAS.

It is reasonable to propose that consumption of drugs of abuse reflects the outcome of an approach-avoidance conflict, in which the BAS responds to the immediate positive-reinforcing properties of the drugs while the BIS responds to the much-delayed negative consequences of drug consumption (e.g., loss of job and friends, legal problems, withdrawal distress, social disapproval). Wise (1988) further argues that the direct pharmacological action of drugs of abuse makes them more potent reinforcers than naturally occurring rewards, such as food and sex. To the extent that this approach-avoidance conflict model applies, appetitive and aversive motivational constructs are particularly useful to the understanding of substance abuse.

DOPAMINE AND BEHAVIORAL ACTIVATION

It was mentioned above that Gray identified dopaminergic pathways as contributing strongly to the BAS and that support for that view is found in the substance abuse literature. Stewart et al. (1984) report a consensus that the incentive effects of opiates are "mediated via the mesolimbic dopamine pathway, probably through activation of a subpopulation of cell bodies in the [ventral tegmental area]" (Stewart et al., 1984, p. 255) and say that stimulant drugs exert their incentive effects via the same pathways. Similarly, it is the A10 dopamine projection system in the ventral tegmental area (which projects to the nucleus accumbens and the frontal cortex) that is most clearly implicated in the effects of stimulants and opioids for Wise (1988; Wise & Rompre, 1989). Wise (1988) concludes that psychomotor activation is especially associated with activity in the nucleus accumbens, a primary target of the dopaminergic mesolimbic pathway originating in the ventral tegmental area. Wise and Bozarth (1987) also suggest that the dopaminergic nigrostriatal projection from the substantia nigra to the caudate nucleus is closely related to the mesolimbic dopamine system and further propose that the mesolimbic and nigrostriatal dopaminergic pathways be viewed as subdivisions of a mesocortical dopaminergic fiber system. These dopamine pathways are seen as playing some fundamental role, possibly that of an intermediate common path for most rewards, but of course they are not the only neurotransmitters involved in mediating the effects of rewards (Wise & Rompre, 1989). This conclusion that dopamine (most clearly the projection from the A10 nucleus in the ventral tegmental area to the nucleus accumbens) is strongly involved in responding to cues for rewards is particularly important (and surprising) in view of the consensus that antipsychotic medications block dopamine receptors—a point to be discussed below.

Affective Disorders

A considerable amount of research indicates that a motivational construct similar to the behavioral activation system is particularly relevant to the affective disorders. Depue's work on bipolar affective disorder provides the most direct and elegant support for this conclusion and also strongly implicates the mesolimbic dopaminergic system just described.

BIPOLAR AFFECTIVE DISORDER AND THE BEHAVIORAL FACILITATION SYSTEM

Depue and his colleagues (e.g., Depue & Iacono, 1988; Depue & Spoont, 1986; Depue et al., 1987, 1989) have described what they call the behavioral facilitation system (BFS), also called the behavioral engagement system. (I will use the term BFS, since that is the more frequently occuring term.) The BFS is seen as a basic biobehavioral system through which bipolar disease factors operate (e.g., Depue et al., 1987).

Depue et al. (1987) demonstrated that the bipolar behavioral dimensions associated with bipolar affective disorder showed high covariation in both normal and bipolar populations and, thus, defined a unitary dimension of behavioral engagement. These component dimensions as seen in mania included high motor activity (hyperactivity, rapid and pressured speech, and expressive facies), high incentive reward activation (excessive interest and pleasure, desire for excitement), a positive mood (elation, euphoria), high nonspecific arousal (manifested in changes in appetite, energy level, need for sleep, thought, attention, and sensory vividness), and cognitive changes (increased optimism and feelings of self-worth). Bipolar depression represents the opposite of mania, an absence of activity in the BFS (e.g., an absence of motor activity, no interest or pleasure).

Depue et al. (1987) distinguished between the overall *level* or strength of the BFS versus *variability* within a subject (increased as a result of poor regulation). They provided considerable evidence that bipolar disorder is attributable to a failure to regulate the BFS (trait variability), thereby permitting unduly wide swings, with mania and hypomania reflecting an elevated or excessive activation of this system and with bipolar depression reflecting an absence of behavioral facilitation. The trait level of the BFS is said to affect the manifestation of bipolar disorder: variations around a strong BFS will more often reach clinical severity for mania, variations around a weak system will more often result in depression, and variations around an average system will produce episodes of both mania and depression. If the BFS is weak enough, manic episodes will not occur and the disorder will present as unipolar depression. Depue et al. (1987) note that this model would account for the appearance of unipolar depression among the relatives of bipolar probands, as is found in the genetics literature (e.g., Nurnberger & Gershon, 1992).

There has been some uncertainty as to which bipolar patients this theory applies. Depue et al. (1989) argued that the winter retarded depression phase of seasonal affective disorder reflects extremely low activity of the BFS, while the summer hyperthymic/hypomanic phase reflects excessively high activity of the same system. Depue et al. (1987) similarly limited this theory to bipolar disorders showing a seasonal pattern. In more recent work, however, the theory appears to have been applied to bipolar disorders more generally (Collins & Depue, 1992; Depue & Iacono, 1989). Thus, it appears to represent a model for bipolar disorders in general, albeit with the reservation that there may be as yet undiscovered etiologic heterogeneity that would circumscribe its application.

Using the work of Tellegen (1985) and Watson and Tellegen (1985) demonstrating that current mood in normal subjects could be resolved into two dimensions of positive affect and negative affect, Depue et al. (1987) were able to show that the positive affect dimension was better described as a locomotor-motivation-energy complex than as a mood dimension per se. They further described this motivational complex as one that integrates a host of biobehavior subsystems, including locomotor behavior and incentive motivation to engage in goal-directed behavior, with the purpose of active engagement of the environment. Arguing that such an important system should be manifested in the personality domain and using the state measures just described as markers, these authors summarized personality measures they found to be related to the BFS. These included positive emotionality (achievement, social potency, social closeness, and well-being), extraversion (sociability), sensation seeking, monotony avoidance, venturesomeness, risk taking, and liveliness. These scales were viewed as representing one or more of the biobehavioral subsystems of the BFS (motor activation, high sensitivity to signals of reward, mood, nonspecific arousal). Interestingly, the desire for excitement and new, rewarding experience embodied in such scales as sensation seeking and monotony avoidance were interpreted as reflecting high sensitivity to cues for reward, but impulsivity scales were not related to the BFS. These results for the personality scales were said to indicate that the BFS represents not simply a motor/energy and nonspecific arousal dimension but rather a goal-oriented activation system that involves both behavioral mastery of the work and social environments and a strong, generalized, incentive-reward activation.

In other studies (e.g., Depue & Iacono, 1988; Depue & Spoont, 1986; Depue et al., 1989) additional characteristics of the BFS have been described. For example, Depue and Iacono (1988) describe two major components to the BFS—the initiation of locomotor activity and incentive-reward motivation. The BFS facilitates two broad categories of behavior: positive engagements with the environment (approach responses) under the control of stimuli for social, sexual, consumatory, and achievement-related rewards and responses to environmental threat, especially active avoidance responses and irritative aggression. The BFS is said to facilitate both conditioned and unconditioned behavior. In both types of behavior, the incentive and locomotor components of the BFS are activated by inherently rewarding stimuli or conditioned signals of these stimuli. In active avoidance, the cues in the safe compartment are viewed as CS for reward. In irritative aggression in response to frustrative nonreward, the BFS is activated by the expectation of rewards after removal of the stimuli that block access to the reward.

This description of the BFS is strikingly similar to Gray's BAS. The only noteworthy difference is that the BFS is said to respond to *un*conditioned reward stimuli (e.g., olfactory stimuli that lead to sexual approach responses in animals), whereas Gray describes the BAS as responding to CSS for rewards. However, even though the BIS largely responds to CSS for punishment and frustrative nonreward, Gray says that it also responds to innate fear stimuli (see above), paralleling Depue's inclusion of innate appetitive stimuli in the case of the BFS. Since Gray has focused on the BIS rather than the

BAS, the failure to include innate appetitive stimuli may be more a matter of oversight than of disagreement.

Depue and Iacono (1988) reviewed evidence that more directly implicates dopamine in bipolar disorder. Evaluation of this literature is made difficult by the severe limitations of assessing neurotransmitter activity in patients and by our limited understanding of the complex effects of pharmacological manipulations. Nevertheless, the evidence to date is consistent with the notion that at least a portion of bipolar patients show an involvement of dopaminergic systems. The success of selective dopamine antagonists in reducing manic symptoms and the precipitation of mania in bipolar patients by dopamine agonists implicate dopamine in bipolar affective disorder (Jimerson, 1987; Nöthen et al., 1992). Cummings (1992) concluded that deficient functioning of mesocortical/prefrontal dopaminergic reward, motivational, and stress-response systems mediates depression seen in Parkinson's disease—a conclusion strikingly similar to Depue's view of bipolar depression.

Depue et al. (1987) noted the similarity of the BFS to Gray's BAS and stated that these functions are known to be coordinated within the mesolimbic dopaminergic pathway. Other articles (Depue et al., 1989; Depue & Iacono, 1988; Depue & Spoont, 1986) reviewed an extensive literature showing that the BFS critically involves the mesolimbic dopaminergic system, especially the projections of the A10 dopamine cell group in the ventral tegmental area to the nucleus accumbens and the prefrontal cortex. Similarly, Panksepp (1992) described his expectancy system (see above) as comparable to Gray's BAS and Depue's BFS and as involving the dopamine system arising in the ventral tegmental area and projecting to the nucleus accumbens (or ventral striatum) and various zones of the frontal cortex.

In summary, Depue's work implicates an appetitive motivational system almost identical to the BAS in the etiology of bipolar disorder. The fundamental problem is a failure of regulation, with mania reflecting excessive activation and bipolar depression (and some unipolar depressions) reflecting the nonactivation of this system. This appetitive motivational system is also manifested in self-reported mood and personality. The identification of the mesolimbic and mesocortical dopamine pathways as the neurobiological substrate for this motivational system is strongly consistent with Wise's concept of psychomotor activation from the literature on substance abuse, as well as Gray's own suggestion. Thus, there appears to be considerable consensus concerning the importance of dopamine pathways for this appetitive motivational system. The dopamine projections from the ventral tegmental area to the nucleus accumbens are cited by all authors, whereas those to the prefrontal cortex are not always mentioned.

UNIPOLAR DEPRESSION

Theories of depression tend to emphasize the disruption of appetitive motivation as the core feature. For example, the common feature in almost all behavioral theories of depression is a blockage of appetitive motivation (e.g., Eastman, 1976). The death of a spouse, which produces a high rate of depression (e.g., Bruce et al., 1990), eliminates many sources of reinforcement (sexual activity, companionship, social support, shared activities, etc.), as well as the cues that activate the behavior leading to that reinforcement. The cognitive theories of Beck (e.g., 1974) and of Abramson et al. (1978) assume that the depressed patient has developed expectations that reward seeking and the ability to avoid punishment will be ineffective (hopelessness). More biological theories, such as the influential paper on endogenomorphic depression by Klein (1974) and Depue's theory just described, emphasize a primary loss of the capacity to experience pleasure or to respond to rewards in some depressed patients. Data from self-report inventories administered to college students suggest that anxiety and depression scales differ in that depression is more strongly associated with the absence of positive affect and anxiety more strongly associated with the presence of negative affect (Tellegen, 1985). More recently, studies with clinical populations found that both depressed and anxious patients reported high negative affect but that only depressed patients reported low positive affect (Watson et al., 1988). Along the same lines, Clark et al. (1990) found that depressed patients expressed concerns about an inability to obtain rewards as indicated by hopelessness and more negative thoughts involving loss and past failure, while anxious patients expressed more fear of punishment in the form of thoughts of anticipated harm and danger. A reasonable way to conceptualize this difference in concerns is to view anxious patients as fearing that they *may* not be able to obtain rewards or avoid punishment (especially the latter), whereas depressed patients are *certain* that they will fail in these efforts (especially in obtaining rewards)—that is, in anxiety the expectancy for success is low enough to be anxiety provoking but well above zero, whereas in depression the expectancy is zero. In other words, on the average, anxious and depressed patients differ on two counts—the perceived probability of negative outcomes (1.0 for depression, less than 1.0 for anxiety) and the nature of the negative outcome (loss of rewards for depression, receipt of punishment for anxiety).

As just noted, depressed patients often report high negative affect, and the concept of dysphoric mood seems to involve something more than simply the absence of positive affect. The motivational perspective suggests sources of negative affect, as well as a probable time course in some cases. In depressive reactions associated with the relatively sudden receipt of bad news, such as the unexpected death of a loved one, the loss of a job, and so on, the phenomenon is that of being placed on extinction. In the initial stage of extinction (frustrative nonreward) there is a strong aversive mood in response to disconfirmed positive expectations, but with continued trials the expectations become negative and the aversive motivation drops out. That is, frustration gives way to hopelessness—an expectation that nothing can be done. When expectations of rewards reach this low point, the appetitive motivational system will not be activated. There is a shift over trials from the activation of aversive motivation to the absence of appetitive motivation. A second source of negative affect in depression, which may be more chronic, is the loss of confidence that one can avoid punishments. Many depressogenic life events carry with them exposure to hardships, as well as the loss of rewards, and a perception of certain punishment will produce a mixture of hopelessness and negative affect. A third source of increased negative affect in depression is the disinhibition of the BIS secondary to the lack of activation of the BAS. In view of the reciprocal antagonism between the two systems, any disruption of appetitive motivation will have the consequence of "releasing" aversive motivation from its normal restraint. These sources of negative affect in depression, therefore, offer an explanation for the common finding that anxiety is frequently seen in depression (Barlow, 1985; Beck et al., 1987; Foa & Foa, 1982; Garber et al., 1980; Gersh & Fowles, 1979; Roth & Mountjoy, 1982; Swinson & Kirby, 1986).

I hope that these comments will show that concepts of appetitive and aversive motivation are found in almost all theories of depression and that they offer an interesting perspective on the complex clinical picture seen in depression. Further, I hope that these comments make it obvious that, although the motivational concepts derive from work with animals, they are entirely compatible with cognitive theories of depression.

Psychopathy

THEORETICAL APPROACHES

Psychopathy is a term popularized by Cleckley (e.g., 1964), whose conceptualization of it has been employed in much of the research literature. The clinical picture portrays psychopaths as engaging in various undersocialized activities, having insufficient regard for potential punishments, showing callous indifference to others and a willingness to exploit them, exhibiting an absence of loyalty to others, having an impersonal sex life, an absence of guilt, shallow emotional reactions, a low tolerance for alcohol, and so on. Cleckley also emphasized the psychopath's lack of anxiety under circumstances that others would find stressful. In a true psychopath, these characteristics date from childhood and are not secondary to such situational factors as alcoholism, drug abuse, and peer pressure (as in "subcultural delinquency").

This pattern has been interpreted as predominantly reflecting reward-seeking behavior with relatively poor restraint by potential punishments and subsequent poor socialization. When these characteristics are combined with the impression of low anxiety in anticipation of potential punishments, this interpretation suggests poor anxiety conditioning. Specifically, early proposals cited Mowrer's (e.g., 1960) two-factor theory of avoidance learning, in which fear responses are acquired through classical conditioning and these conditioned fear responses, in turn, serve to motivate and reinforce both active and passive avoidance (e.g., Hare, 1970, chap. 6). Of the two forms of avoidance, passive avoidance (in which response-contingent punishment is avoided by not approaching the reward) was theoretically more important. The hypothesis of poor passive avoidance accounts for the psychopath's inability to resist temptation in approach-avoidance conflict situations—for example, opportunities for theft, abusing credit, and engaging in excessive drinking.

More recent theoretical treatments have suggested that psychopaths suffer from a quantitative deficiency in Gray's BIS (Fowles, 1980; Gray, 1970; Quay, 1990, 1993; see esp. Trasler, 1978) or the functioning of the closely related septo-hippocampal system (Gorenstein & Newman, 1980) and possibly a strong BAS as well (e.g., see the suggestion by Quay, 1988a, that conduct-disordered children suffer from an overactive BAS). The weak-BIS hypothesis predicts the following cluster of behaviors: impulsivity in the form of poor passive avoidance and poor extinction, reduced anxiety in response to CSS for punishment or failure, and normal active avoidance of punishment. The prediction of normal active avoidance is important, since psychopaths are often viewed as being skilled at avoiding punishment, for example, by lying and feigning remorse. Gray's model of the lessened role of the BIS (and anxiety) in active avoidance is an advantage over the earlier interpretation in terms of Mowrer's two-factor theory, in which anxiety conditioning was viewed as essential to both active and passive avoidance (thereby predicting an active avoidance deficit as well).

LABORATORY STUDIES OF PSYCHOPATHS

The experimental literature supporting these two theoretical approaches has fallen largely in two areas, one demonstrating passive avoidance deficits in laboratory tasks and the other showing deficient electrodermal responding (skin conductance responding because of sweat gland activity on the palms; see, e.g., Fowles, 1986) in the anticipation of aversive stimulation. The passive-avoidance deficits date from Lykken's (1957) demonstration that psychopaths showed poor passive avoidance of a shock received through an incorrect alternative choice in a "mental maze" with 20 choice points and four alternatives at each choice point. The manifest task, which the psychopaths and nonpsychopaths performed equally well, was to get through the maze by selecting the correct alternative at each choice point. Of the three incorrect alternatives, one was associated with shock to the subject, and psychopaths were inferior to non-psychopaths in avoiding the shock. There was no reward for choosing the correct alternative other than advancing to the next choice point. Lykken's mental-maze results were replicated by Schacter & Latane (1964) and by Schmauk (1970). Schmauk also found a similar result when social punishment (having the experimenter say "wrong") was substituted for the shock. However, in yet another condition, Schmauk gave subjects a stack of quarters at the outset and substituted the loss of a quarter for shock in the punished alternative. In this condition, the psychopaths avoided the punishment (loss of money) as well as the controls. For a while, Schmauk's finding seemed to challenge the hypothesis of a general deficit in avoiding punishment and to suggest the much less attractive hypothesis that psychopaths were less sensitive only to physical and social punishment. Fortunately for the theory, Newman and his colleagues (Newman & Kosson, 1986; Newman et al., 1985, 1987) have been able to show passive-avoidance deficits with loss of money as the punishment, as has Siegel (1978). Waid and Orne (1982) noted that the money in Schmauk's study was more important to the psychopathic prisoners than to the nonprisoner normal controls, who had income from employment—that is, the greater severity of the punishment for psychopaths may have offset their deficit—and Newman and Kosson (1986) suggested other methodological variables that may have contributed to Schmauk's results. Whatever the explanation for Schmauk's anomalous finding, the literature has generally demonstrated a passive-avoidance deficit in psychopaths, which is consistent with the hypothesis that they are less sensitive to cues for potential punishments.

The finding that psychopaths show electrodermal hyporeactivity during the anticipation of punishment has been even more consistent. Hare (1978) provided an extensive review of this literature, which I have updated (Fowles, 1993b). Both reviews found that differences in electrodermal activity between psychopaths and control subjects are small or nonexistent under conditions of minimal stimulation but are repeatedly found in classical aversive conditioning or during a period prior to an *anticipated* stressor. The anticipated stressor usually was electric shock, but individual studies employed aversive tones, mental arithmetic, social disapproval, and shock to another subject (see Fowles, 1993b). Since electrodermal responses reflect activity of the sweat glands on the palm, which are innervated by the sympathetic branch of the autonomic nervous system, these findings have been taken to indicate a deficient emotional response to anticipated punishment that is consistent with the poor fear-conditioning or weak-BIS hypotheses.

Although the electrodermal data have shown hyporeactivity, heart rate data have not. Hare (1978) cited studies in which cardiac acceleration in the anticipation of noxious stimuli was *greater* for criminal psychopaths than for control subjects (Hare & Craigen, 1974; Hare et al., 1978) as well as for noncriminal subjects scoring low on the Gough's Socialization scale (Hare, 1978, n. 6; Schalling, 1975), often taken as an index of psychopathy, or on an anxiety scale used in Lykken's (1957) study (Lykken et al., 1972). These results precluded a simple autonomic hyporesponsivity hypothesis and required an explanation for the specificity of heart rate and electrodermal activity.

GRAY'S THEORY, ELECTRODERMAL ACTIVITY, AND HEART RATE

My (1980) paper offered an explanation in terms of Gray's motivational constructs. Specifically, I proposed that heart rate is more closely tied to activation of the BAS, whereas electrodermal activity reflects the emotional response to threats of punishment and can, in that sense, serve as an index of BIS reactivity. The heart rate aspect of this theory was based, in part, on Obrist's (1976) concept of active coping, which holds that attempts to actively cope with an impending aversive stimulus (by making some response) will produce cardiac acceleration, whereas passively accepting the punishment is associated with cardiac deceleration, or at least an absence of acceleration. This active-coping hypothesis evolved from earlier literature on the tight coupling between heart rate and somatic activity (the cardiac-somatic coupling hypothesis), which was attributed to metabolic need (the heart must pump more blood to active muscles) and was not seen as reflecting psychological processes. Active coping was thus seen as related to cardiac-somatic coupling, in the sense that it was an exaggerated "exercise response," but because the cardiac acceleration exceeded any metabolic need active coping was seen as more psychological than physiological. I reviewed other evidence that heart rate responds to reward incentive stimuli, and stronger evidence was reported later (e.g., Fowles, 1988). Thus, heart rate has been found to increase in connection with somatic activation, active-avoidance responding (active coping), and the anticipation of rewards. Since these are the three major features of the BAS, I proposed (Fowles, 1980) that heart rate increases in connection with activation of the BAS.

With this hypothesis, it was possible to account for the differences between heart rate and electrodermal activity in the studies with psychopaths. Psychopaths show lower electrodermal responding in anticipation of punishment due to a weak BIS. The dgreater cardiac acceleration in anticipation of punishment may reflect a dominance of active-avoidance tendencies (BAS) over inhibitory processes associated with passively accepting the punishment. This proposal is attractive because it accounts for the divergent electrodermal and heart rate patterns while retaining the original link between deficient anxiety and impulsivity. Although the post hoc quality of the explanation for the cardiac acceleration is a weakness, it is not unreasonable in view of data on animals and humans facing an impending punishment: both cardiac acceleration and deceleration can be seen, with deceleration emerging as animals stop struggling to escape and as human subjects become resigned to the punishment. Consequently, the sharp distinction between active and passive avoidance in Gray's model is helpful in understanding a degree of motivational specificity for heart rate and electrodermal activity. Also, as noted above, clinical features suggest that psychopaths show a passive-avoidance deficit but not an active-avoidance deficit.

TWO TYPES OF ANXIETY

To this point in the discussion of psychopathy, the term anxiety has been used as if there were only one type of anxiety. As noted above in connection with Barlow's work, one should distinguish between anxious apprehension (BIS) and acute anxiety in the form of the alarm reaction (fight/flight). With the advantage of this perspective,

Schalling's (1978) review of her own work on psychopathy assumes new importance. On the basis of a cluster analysis of ratings of psychiatric patients, Schalling contrasted *psychic anxiety* with *somatic anxiety*. In line with additional studies, she offered a description of psychic anxiety that is remarkably similar to Barlow's anxious apprehension: it includes "worry, anticipatory anxiousness, slow recuperation after stress, sensitivity, insecurity, and social anxiety" (Schalling, 1978, p. 88). In contrast, somatic anxiety consists of "autonomic disturbances, vague distress and panic attacks, and distractibility" (Schalling, 1978, p. 88). The panic attacks, the autonomic disturbances, and the vagueness of the stimulus for distress all point to a similarity between Schalling's somatic anxiety and Barlow's alarm reaction.

Schalling (1978, p. 89) found that psychopaths "tend to have *more* vague distress and panic, more cardiovascular symptoms and muscular tenseness, but *less* worry and anticipatory concern than non-psychopaths have" (emphasis added)—that is, psychopaths are *low* on the BIS-related psychic anxiety, as suggested above, but they are *high* on somatic anxiety. In the light of Barlow's theory, Schalling's work points to a severe limitation of the statement that psychopaths are deficient in anxiety. The theory suggests that they are deficient in only one type of anxiety and may even be high in the other type. The failure to note such a distinction has undoubtedly caused confusion in studies of "anxiety" in psychopaths. Moreover, Schalling reported that somatic anxiety is positively correlated with impulsivity. This finding is consistent with the old idea that a state of arousal (from somatic anxiety) might energize behavior and thereby increase impulsivity in some individuals (tension discharge), as well as with Gray's emphasis on the activation of vigorous behavior in connection with the fight/flight system. Further, Gray (1987b, p. 355) describes impulsive individuals who score high on neuroticism scales as merely tending "to act on the spur of the moment" (cf. somatic anxiety being positively correlated with impulsivity), whereas impulsive individuals who score low on neuroticism are prepared to take real risks because they lack fear. Note the complexity of this revision of the motivational theory of psychopathy: possibly a weak BIS (psychic anxiety) combined with high fight/flight anxiety (somatic anxiety) results in spur-of-the-moment impulsivity, whereas individuals low on both types of anxiety will show a different type of impulsivity—one based on fearlessness.

If this interpretation is valid, it may offer a significant advance in studies of the role of anxiety in antisocial behavior. It possibly could shed light on the differences between children with attention deficit disorder (ADD), who show the spur-of-the-moment type of impulsivity (Whalen, 1989), versus children with undersocialized aggressive conduct disorder, whose antisocial behavior may reflect fearlessness (Quay, 1990, 1993). In view of the substantial comorbidity of ADD and conduct disorder (Hinshaw, 1987; Whalen, 1989), an interesting speculation is that a weak BIS is a common factor, whereas greater fight/flight anxiety among some ADD children could account for their spur-of-the-moment impulsivity and lesser tendency toward aggression.

ANTISOCIALITY AS A PERSONALITY DIMENSION

An additional theoretical loose end should be noted. Crider (1993) has postulated that an electrodermal dimension of lability-stability relates to a personality dimension of antisociality (stabiles are antisocial). Lability stability is defined primarily in terms of electrodermal responding at rest and in response to simple tones, with stabiles being hyporeactive. While the direction of this hypothesis is similar to that for psychopaths (antisocial stabiles are hyporeactive), the problem is that stability is assessed under experimental conditions of minimal stimulation in which few differences have been obtained with psychopaths. On the other hand, Crider cites evidence (O'Gorman & Horneman, 1979) that such resting measures are correlated with electrodermal responding in more stimulating experimental conditions, supporting a continuity between resting and stimulated electrodermal responding. Additionally, stabiles do poorly on vigilance tasks and may become drowsy during boring experimental conditions (Schell et al., 1988), descriptions perhaps also characteristic of psychopaths (Hare, 1978, pp. 109–110, 112). More work will be needed to determine whether lability stability relates to the dimension of hyporeactivity to threats of punishment seen in psychopaths.

Schizophrenia

Schizophrenia has been left until last, because the three motivational systems under discussion are not seen as contributing specifically to the etiology of schizophrenia. Rather, I propose that they contribute in a nonspecific way. Perhaps this perspective can be best introduced by observing that, if the systems in question are of fundamental importance in emotional and motivational processes, it should be possible to identify their contribution to etiology and their influence on the clinical picture in schizophrenia. In that spirit I (Fowles, 1992b) proposed the hypotheses that are summarized in brief below.

GENETIC MODELS

The starting point is the development of genetic models for the etiology of schizophrenia. More than for any other disorder, a massive data base of family risk, twin, and adoption studies have documented the importance of genetic contributions to etiology. On the basis of this type of evidence, Rosenthal (1970) proposed that the etiology of schizophrenia should be conceptualized in the context of the *diathesis-stress* model. The genetic endowment produces the diathesis or vulnerability, which is then transformed into schizophrenia through exposure to environmental stress.

Given the extent of the family, twin, and adoption data, it is possible to make inferences concerning the appropriate genetic model. In spite of vigorous attempts to fit the data to a single major locus model (i.e., single locus with two alleles for the gene—one healthy allele and one conveying vulnerability to schizophrenia) with high penetrance (meaning that the gene accounts for most of the phenotypic variance), the evidence is strongly against this model (e.g., Faraone & Tsuang, 1985; McGue & Gottesman, 1989; Risch, 1990). Similarly, a limited-loci-polygenic model (e.g., two loci with two alleles each) with high penetrance also fails to fit the data (Faraone & Tsuang, 1985). Whatever the precise model involving a small number of genes, tests of such models against the extant data show that nongenetic factors—either physical or psychosocial environmental—strongly influence whether schizophrenia develops in a person with genetic vulnerability (Gottesman & McGue, 1991).

INTEGRATIVE VIEWS OF MOTIVATION, COGNITION, AND EMOTION

In contrast to the strains of research that attempt to fit single major locus or limited-loci-polygenic models to the data, the multifactorial polygenic model fits the data well (Faraone & Tsuang, 1985; Gottesman, 1991; Gottesman et al., 1987; Kendler, 1987; Plomin, 1990; Reiss et al., 1991; Risch, 1990). That is, whereas the single major locus and the limited-loci-polygenic models *with high penetrance* can be rejected, the multifactorial threshold model cannot. Mixed models, in which a single gene might exert quantitatively modest effects embedded in a polygenic context, are also possible. For example, Gottesman and McGue (1991) tested several models and found that a standard multifactorial threshold model provides an excellent fit to the data but that two mixed models were not inconsistent with the genetic data. In the first of these models, a major gene with relatively high penetrance (0.6) has a low frequency in the population and accounts for a small portion (20%) of schizophrenics, the rest being accounted for by a multifactorial loading. In this model, the percentage of total variance (in phenotypic outcome) attributable to the single major gene was only 2.2%, compared with 78.2% for polygenic inheritance and 19.5% for environmental factors. Thus, it is not impossible that there is genetic heterogeneity, involving a single major gene with relatively high penetrance that contributes to the etiology in a minority of schizophrenics but that accounts for a very small portion of the total variance in phenotypic outcome. The second mixed model assumed a single gene with low penetrance (e.g., 0.10) and a large residual polygenic inheritance (e.g., 60–80%). This model was consistent with either a large or small portion of schizophrenics carrying the single gene. In this model, the percentage of variance in phenotypic outcome attributable to the single gene varies with its frequency. In the important case in which the gene is present in almost all schizophrenics, it accounts for a sizable portion of the variance (32.9%), leaving 40.3% for polygenic and 27.8% for environmental contributions. It is important to emphasize that in this model in which a single gene contributes to almost all cases of schizophrenia, its penetrance is very low, leaving considerable room for other influences. Thus, the current status of genetic models is that a multifactorial polygenic model fits the data well but that some mixed models cannot be rejected. In these mixed models, the single gene either is infrequent with high (although by no means complete) penetrance or is common with very low penetrance. In all cases, there is ample room for environmental influences—consistent with the diathesis-stress model. For the sake of simplicity, the polygenic model will be assumed in the argument that follows, but it should be noted that mixed models such as those just described would not alter the fundamental argument.

First applied to schizophrenia by Gottesman and Shields (1967), the multifactorial polygenic model assumes that a large number of genes—each of small effect—contribute in an additive fashion to the overall liability for schizophrenia and that phenotypic schizophrenia is seen when the liability exceeds a given threshold. Gottesman and Shields (e.g., 1982, pp. 63–69, pp. 220–229) presented the major features of a polygenic model. The key features are a liability to the development of schizophrenia, derived from both genetic and environmental sources, that is continuously and normally distributed in the population with a threshold for the development of schizophrenia. Individuals whose liability exceeds the threshold develop (phenotypic) schizophrenia. The sources of liability include *specific* genetic liability, *general* genetic liability, and *general* environmental liability. Provision is also made for genetic assets and environmental assets to subtract from the liability, but these are of little interest in this context. The term *specific genetic liability* refers to the genetic contribution that conveys a specific risk for schizophrenia. The general sources of liability, which are critical to the present argument, have nothing to do with schizophrenia per se but represent *modifiers* or *potentiators* (cf. Meehl, 1962) of the specific liability—that is, they are nonspecific contributors to etiology, and they necessarily include the components that mediate the effects of stress in the diathesis-stress model (see Fig. 1).

Estimates of the heritability of schizophrenia in the context of the polygenic model tend to be high. For example, employing path-analytic multifactorial polygenic models, Faraone and Tsuang (1985) estimated the genetic contribution to be 60–70%. To understand that even higher estimates of heritability would be entirely compatible with an important environmental contribution, one must consider that in a threshold model the role of the environment varies with the severity of the total genetic liability (Gottesman & Shields, 1982, pp. 63–69, 220–221; Zubin & Spring, 1977), as shown in Figure 1 (in which the x-axis shows an increasing genetic contribution to liability and the y-axis shows the total liability, with a horizontal line indicat-

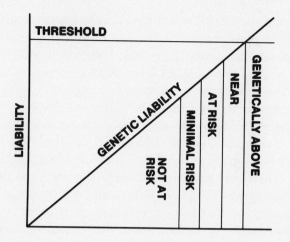

FIGURE 1. Effect of increasing genetic liability (x-axis) on the amount of environmental liability required to reach the threshold for schizophrenia (y-axis).

ing the threshold for the appearance of symptoms). It is at least a theoretical possibility that a small number of individuals are genetically above threshold—that is, they have such a high genetic contribution that environmental contributions are not needed to develop schizophrenia. Next, it seems quite likely that a larger number of individuals will have a genetic liability that is near threshold. They are likely to reach threshold (develop schizophrenia) from the additional environmental liability in most environments and are, for that reason, likely to be chronic. For them, the environmental contribution is relatively small. An important third group will have a genetic liability that places them close enough to threshold to be at risk but that is low enough to require a significant environmental contribution. Often they will show episodes in response to a recognizable increase in environmental liability, for example, a life event or a relapse in connection with a return to an aversive family interaction (see below). If they are unfortunate enough to live in chronically harsh environments, they might also be chronic or at least manifest recurring episodes. For this group the environmental contributions are quite important. As the genetic liability decreases even more, a fourth group might be said to be at minimal risk, meaning that schizophrenic symptoms could develop in response to very severe environments but that such environments are infrequently encountered. They might well develop a brief reactive psychosis in response to major stressors, but this reaction would not be considered true schizophrenia because of its brevity. The environmental contribution for this group, although important for the infrequent episodes of schizophrenia, is quantitatively small in a population variation sense, because these individuals are largely not schizophrenic for genetic reasons. Finally, a large proportion of the population will have such a low genetic liability as to be not at risk—that is, they are not schizophrenic for genetic reasons and the environment is unimportant to them with respect to developing schizophrenia. From this analysis one can see that, since only in the "at-risk" group would one expect to observe an appreciable contribution of recognizable life events among those conventionally seen as schizophrenic, the total contribution of environmental liability to population phenotypic variance need not be large. This environmental contribution is, however, focused on the population of most interest—those who are at risk for developing schizophrenia and, to a lesser extent, those near threshold. Much of the genetic contribution to population phenotypic variance is to the *absence* of schizophrenia—that is, to the large portion of the population not at risk or minimally at risk for schizophrenia, because of a minimal genetic liability.

ENVIRONMENTAL CONTRIBUTIONS

The data on genetics strongly implicate environmental factors, but they are neutral with respect to whether these factors are physical or psychosocial in nature. Although psychosocial contributions are the focus of this review, it should be noted that Gottesman (1991, pp. 93, 95, 162–164) suggests that head injuries constitute a physical contribution to nonspecific environmental liability. Fortunately, there is positive evidence for the importance of psychosocial factors. With respect to life events, Brown and Birley (1968; Birley & Brown, 1970) found an increased number of life events in the 3 wk before a datable onset of symptoms relative to three previous 3-wk periods among the schizophrenic patients and to all four 3-wk periods among community controls. The same results were obtained for events that were clearly not secondary to incipient symptomatology (independent events). The increased rate of total and of independent life events in the 3 wk before the onset of symptoms relative to earlier 3-wk periods was replicated by Day et al. (1987) at eight field research centers located in developed and developing countries in a World Health Organization–sponsored cross-national study. This study did not include nonpatient community controls. Finally, Ventura et al. (1989) conducted a prospective longitudinal study of relapse among 30 recent-onset schizophrenic patients and also found a significant association of life events with relapse. In both the Brown and Birley and the Day et al. studies, the critical methodological variable was the likely restriction of the sample to patients with a datable onset, which has the effect of selecting for "reactive" schizophrenics and against "process" schizophrenics with a slow, insidious onset. The concept of reactive schizophrenia (Chapman & Chapman, 1973; Garmezy, 1968; Neale & Oltmanns, 1980, p. 8), with a good premorbid adjustment, a life event, and a datable onset, describes just the type of patients described above as being "at risk" because of a substantial but not overwhelming genetic liability. Thus, these studies support the expectation that, for a subset of schizophrenics, psychosocial factors contribute to the onset of episodes.

Positive evidence for psychosocial factors has also been forthcoming from studies of relapse among schizophrenic patients subjected to aversive family interactions. On the basis of an interview with key relatives (spouse or parent) at the index admission, families who score high on the number of critical comments and/or on emotional overinvolvement are labeled as high "expressed emotion" (EE) families. Patients who return after discharge from the hospital to high-EE families relapse at a substantially higher rate than those who return to live with low-EE families. In the original British studies (see Leff & Vaughn, 1985, for a summary), the relapse rate among those who returned to high-EE homes was lower if they spent fewer than 35 h per week in face-to-face contact with their relative, which is consistent with attributing relapse to the stressfulness of the aversive interaction. Similarly, the relationship between relapse and EE does not appear to be secondary to the patient's disturbed behavior (Leff & Vaughn, 1985; Vaughn et al., 1984). Attempts to reduce the family's expressed emotion and/or to reduce contact between the patient and the family have met with success (Falloon et al., 1985; Hogarty et al., 1986; Leff et al., 1982; Tarrier et al., 1988). The basic finding of differential relapse rates as a function of expressed emotion in families has been widely replicated (see, e.g., Barrelet et al., 1990).

Gottesman (1991, pp. 141–142) has further argued for the importance of family interactions. By comparing the risk of schizophrenia (27%) among the illegitimate offspring reared by their own severely ill schizophrenic mothers (as reported by Kallmann, 1938) with the risk of schizophrenia (17%) among adopted-away children with similar parental background (as reported by Heston, 1966), Gottesman found support for a familial environmental contribution to liability for schizophrenia.

This evidence provides positive support for the importance of the easily identified variables of life events and aversive family interactions. Wing (e.g., 1978) has argued for the importance of such extrinsic factors as poor education, lack of vocational skills, low intelligence, and minimal social support (all of which make the environment more stressful) and handicaps secondary to the disorder such as altered self-attitudes and the development of maladaptive behaviors associated with institutionalism. Additionally, Bleuler (1974) describes his own lifetime longitudinal study of environmental influences on schizophrenia. Overall, then, there is sufficient positive evidence to warrant an argument that a substantial portion of the nonspecific liability for schizophrenia is attributable to psychosocial factors (see Breier et al., 1991; and Lukoff et al., 1984, for additional support for the contribution of stress to schizophrenia).

MOTIVATIONAL CONTRIBUTIONS TO LIABILITY FOR SCHIZOPHRENIA

Thus, the genetic data strongly implicate nonspecific contributions to etiology at both the genetic and the environmental levels, and factors that influence the amount and impact of environmental stress constitute a significant part of this nonspecific contribution to etiology. Motivational systems are implicated, given the intimate connection they share with stress. At a gross level, it can be suggested that both the BIS and BAS are centrally involved in the response to stressful environmental events. In the case of the BIS, its identification as an anxiety system that processes cues for potential punishments and frustrations makes this obvious. The diathesis-stress model implies that, in some way, activation of the BIS contributes to nonspecific liability for schizophrenia. Individuals with a particularly reactive BIS (cf. generalized anxiety disorder above) will find their environment generally more stressful than those with a less reactive BIS, thereby increasing their risk of developing schizophrenia if they also have other sources of liability.

The conclusion that the BAS contributes to the etiology of schizophrenia rests on two arguments, both of which draw on the link between the BAS and dopaminergic activity. First, the central role of the BAS in active avoidance (active coping) indicates that it will be strongly activated in the face of threats of punishment (and loss of reward). Consistent with this view, Depue and Iacono state that the behavioral facilitation system (their equivalent of the BAS) is activated during stress and defensive aggression. Observations of increased dopaminergic activity in response to stress (e.g., Braden, 1984; Breier et al., 1991; Glowinski et al., 1984; Gray, 1987b, p. 337; Trulson & Preussler, 1984) provide further support. Second, increased dopaminergic activity is implicated in schizophrenia by three lines of evidence:

- The therapeutic efficacy of the antipsychotic drugs relates especially to their ability to block dopamine receptors, especially D-2 receptors (e.g., Haracz, 1982; Losonczy et al., 1987; Snyder, 1978).
- Large doses of drugs that increase dopamine activity (e.g., amphetamines) can produce a clinical syndrome indistinguishable from paranoid schizophrenia in otherwise nonschizophrenic individuals (Snyder, 1978).
- Small doses of the same drugs will exacerbate schizophrenic symptoms in a patient who is actively schizophrenic at the time (Andreasen, 1985; Davis, 1978) or will produce transient symptoms in schizophrenic patients in remission (Losonczy et al., 1987).

These findings converge to support the well-known dopamine theory of schizophrenia. Thus, there is reason to believe that the BAS is activated in response to stressful events and that such activation would promote episodes of schizophrenia in vulnerable individuals (see also Breier et al., 1991). It is worth noting as well that the role of dopamine in appetitive behavior accounts for the tendency of neuroleptic medications to produce a broad range of negative symptoms—that is, the syndrome of akinesia, consisting of a lack of emotional reactivity, lack of goal directedness, reduced or retarded speech, diminished social and vocational initiative, and so on (Sommers, 1985).

It is not clear how strongly the fight/flight response contributes to liability in schizophrenia. The phasic nature of this response would seem to minimize a contribution to relatively stable levels of liability. On the other hand, in anxiety disorders panic attacks serve as a source of anxiety for individuals with high levels of anxious apprehension. Additionally, the state of acute anxiety associated with the fight/flight response might contribute to symptomatic behavior. There may then be some possible contribution of the fight/flight system to liability for schizophrenia, but at the present the extent of the contribution is unclear, and the BIS appears to be the most relevant anxiety system—an importance parallel to Barlow's specification of anxious apprehension as the key factor in anxiety disorders.

MOTIVATION AND SCHIZOAFFECTIVE DISORDERS

In addition to this global argument concerning the likely importance of motivational systems in schizophrenia, there are more specific implications that center around the problems of schizoaffective disorders and heterogeneity in behavioral features (activity withdrawal, positive vs. negative symptoms) that are associated with differences in the course of schizophrenia. Of these topics, the most interesting perspective derives from the juxtaposition of the dopamine theory of schizophrenia with Depue's theory that an overactive BAS is implicated in mania.

The traditional view that schizophrenia and affective disorders constitute unrelated diseases is challenged by the existence of large numbers of patients with both schizophrenic and affective disorders, termed *schizoaffective disorders*. When patients are arranged along the continuum from schizophrenia to affective disorders, no discontinuity allows easy separation into two categories. Indeed, the distribution is unimodal—that is, patients with schizoaffective symptoms outnumber those with purely schizophrenic or purely affective symptoms (Kendell, 1982). The importance of this fundamental theoretical problem has been increasingly recognized in recent years (Baron & Gruen, 1991; Crow, 1986, 1991; Delva & Letemendia, 1982; Kendell, 1982; Kerr & McClelland, 1991; Levinson & Levitt, 1987; Meltzer, 1984; Procci, 1989; Taylor, 1992; Taylor et al., 1993; Williams & McGlashan, 1987).

In the case of schizoaffective disorder with manic symptoms, Depue's dopamine theory of mania and the dopamine theory of schizophrenia point to the obvious possibility that activation of the dopaminergically based BAS in manic individuals contributes substantial nonspecific liability to the development of schizophrenic symptoms in vulnerable individuals. That is, in a simple additive model, a person with other sources of liability for schizophrenia (including specific genetic liability) would be brought above threshold for schizophrenic symptoms by the massive amounts of dopaminergic activity associated with a manic episode. (It should be noted that, in this approach, dopaminergic activity constitutes a nonspecific contributor to liability for schizophrenia and is not viewed as the primary [specific] etiological factor). The relative prominence of schizophrenic versus manic symptoms would be determined by the size of the two contributions to liability. Individuals with a reasonably large liability for schizophrenia would require only a modest amount of BAS-dopaminergic activation and thus frequently would manifest schizoaffective mania, mainly of the schizophrenic subtype (although nothing would prevent them from also suffering at times from a major BAS-dopaminergic activation with more prominent manic symptoms). Toward the other end of the continuum, those with a more moderate liability for schizophrenia would only show such symptoms in the presence of strong BAS activation and would, therefore, appear to be schizoaffective manic, mainly of the manic subtype. Intermediate cases would show a generally equal prominence of schizophrenic and manic symptoms. This hypothesis is attractive because it offers an explanation for the fusion of the boundaries of schizophrenia and the affective disorders and because it brings together the dopamine theories of schizophrenia and mania.

A parallel argument can be made for the nonspecific contribution of depression to liability for schizophrenia in accounting for the continuum of schizoaffective, depressed disorders. This argument proceeds from the assumption that aversive arousal (from activation of the BIS and, possibly, the fight/flight system) is frequently associated with depression, as argued above, and contributes to the liability for schizophrenia. To the extent that this assumption is valid, either genetic or environmental factors promoting depression will contribute to the development of schizophrenia in otherwise vulnerable individuals.

MOTIVATION AND POSITIVE AND NEGATIVE SYMPTOMS

This perspective also leads to suggestions regarding the heterogeneity of symptomatology in schizophrenia (see Fowles, 1992b, esp. pp. 329–332, for a more complete discussion of this complex topic). In particular, much interest has centered on positive versus negative symptoms (e.g., Lewine, 1985), a distinction introduced by Strauss et al. (1974). It is generally agreed that positive and negative symptoms are independent symptom dimensions within schizophrenia (e.g., Carpenter, 1992; Carpenter et al., 1988; Crow, 1980, 1985; Sommers, 1985). A prominent theory (Crow, 1985) attributes positive symptoms primarily to a neurochemical disturbance involving excessive dopaminergic activity, and a better response of positive than negative symptoms to antipsychotics (which block dopamine) is widely accepted (e.g., Andreasen, 1985; Crow, 1985; Losonczy et al., 1987; Lydiard & Laird, 1988; Reynolds, 1989). Further, positive symptoms tend also to be associated with an acute onset, an episodic course, and good premorbid adjustment (Crow, 1985).

In contrast, negative symptoms tend to be associated with chronicity, an insidious onset, poor premorbid adjustment, intellectual deterioration, and a poorer response to antipsychotics (Crow, 1985). It has been further established that the withdrawn end of an activity-withdrawal dimension (based on ratings of ward behavior among hospitalized schizophrenics) is related to chronicity, poor premorbid adjustment, negative symptoms, anhedonia, and high levels of (purportedly cortical) arousal as measured by skin potential and two perceptual measures (Depue, 1976; Venables, 1963a, 1963b; 1967; Venables & Wing, 1962; Wing, 1961). Individuals assessed at the active end of the dimension are characterized as restless, loud, overtalkative, overactive, and as having many friends and interests. Withdrawn patients showed an absence of these features.

The activity-withdrawal dimension is particularly important in this context, since it should be influenced by the BAS and BIS. That is, the balance between these two systems should influence the degree of activity versus withdrawal. This perspective in combination with the findings of high arousal suggests that negative-symptom, withdrawn patients suffer from high aversive arousal with behavioral inhibition or passive avoidance due to activation of the BIS and, quite possibly, a deficiency in BAS activity. The latter could be due to a temperament-based weak BAS or to depression from various sources (genetic factors, life events, demoralization, institutionalism, etc.). On the other hand, positive-symptom, active schizophrenics would presumably have a contribution to liability from activation of the BAS, which would respond better to antipsychotics.

An assumption of the foregoing analysis is that aversive motivational arousal contributes to the production of schizophrenic symptoms but in a manner at least somewhat distinct from the contribution of dopamine/behavioral activation. In addition to a contribution to negative symptoms (behavioral inactivity), it seems likely that BIS activity will produce nonspecific arousal that in turn will contribute to some florid symptoms and, if severe enough, possibly to motor agitation. (This motor agitation is to be distinguished from the goal-oriented, incentive-based psychomotor activation associated with BAS activity and characteristic of active schizophrenic patients.) From this perspective, psychotic symptoms might reflect a more dopaminergic contribution in some patients and a more aversive arousal contribution in others. There might well be a degree of specificity, in which some types of symptoms were more strongly related to dopamine activity, others to aversive arousal, and still others to either factor equally (e.g., thought disorder appears to be common to both positive- and negative-symptom syndromes).

Given the hypothesized contribution of the BIS to schizophrenic symptoms and the efficacy of anxiolytics in reducing BIS activity, one would expect that anxiolytics would produce a degree of symptom improvement in a subset of patients (i.e., those in which BIS activation provides a strong contribution to liability). Although the contribution of anxiolytics to the treatment of schizophrenia is not heavily researched, a recent review by Wolkowitz and Pickar (1991) provides support for this expectation in the case of benzodiazepines. These authors emphasize the variability of response across patients but estimate that 30–50% of schizophrenic patients show a favorable response. Several studies in each case supported a beneficial effect on negative-affect symptoms (anxiety, tension, irritability, hostility), depressive symptoms, core psychotic symptoms (hallucinations, delusions, thought disorder), negative symptoms (lack of spontaneity, emotional withdrawal, blunted affect, passivity, apathy, negativism), and motor disturbances (motor unrest, agitation). In addition to prominent initial psychotic symptoms, predictors of good response to benzodiazepines include anxiety or panic symptoms or high levels of motor tension, agitation, or retardation. Responsivity of psychotic symptoms in individual patients was associated with responsivity of other symptoms—for example, anxiety and depressive symptoms—consistent with a common mechanism across symptoms. Many of these findings are consistent with the notion that BIS activation may contribute to a wide range of symptoms.

Thus, an examination of motivational factors in schizophrenia suggests several potential contributions. First, appetitive and aversive motivations contribute to nonspecific liability in schizophrenia, including responses to stressful environments. Second, activation of the BAS may be implicated in schizoaffective mania, and a combination of low BAS activation/high BIS activation may be implicated in schizoaffective depression. Third, BAS activation may be associated with positive symptoms of schizophrenia and a good response to neuroleptics, while BIS activation (and possibly weak BAS activation) may be associated with negative symptoms, behavioral withdrawal, and poor response to neuroleptics.

Caveats and Comments

Having offered such a grandiose perspective on a motivational approach to psychopathology, I must now backpedal a bit and close with an acknowledgment of the tentativeness of what has been proposed and of the many remaining uncertainties. I intend this chapter to be very much a "work in progress" and offer it for its heuristic value. The major point here is that a motivational approach to understanding psychopathology has much to offer and may ultimately provide a general theoretical framework, such as is suggested in this chapter. I am mindful of the potential errors that may be contained in any attempt to understand a single form of psychopathology and that these are compounded many times when several forms of psychopathology are considered. Thus, it is hoped that others with various types of special expertise will examine these same issues and attempt to make improvements on the theory that has been offered.

AROUSAL

Attention should be directed to one particular problem that will be obvious to many readers: the problem of too many types of "arousal" and the difficulty of sorting them out. The original arousal concept combined several traditions (e.g., Malmo, 1959), elements of which can be seen in the four different constructs of Gray's theory. Activity in the BIS is said to represent anxiety and to involve a negative affective state. In past theories, anxiety has been assumed to contribute to arousal, a position made explicit in the use of the Taylor Manifest Anxiety Scale to select subjects with high "generalized drive" in the context of Hullian theory. Activity in the BAS is said to energize behavior, thereby subserving one of the functions attributed to arousal or drive in the older theories. Gray's concept of nonspecific arousal constitutes a third aspect of arousal—one that also energizes behavior in the sense of contributing to behavioral vigor but without the steering or directional quality associated with the BAS response to incentive stimuli. For these reasons, I have referred to Gray's theory as a three-arousal model (Fowles, 1980). With the addition of the fight/flight system as relevant to psychopathology, it must be considered a four-arousal model, since this system relates directly to Cannon's work on the massive activation of the sympathetic nervous system that also inspired the original theories of arousal.

Although the differences among these arousal components may be clear enough at the behavioral level in controlled experiments with animals, it is difficult to be sure how to assess them with physiological measures in humans. For example, which (or how many) of them influence responding in the electrodermal system used so extensively in research with psychopaths, in Lang's startle response used in studies of positive and negative affect, and in the perceptual measures used by Venables and Wing in their studies of withdrawal in schizophrenia? It is also difficult to know at a theoretical level which components are doing what. In the discussion above of contributors to liability in schizophrenia, it was suggested that both the BAS and the BIS contribute. Even if this suggestion is valid, it is difficult to know how much contribution there may be from activity in the BAS and the BIS, as opposed to the nonspecific arousal component that is common to both, and the contribution of the fight/flight system is unclear. Similarly, in depression, it is possible that all four systems are involved at one point or another (the fight/flight response to frustration UCSS, the BIS to CSS for frustration and possibly punishment at the beginning of experiences of loss or failure, and nonspecific arousal in connection with the BIS activation; a declining activation of the BAS over time as the expectancies of being able to cope diminish). These uncertainties contribute to the difficulty of making clear theoretical predictions in the context of clinical research.

COGNITIVE COMPONENTS OF MOTIVATION

A different limitation of this chapter can be seen by a consideration of the concept of executive function. As described by Tranel et al. (1993), executive functions refer to a variety of cognitive capacities, including judgment, planning, decision making, and social conduct, that have been employed to account for behavioral deficits produced by damage to the frontal lobes. Although these authors emphasize that executive functions are not limited to the frontal lobes, it is clear that many of the cognitive capacities designated by that term are influenced by the functioning of the frontal lobes.

The cognitive nature of these executive functions is further underscored by their description as being at the most supraordinate level in the cognitive hierarchy. Such cognitive abilities as memory, perception, and linguistic functions are employed by executive functions to achieve the desired goal. At the same time, central aspects of what are being called executive functions appear to overlap with motivational concepts. Tranel et al. (in press) cite Lezak's (1983) enumeration of executive-function disturbances, among which are problems of starting (e.g., decreased spontaneity and lost initiative) and of stopping (e.g., disinhibition and impulsivity). They also cite Fuster's (1989) statement that an inability to initiate and carry out

226

INTEGRATIVE VIEWS OF MOTIVATION, COGNITION, AND EMOTION

goal-directed behavior is the most distinctive disorder associated with damage to the prefrontal cortex. Fuster (1989) further describes an "apathetic syndrome" with a lack of initiative and affective and emotional bluntness—apparently a consequence of the inability to carry out goal-directed behavior. These descriptions appear to correspond strongly to the amotivational syndrome seen in chronic, withdrawn schizophrenics, which was attributed above to poor functioning of the BAS. Similarly, Tranel et al. (in press), again citing Fuster (1989), describe a "euphoric syndrome" that involves an abnormal elevation of mood, disinhibition, and in extreme form a clear disorder of social conduct that they term "acquired sociopathy" (see also Damasio et al. 1990, 1991). Of course, impulsivity was attributed above to weak functioning of Gray's BIS.

These comments clearly indicate a substantial overlap between clinical syndromes that neuropsychologists attribute to executive-function deficits and those that have been viewed as motivational deficits in this chapter (see also Pervin, 1992). These views are not inherently incompatible, but they do point to the complexity of motivation. One way to account for these differences is to suggest that major aspects of motivation discussed in this chapter have implicitly been concerned with the evaluation of whether certain goals are important and with the activation of behavior, whereas cognitive processes or executive functions are involved in attaining those goals (i.e., through judgment, planning, and decision making) once they are seen as desirable. Alternatively, one could embrace the vertical integration model of the brain (e.g., Derryberry & Tucker, 1990). In contrast to the traditional model that places the cortex at the highest level of control in the central nervous system, this model views the motivational components of the brain stem and limbic system as regulating the cortical functions. In either case, a more complete view probably considers behavioral activation and inhibitory control as mediated by a complex and integrated system that involves important cognitive components in achieving the goals. It has already been noted that Gray described the BIS as having projections to neocortical structures (including the prefrontal cortex; see esp. Gray, 1987b, Fig. 13.14, p. 295, which relates the prefrontal cortex projection to planning, and p. 354, in which severing the connections between the prefrontal cortex and the rest of the BIS is said to reduce trait anxiety) and that the dopaminergic pathways from the ventral tegmental area associated with the BAS project to the frontal cortex, which is consistent with the view of an articulation between these motivational systems and executive functions. Of course, the more complex a system, the greater the number of individual components that could malfunction and produce defective functioning.

PSYCHOLOGICAL VERSUS NEUROCHEMICAL LEVELS OF ANALYSIS

A basic tenet of this effort is that it is reasonable to expect some degree of isomorphism between motivational concepts derived from animal behavior and the underlying neurochemical substrates of behavior. Although it is not troublesome to anticipate that modifications of the concepts will be required as the two levels of analysis are examined more closely, another likely mismatch must be considered. It is not at all inconceivable that a deficiency might occur in the functioning of a given neurotransmitter (e.g., acetylcholine, norepinephrine, dopamine, serotonin). Any neurotransmitter may be involved in a number of different functional systems, with the result that alterations in its overall functioning may have multiple effects, not just an effect on a single motivational system. Serotonin is a case in point. Depue and Spoont (1986) described serotonin as heavily involved in the inhibition of behavior by the BIS, with the result that a serotonin deficiency reduces sensitivity to cues for punishment and nonreward. However, they also noted that low levels of serotonin produce hyperirritability, hyperexcitability, and hypersensitivity in the form of an exaggerated emotional arousal to relatively mild stimuli. McBurnett (1992) concluded that, although serotonergic fibers are involved in the inhibition of motor behavior by the BIS, a serotonin deficiency more generally "results in hypersensitivity to virtually all environmental stimuli and hyperactivity in virtually all situations" (p. 129). Thus, although temperament-based or pharmacologically produced serotonin deficiencies would impair aspects of BIS functioning, that would be only part of the effects. A particularly interesting implication in the case of serotonin deficiency is that, according to McBurnett, it would also increase the reactivity of the fight/flight system to aversive stimulation. He describes such individuals as exhibiting excessive motor behavior and impulsiveness and also reacting to unconditioned frustration or punishment with irritability, aggression, or otherwise unreflective (or perhaps disinhibited) behavior. Spoont (1992) similarly argues that low serotonin activity may produce a combination of reduced behavioral inhibition and increased vulnerability to stressful stimuli, causing such individuals to be impulsive and show a high stress reactivity. The implication of this conclusion from a motivational perspective is that a serotonin deficiency would produce a person weak in passive avoidance (the inhibitory aspects of the BIS), but also high in anxiety mediated by the fight/flight system. This combination, similar to Schalling's description of some impulsive psychopaths as having high somatic anxiety, would reflect a serotonin deficiency syndrome, rather than the combination of two independently distributed motivational systems that happen to combine in a certain fashion. Yet another perspective is offered by Gray (1987b, p. 334), who notes that motor inhibition is the major contribution of serotonergic systems. He suggests that impaired serotonergic transmission would interfere with punishment-induced response suppression but would leave the person still anxious in response to anxiogenic stimuli—that is, the effects of impairment of the serotonergic transmission occur after the BIS produces anxiety but before BIS activation results in motor inhibition. Thus, alterations in serotonergic functioning could uncouple two major aspects of the BIS, creating impulsivity but not reducing anxiety. Even though the motivational concepts are still useful in this context, one must be alert to the likelihood that malfunctions at the neurochemical level may have complex effects.

Advantages of a Motivational Approach

In spite of these acknowledgments of potential weaknesses of the perspective adopted here, it is worth stating again that motivational approaches to psychopathology have the numerous advantages described in the Introduction: they are relevant to emotional disorders, easily related to neurochemical processes through animal research and, therefore, to pharmacological and genetic contributions, provide a framework for environmental and learning-history influences, and are compatible with cognitive approaches to psychopathology. Few approaches can claim such scope.

REFERENCES

Abramson, L. Y., Seligman, M. E. P., & Teasdale, J. D. (1978). Learned help-lessness in humans: Critique and reformulation. *Journal of Abnormal Psychology, 87*, 49–74.

Andreasen, N. C. (1985). Positive vs. negative schizophrenia: A critical evaluation. *Schizophrenia Bulletin, 11*, 380–389.

Barlow, D. H. (1985). The dimensions of anxiety disorders. In A.H. Tuma & J. D. Maser (Eds.), *Anxiety and anxiety disorders* (pp. 479–500). Hillsdale, NJ: Erlbaum.

Barlow, D. H. (1988). *Anxiety and its disorders.* New York: Guilford.

Baron, M., & Gruen, R. S. (1991). Schizophrenia and affective disorder: Are they genetically linked? *British Journal of Psychiatry, 159*, 267–270.

Barrelet, L., Ferrero, F., Szigethy, L., Giddey, C., & Pellizzer, G. 1990. Expressed emotion and first-admission schizophrenia. Nine-month follow-up in a French cultural environment. *British Journal of Psychiatry, 156*, 357–362.

Beck, A. T. (1974). The development of depression: A cognitive model. In R. J. Friedman & M. M. Katz (Eds.), *The psychology of depression* (pp. 3–27). Washington, DC: Winston.

Beck, A. T., Brown, G., Steer, R. A., Eidelson, J. I., & Riskind, J. H. (1987). Differentiating anxiety and depression: A test of the cognitive content-specificity hypothesis. *Journal of Abnormal Psychology, 96*, 179–183.

Birley, J., & Brown, G. W. (1970). Crisis and life changes preceding the onset or relapse of acute schizophrenia: Clinical aspects. *British Journal of Psychiatry, 16*, 327–333.

Bleuler, M. (1974). The long-term course of schizophrenic psychoses. *Psychological Medicine, 4*, 244–254.

Braden, W. (1984). Vulnerability and schizoaffective psychosis: A two-factor model. *Schizophrenia Bulletin, 10*, 71–86.

Breier, A., Wolkowitz, O. M., & Pickar, D. (1991). Stress and schizophrenia. In C. A. Tamminga & S. C. Schulz (Eds.), *Advances in neuropsychiatry and psychopharmacology: Vol. 1. Schizophrenia research* (pp. 141–152). New York: Raven.

Brown, G. W., & Birley, J. L. T. (1968). Crisis and life change and the onset of schizophrenia. *Journal of Health and Social Behavior, 9*, 203–214.

Bruce, M. L., Kim, K., Leaf, P. J., & Jacobs, S. (1990). Depressive episodes and dysphoria resulting from conjugal bereavement in a prospective community sample. *American Journal of Psychiatry, 147*, 608–611.

Cannon, W. B. (1929). *Bodily changes in pain, hunger, fear, and rage* (2nd ed.). New York: Appleton-Century-Crofts.

Carpenter, W. T., Jr. (1992). The negative symptom challenge. *Archives of General Psychiatry, 49*, 236–237.

Carpenter, W. T., Jr., Heinrichs, D. W., & Wagman, A. M. I. (1988). Deficit and nondeficit forms of schizophrenia: The concept. *American Journal of Psychiatry, 145*, 578–583.

Chapman, L. J., & Chapman, J. P. (1973). *Disordered thought in schizophrenia*. Englewood Cliffs, NJ: Prentice-Hall.

Clark, D. A., Beck, A. T., & Stewart, B. (1990). Cognitive specificity and positive-negative affectivity: Complementary or contradictory views on anxiety and depression? *Journal of Abnormal Psychology, 99,* 148–155.

Cleckley, H. (1964). *The mask of sanity* (4th ed.). St. Louis: Mosby.

Collins, P., & Depue, R. (1992). A neurobehavioral systems approach to developmental psychopathology: Implications for disorders of affect. In D. Cichetti (Ed.), *Developmental psychopathology* (Vol. 4). Hillsdale, NJ: Erlbaum.

Crider, A. (1993). Electrodermal response lability-stability: Individual difference correlates. In J.-C. Roy, W. Boucsein, D. Fowles, & J. Gruzelier (Eds.), *Progress in electrodermal research* (pp. 173–186). London: Plenum.

Crow, T. (1980). Molecular pathology of schizophrenia: More than one disease process? *British Medical Journal, 280,* 66–68.

Crow, T. J. (1985). The two-syndrome concept: Origins and current status. *Schizophrenia Bulletin, 11,* 471–486.

Crow, T. J. (1986). The continuum of psychosis and its implications for the structure of the gene. *British Journal of Psychiatry, 149,* 419–429.

Crow, T. J. (1991). The search for the psychosis gene. *British Journal of Psychiatry, 158,* 611–614.

Cummings, J. L. (1992). Depression and Parkinson's disease: A review. *American Journal of Psychiatry, 149,* 443–454.

Damasio, A. R., Tranel, D., & Damasio, H. (1990). Individuals with sociopathic behavior caused by frontal lobe damage fail to respond autonomically to social stimuli. *Behavioural Brain Research, 41,* 81–94.

Damasio, A. R., Tranel, D., & Damasio, H. (1991). Somatic markers and the guidance of behavior: Theory and preliminary testing. In H. S. Levin, H. M. Eisenberg, & A. Benton (Eds.), *Frontal lobe function and dysfunction* (pp. 217–229). New York: Oxford University Press.

Davis, J. M. (1978). Dopamine theory of schizophrenia: A two-factor theory. In L. C. Wynne, R. L. Cromwell, & S. Matthysse (Eds.), *The nature of schizophrenia* (pp. 105–115). New York: Wiley.

Day, R., Nielsen, J. A., Korten, A., Ernberg, G., Dube, K. C., Gebhart, J., Jablensky, A., Leon, C., Marsella, A., Olatawura, M., Sartorius, N., Stromgren, E., Takahashi, R., Wig, N., & Wynne, L. C. (1987). Stressful life events preceding the acute onset of schizophrenia: A cross-national study from the World Health Organization. *Culture, Medicine, and Psychiatry, 11,* 123–205.

Delva, N. J., & Letemendia, F. J. J. (1982). Lithium treatment in schizophrenia and schizoaffective disorders. *British Journal of Psychiatry, 141,* 387–400.

Depue, R. A. (1976). An activity-withdrawal distinction in schizophrenia: Behavioral, clinical brain damage, and neurophysiological correlates. *Journal of Abnormal Psychology, 85,* 174–185.

Depue, R. A., Arbisi, P., Spoont, M. R., Leon, A., & Ainsworth, B. (1989). Dopamine functioning in the Behavioral Facilitation System and seasonal variation in behavior: Normal population and clinical studies. In N. Rosenthal & M. Blehar (Eds.), *Seasonal affective disorder* (pp. 230–259). New York: Guilford.

Depue, R. A., & Iacono, W. G. (1988). Neurobehavioral aspects of affective disorders. *Annual Review of Psychology, 40*, 457–492.

Depue, R. A., Krauss, S. P., & Spoont, M. R. 1987. A two dimensional threshold model of seasonal bipolar affective disorder. In D. Magnusson & A. Ohman (Eds.), *Psychopathology: An interactional perspective* (pp. 95–123). New York: Academic Press.

Depue, R. A., & Spoont, M. R. (1986). Conceptualizing a serotonin trait: A behavioral dimension of constraint. *Annals of the New York Academy of Sciences, 487*, 47–62.

Derryberry, D., & Tucker, D. M. (1990). The adaptive base of the neural hierarchy: Elementary motivational controls on network function. *Nebraska Symposium on Motivation, 1991*, 289–342.

Eastman, C. (1976). Behavioral formulations of depression. *Psychological Review, 83*, 277–291.

Falloon, I. R. H., Boyd, J. L., McGill, C. W., Williamson, M., Razani, J., Moss, H. B., Gilderman, A. M., & Simpson, G. M. (1985). Family management in the prevention of morbidity of schizophrenia. *Archives of General Psychiatry, 42*, 887–896.

Falk, J. L., Schuster, C. R., Bigelow, G. E., & Woods, J. H. (1982). Progress and needs in the experimental analysis of drug and alcohol dependence. *American Psychologist, 37*, 1124–1127.

Faraone, S. V., & Tsuang, M. T. (1985). Quantitative models of the genetic transmission of schizophrenia. *Psychological Bulletin, 98*, 41–66.

Foa, E. B., & Foa, U. G. (1982). Differentiating depression and anxiety: Is it possible? Is it useful? *Psychopharmacology Bulletin, 18*, 62–68.

Fowles, D. C. (1980). The three arousal model: Implications of Gray's two-factor learning theory for heart rate, electrodermal activity, and psychopathy. *Psychophysiology, 17*, 87–104.

Fowles, D. C. (1986). The eccrine system and electrodermal activity. In M. G. H. Coles, S. W. Porges, & E. Donchin (Eds.), *Psychophysiology: Systems, processes, and applications* (Vol. 1, pp. 51–96). New York: Guilford.

Fowles, D. C. (1988). Psychophysiology and psychopathology: A motivational approach. *Psychophysiology, 25*, 373–391.

Fowles, D. C. (1992a). Motivational approach to anxiety disorders. In D. G. Forgays, T. Sosnowski, & K. Wrzesniewski (Eds.), *Anxiety: Recent developments in cognitive, psychophysiological, and health research* (pp. 181–192). Washington, DC: Hemisphere.

Fowles, D. C. (1992b). Schizophrenia: Diathesis-stress revisited. *Annual Review of Psychology, 43*, 303–336.

Fowles, D. C. (1993a). Biological variables in psychopathology: A psychobiological perspective. In P. B. Sutker & H. E. Adams (Eds.), *Comprehensive handbook of psychopathology* (2nd ed., pp. 57–82). New York: Plenum.

Fowles, D. C. (1993b). Electrodermal activity and antisocial behavior: Empirical findings and theoretical issues. In J.-C. Roy, W. Boucsein, D.

Fowles, & J. Gruzelier (Eds.), *Progress in electrodermal research* (pp. 223–237). London: Plenum.

Fuster, J. M. (1989). *The prefrontal cortex: Anatomy, physiology, and neuropsychology of the frontal lobe* (2nd ed.). New York: Raven.

Garber, J., Miller, S. M., & Abramson, L. Y. (1980). On the distinction between anxiety and depression: Perceived control, certainty, and probability of goal attainment. In J. Garber & M. E. P. Seligman (Eds.), *Human helplessness* (pp. 131–169). New York: Academic Press.

Garmezy, N. (1968). Process and reactive schizophrenia: Some conceptions and issues. In M. M. Katz, J. O. Cole, & W. E. Barton (Eds.), *The role and methodology of classification in psychiatry and psychopathology* (pp. 419–466) (Public Health Service Publication No. 1584). Washington, DC: U. S. Government Printing Office.

Gersh, F., & Fowles, D. C. (1979). Neurotic depression: The concept of anxious depression. In R. A. Depue (Ed.), *The psychobiology of the depressive disorders: Implications for the effects of stress* (pp. 81–104). New York: Academic Press.

Glowinski, J., Tassin, J. P., & Thierry, A. M. (1984). The mesocortical-prefrontal dopaminergic neurons. *Trends in Neuroscience, 7,* 415–418.

Gorenstein, E. E., & Newman, J. P. (1980). Disinhibitory psychopathology: A new perspective and a model for research. *Psychological Review, 87,* 301–315.

Gottesman, I. I. (1991). *Schizophrenia genesis.* New York: Freeman.

Gottesman, I. I., & McGue, M. (1991). Mixed and mixed-up models for the transmission of schizophrenia. In D. Cichetti & W. Grove (Eds.), *Thinking clearly about psychology: Essays in honor of Paul E. Meehl.* Minneapolis: University of Minnesota Press.

Gottesman, I. I., McGuffin, P., & Farmer, A. E. (1987). Clinical genetics as clues to the "real" genetics of schizophrenia (a decade of modest gains while playing for time). *Schizophrenia Bulletin, 13,* 23–47.

Gottesman, I. I., & Shields, J. A. (1967). A polygenic theory of schizophrenia. *Proceedings of the National Academy of Sciences of the USA.* 58:199–205.

Gottesman, I. I., & Shields, J. A. (1982). *Schizophrenia: The epigenetic puzzle.* New York: Cambridge University Press.

Gray, J. A. (1970). The psychophysiological basis of intraversion-extraversion. *Behavior Research and Therapy, 8,* 249–266.

Gray, J. A. (1975). *Elements of a two-process theory of learning.* New York: Academic Press.

Gray, J. A. (1976). The behavioural inhibition system: A possible substrate for anxiety. In M. P. Feldman & A. Broadhurst (Eds.), *Theoretical and experimental bases of the behaviour therapies* (pp. 3–41). London: Wiley.

Gray, J. A. (1977). Drug effects on fear and frustration: Possible limbic site of action of minor tranquilizers. In L. L. Iversen, S. D. Iversen, & S. H. Snyder (Eds.), *Handbook of psychopharmacology: Vol. 8. Drugs, neurotransmitters, and behavior* (pp. 433–529). New York: Plenum.

Gray, J. A. (1978). The neuropsychology of anxiety. *British Journal of Psychology, 69*, 417–434.

Gray, J. A. (1979). A neuropsychological theory of anxiety. In C. E. Izard (Ed.), *Emotions in personality and psychopathology* (pp. 303–335). New York: Plenum.

Gray, J. A. (1982). *The neuropsychology of anxiety: An enquiry into the functions of the septo-hippocampal system.* Oxford: Oxford University Press.

Gray, J. A. (1987a). Perspectives on anxiety and impulsivity: A commentary. *Journal of Research in Personality, 21*, 493–509.

Gray, J. A. (1987b). *The psychology of fear and stress* (2nd ed.). Cambridge: Cambridge University Press.

Haracz, J. L. (1982). The dopamine hypothesis: An overview of studies with schizophrenic patients. *Schizophrenia Bulletin, 8*, 438–469.

Hare, R. (1970). *Psychopathy.* New York: Wiley.

Hare, R. D. (1978). Electrodermal and cardiovascular correlates of psychopathy. In R. D. Hare & D. Schalling (Eds.), *Psychopathic behavior: Approaches to research* (pp. 107–144). New York: Wiley.

Hare, R. D., & Craigen, D. (1974). Psychopathy and physiological activity in a mixed-motive game situation. *Psychophysiology, 11*, 197–206.

Hare, R. D., Frazelle, J., & Cox, D. N. (1978). Psychopathy and physiological responses to threat of an aversive stimulus. *Psychophysiology, 15*, 165–172.

Heston, L. L. (1966). Psychiatric disorders in foster home reared children of schizophrenic mothers. *British Journal of Psychiatry, 112*, 819–825.

Hinshaw, S. P. (1987). On the distinction between attentional deficits/hyperactivity and conduct problems/aggression in child psychopathology. *Psychological Bulletin, 101*, 443–463.

Hogarty, G. E., Anderson, C. M., Reiss, D. J., Kornblith, S. J., Greenwald, D. P., Javna, C. D., & Madonia, M. J. (1986). Family psychoeducation, social skills training, and maintenance chemotherapy in the aftercare treatment of schizophrenia. *Archives of General Psychiatry, 43*, 633–642.

Jaffe, J. H. (1990). Drug addiction and drug abuse. In A. G. Gilman, T. W. Rall, A. S. Nies, & P. Taylor (Eds.). *Goodman and Gilman's pharmacological basis of therapeutics* (8th ed., pp. 522–573). New York: Macmillan.

Jimerson, D. C. 1987. Role of dopamine mechanisms in the affective disorders. In H. Meltzer (Ed.), *Psychopharmacology: The third generation of progress* (pp. 505–512). New York: Raven.

Kallmann, F. J. (1938). *The genetics of schizophrenia.* New York: Augustin.

Kendell, R. E. (1982). The choice of diagnostic criteria for biological research. *Archives of General Psychiatry, 39*, 1334–1339.

Kendler, K. S. (1987). The genetics of schizophrenia: A current perspective. In H. Y. Meltzer (Ed.), *Psychopharmacology: The third generation of progress* (pp. 705–713). New York: Raven.

Kerr, A., & McClelland, H. (Eds.). (1991). *Concepts of mental disorder.* London: Gaskell.

Klein, D. F. (1974). Endogenomorphic depression: A conceptual and terminological revision. *Archives of General Psychiatry, 31*, 447–454.

234

Konorski, J. (1967). *Integrative activity of the brain: An interdisciplinary approach.* Chicago: University of Chicago Press.

Lang, P. J., Bradley, M., & Cuthbert, B. N. (1990). Emotion, attention, and the startle reflex. *Psychological Review, 97,* 377–395.

Lang, P. J., Bradley, M., Cuthbert, B. N., & Patrick, C. J. (1993). Emotion and psychopathology: A startle probe analysis. In L. J. Chapman, J. P. Chapman, & D. C. Fowles (Eds.), *Models and methods of psychopathology* (pp. 163–199). New York: Springer.

Leff, J. P., Kuipers, L., Berkowitz, R., Eberlein-Vries, R., & Sturgeon, D. 1982. A controlled trial of social intervention in the families of schizophrenic patients. *British Journal of Psychiatry, 141,* 121–134.

Leff, J. P., & Vaughn, C. E. (1985). *Expressed emotion in families: Its significance for mental illness.* New York: Guilford.

Levinson, D. F., & Levitt, M. E. M. (1987). Schizoaffective mania reconsidered. *American Journal of Psychiatry, 144,* 415–425.

Lewine, R. R. J. (1985). Negative symptoms in schizophrenia: Editor's introduction. *Schizophrenia Bulletin, 11,* 361–363.

Lezak, M. D. (1983). *Neuropsychological assessment* (2nd ed.). New York: Oxford University Press.

Losonczy, M. F., Davidson, M., & Davis, K. L. (1987). The dopamine hypothesis of schizophrenia. In H. Y. Meltzer (Ed.), *Psychopharmacology: The third generation of progress* (pp. 715–726). New York: Raven.

Lukoff, D., Snyder, K., Ventura, J., & Nuechterlein, K. H. (1984). Life events, familial stress, and coping in the developmental course of schizophrenia. *Schizophrenia Bulletin, 10,* 258–292.

Lydiard, R. B., & Laird, L. K. (1988). Prediction of response to antipsychotics. *Journal of Clinical Psychopharmacology, 8,* 3–13.

Lykken, D. T. (1957). A study of anxiety in the sociopathic personality. *Journal of Abnormal Psychology, 55,* 6–10.

Lykken, D. T., MacIndoe, I., & Tellegen, A. (1972). Autonomic response to shock as a function of predictability in time and locus. *Psychophysiology, 9,* 318–333.

Mackintosh, N. J. (1974). *The psychology of animal learning.* New York: Academic Press.

Malmo, R. (1959). Activation: A neuropsychological dimension. *Psychological Review, 66,* 367–386.

Martin, I. (1983). Human classical conditioning. In A. Gale & J. A. Edward (Eds.), *Physiological correlates of human behavior: Vol. 2. Attention and performance.* London: Academic Press.

McBurnett, K. (1992). Psychobiological approaches to personality and their applications to child psychopathology. In B. B. Lahey & A. E. Kazdin (Eds.), *Advances in clinical child psychology* (Vol. 14, pp. 107–164). New York: Plenum.

McGue, M., & Gottesman, I. I. (1989). Genetic linkage in schizophrenia: Perspectives from genetic epidemiology. *Schizophrenia Bulletin, 15,* 453–464.

Meehl, P. (1962). Schizotaxia, schizotypy, schizophrenia. *American Psychologist, 17,* 827–838.

Meltzer, H. Y. (1984). Schizoaffective disorder; Editor's introduction. *Schizophrenia Bulletin, 10,* 11–13.

Mineka, S. (1985). Animal models of anxiety-based disorders: Their usefulness and limitations. In A.H. Tuma & J. D. Maser (Eds.), *Anxiety and anxiety disorders* (pp. 199–244). Hillsdale, NJ: Erlbaum.

Mineka, S., Gunnar, M., & Champoux, M. (1986). Control and early socioemotional development: Infant rhesus monkeys reared in controllable versus uncontrollable environments. *Child Development, 57,* 1241–1256.

Mineka, S., & Kelly, K. A. (1989). The relationship between anxiety, lack of control and loss of control. In A. Steptoe and A. Appels (Eds.), *Stress, personal control and worker health.* New York: Wiley.

Mowrer, O. H. (1960). *Learning and behavior.* New York: Wiley.

Neale, J. M., & Oltmanns, T. F. (1980). *Schizophrenia.* New York: Wiley.

Newman, J. P., & Kosson, D. S. (1986). Passive avoidance learning in psychopathic and nonpsychopathic offenders. *Journal of Abnormal Psychology, 95,* 252–256.

Newman, J. P., Patterson, C. M., & Kosson, D. S. (1987). Response perseveration in psychopaths. *Journal of Abnormal Psychology, 96,* 145–148.

Newman, J. P., Widom, C. S., & Nathan, S. (1985). Passive-avoidance in syndromes of disinhibition: Psychopathy and extraversion. *Journal of Personality and Social Psychology, 48,* 1316–1327.

Nöthen, M. M., Erdmann, J., Körner, J., Lanczik, M., Fritze, J., Fimmers, R., Grandy, D. K., O'Dowd, B., & Propping, P. (1992). Lack of association between dopamine D1 and D2 receptor genes and bipolar affective disorder. *American Journal of Psychiatry, 149,* 199–201.

Nurnberger, J. I., Jr., & Gershon, E. S. (1992). Genetics. In E. S. Paykel (Ed.), *Handbook of affective disorders* (pp. 131–148). New York: Guilford.

Obrist, P. A. (1976). The cardiovascular-behavioral interaction—as it appears today. *Psychophysiology, 13,* 95–107.

O'Gorman, J. G., & Horneman, C. (1979). Consistency of individual differences in non-specific electrodermal activity. *Biological Psychology, 9,* 13–21.

Panksepp, J. (1992). A critical role for "affective neuroscience" in resolving what is basic about basic emotions. *Psychological Review, 99,* 554–560.

Pervin, L. A. (1992). The rational mind and the problem of volition. *Psychological Science, 3,* 162–164.

Plomin, R. (1990). The role of inheritance in behavior. *Science, 248,* 183–188.

Procci, W. R. (1989). Psychotic disorders not elsewhere classified. In H. I. Kaplan and B. J. Sadock (Eds.), *Comprehensive textbook of psychiatry* (Vol. 5, pp. 830–842). Baltimore: Williams & Williams.

Quay, H. C. (1988a). Attention deficit disorder and the behavioral inhibition system: The relevance of the neuropsychological theory of Jeffrey A. Gray. In L. M. Bloomingdale & J. A. Sergeant (Eds.), *Attention deficit disorder: Criteria, cognition, intervention* (pp. 117–125). Oxford: Pergamon.

Quay, H. (1988b). The behavioral reward and inhibition systems in childhood behavior disorder. In L. M. Bloomingdale (Ed.), *Attention deficit disorder: Research in treatment, psychopharmacology & attention.* (Vol. 3, pp. 176–186). New York: Spectrum.

Quay, H. C. (October, 1990). Electrodermal responding, inhibition, and re-ward-seeking in undersocialized aggressive conduct disorder. Paper presented at the annual meeting of the American Academy of Child and Adolescent Psychiatry, Chicago.

Quay, H. C. (1993). The psychobiology of undersocialized aggressive con-duct disorder: A theoretical perspective. *Development and Psychopathology, 5,* 165–180.

Razran, G. (1961). The observable unconscious and the inferable conscious in current Soviet psychophysiology: Interoceptive conditioning, seman-tic conditioning, and the orienting reflex. *Psychological Review, 68,* 81–150.

Reiss, D., Plomin, R., & Hetherington, E. M. (1991). Genetics and psychia-try: An unheralded window on the environment. *American Journal of Psychiatry, 148,* 283–291.

Reynolds, G. P. (1989). Beyond the dopamine hypothesis: The neurochemi-cal pathology of schizophrenia. *British Journal of Psychiatry, 155,* 305–316.

Risch, N. (1990). Genetic linkage and complex diseases, with special refer-ence to psychiatric disorders. *Genetic Epidemiology, 7,* 3–16.

Rosenthal, D. (1970). *Genetic theory and abnormal behavior.* New York: McGraw-Hill.

Roth, M., & Mountjoy, C. Q. (1982). The distinction between anxiety states and depressive disorders. In E. S. Paykel (Ed.), *Handbook of affective disor-ders.* Edinburgh: Churchill Livingstone.

Schachter, S., & Latane, B. (1964). Crime, cognition, and the autonomic ner-vous system. In M. R. Jones (Ed.), *Nebraska Symposium on Motivation 1963.* Lincoln: University of Nebraska Press.

Schalling, D. (1975). The role of heart rate increase for coping with pain as related to impulsivity. Unpublished manuscript, University of Stock-holm.

Schalling, D. (1978). Psychopathy-related personality variables and the psy-chophysiology of socialization. In R. D. Hare & D. Schalling (Eds.), *Psy-chopathic behavior: Approaches to research* (pp. 85–106). New York: Wiley.

Schell, A. M., Dawson, M. E., & Filion, D. L. (1988). Psychophysiological correlates of electrodermal lability. *Psychophysiology, 25,* 619–632.

Schmauk, F. J. (1970). Punishment, arousal, and avoidance learning in so-ciopaths. *Journal of Abnormal Psychology, 76,* 325–335.

Siegel, R. A. (1978). Probability of punishment and suppression of behavior in psychopathic and non-psychopathic offenders. *Journal of Abnormal Psychology, 87,* 514–522.

Snyder, S. H. (1978). Dopamine and schizophrenia. In L. C. Wynne, R. L. Cromwell, & S. Matthysse (Eds.), *The nature of schizophrenia* (pp. 87–94). New York: Wiley.

Solomon, R. L. (1980). The opponent-process theory of acquired motiva-tion. *American Psychologist, 35,* 691–712.

Sommers, A. A. (1985). "Negative symptoms": Conceptual and meth-odological problems. *Schizophrenia Bulletin, 11,* 364–379.

Spoont, M. R. (1992). Modulatory role of serotonin in neural information processing: Implications for human psychopathology. *Psychological Bulletin, 112*, 330–350.

Stewart, J., de Witt, H., & Eikelboom, R. (1984). Role of unconditioned and conditioned drug effects in the self-administration of opiates and stimulants. *Psychological Review, 91*, 251–268.

Strauss, J., Carpenter, W. T., Jr., & Bartko, J. (1974). The diagnosis and understanding of schizophrenia: 3. Speculations on the processes that underlie schizophrenic symptoms and signs. *Schizophrenia Bulletin, 1*, (experimental issue 11), 61–69.

Swinson, R. P., & Kirby, M. (1986). The differentiation of anxiety and depressive syndromes. In B. F. Shaw, Z. V. Segal, T. M. Vallis, & F. E. Cashman (Eds.), *Anxiety disorders: Psychological and biological perspectives* (pp. 21–34). New York: Plenum.

Tarrier, N., Barrowclough, C., Vaughn, C., Bamrah, J. S., Porceddu, K., Watts, S., & Freeman, H. L. 1988. The community management of schizophrenia: A controlled trial of a behavioural intervention with families to reduce relapse. *British Journal of Psychiatry, 153*, 532–542.

Taylor, M. A. (1992). Are schizophrenia and affective disorder related? A selective review of the literature. *American Journal of Psychiatry, 149*, 22–32.

Taylor, M. A., Berenbaum, S. A., Jampala, V. C., & Cloninger, C. R. (1993). Are schizophrenia and affective disorder related? Preliminary data from a family study. *American Journal of Psychiatry, 150*, 278–285.

Tellegen, A. (1985). Structures of mood and personality and their relevance to assessing anxiety, with an emphasis on self-report. In A. H. Tuma & J. D. Maser (Eds.), *Anxiety and the anxiety disorders* (pp. 681–706). Hillsdale, NJ: Erlbaum.

Tranel, D., Anderson, S. W., & Benton, A. (in press). Development of the concept of "executive function" and its relationship to the frontal lobes. In S. Boller & J. Grafman (Eds.), *Handbook of neuropsychology* (Vol. 9). Amsterdam: Elsevier.

Trasler, G. (1978). Relations between psychopathy and persistent criminality: Methodological and theoretical issues. In R. D. Hare & D. Schalling (Eds.), *Psychopathic behavior: Approaches to research* (pp. 273–298). New York: Wiley.

Trulson, M. E., & Preussler, D. W. (1984). Dopamine-containing ventral tegmental area neurons in freely moving cats: Activity during the sleep-waking cycle and effects of stress. *Experimental Neurology, 83*, 367–377.

Vaughn, C. E., Snyder, K., Jones, S., Freeman, W. B., & Falloon, I. R. H. (1984). Family factors in schizophrenic relapse. *Archives of General Psychiatry, 41*, 1169–1177.

Venables, P. H. (1963a). The relationship between level of skin potential and fusion of paired light flashes in schizophrenic and normal subjects. *Journal of Psychiatric Research, 1*, 279–287.

Venables, P. H. (1963b). Selectivity of attention, withdrawal, and cortical activation. *Archives of General Psychiatry, 9*, 74–78.

Venables, P. H. (1967). The relation of two flash and two click thresholds to withdrawal in paranoid and non-paranoid schizophrenics. *British Journal of Social and Clinical Psychology, 6*, 60–62.

Venables, P. H., & Wing, J. K. (1962). Level of arousal and the subclassification of schizophrenia. *Archives of General Psychiatry, 7*, 114–119.

Ventura, J., Nuechterlein, K. H., Lukoff, D., & Hardesty, J. P. (1989). A prospective study of stressful life events and schizophrenic relapse. *Journal of Abnormal Psychology, 98*, 407–411.

Waid, W. M., & Orne, M. T. (1982). Reduced electrodermal response to conflict, failure to inhibit dominant behaviors, and delinquency proneness. *Journal of Personality and Social Psychology, 43*, 769–774.

Watson, D., & Clark, L. A. (1984). Negative affectivity: The disposition to experience aversive emotional states. *Psychological Bulletin, 96*, 465–490.

Watson, D., Clark, L. A., & Carey, G. (1988). Positive and negative affectivity and their relation to anxiety and depressive disorders. *Journal of Abnormal Psychology, 97*, 346–353.

Watson, D., & Tellegen, A. (1985). Toward a consensual structure of mood. *Psychological Bulletin, 98*, 219–235.

Whalen, C. K. (1989). Attention deficit and hyperactivity disorders. In T. H. Ollendick & M. Hersen (Eds.), *Handbook of child psychopathology*, (2nd ed., pp. 131–169). New York: Plenum.

Williams, P. V., & McGlashan, T. H. (1987). Schizoaffective psychosis. *Archives of General Psychiatry, 44*, 130–137.

Wing, J. K. (1961). A simple and reliable subclassification of chronic schizophrenia. *Journal of Mental Science, 107*, 862–875.

Wing, J. K. (1978). Social influences on the course of schizophrenia. In L. C. Wynne, R. L. Cromwell, & S. Matthysse (Eds.), *The nature of schizophrenia* (pp. 599–616). New York: Wiley.

Wise, R. A. (1988). The neurobiology of craving: Implications for the understanding and treatment of addiction. *Journal of Abnormal Psychology, 97*, 118–132.

Wise, R. A., & Bozarth, M. A. (1987). A psychomotor stimulant theory of addiction. *Psychological Review, 94*, 469–492.

Wise, R. A., & Rompre, P.-P. (1989). Brain dopamine and reward. *Annual Review of Psychology, 40*, 191–225.

Wolkowitz, O. M., & Pickar, D. (1991). Benzodiazepines in the treatment of schizophrenia: A review and reappraisal. *American Journal of Psychiatry, 148*, 714–726.

Zubin, J., & Spring, B. (1977). Vulnerability: A new view of schizophrenia. *Journal of Abnormal Psychology, 86*, 103–126.

Abstracts for Poster Presentations

Learning Unbinds Bounded Rationality

Gordon M. Becker, University of Nebraska–Omaha

Raising the aspiration level (Simon, 1957, 1982) to the most preferred outcome is likely to result in failure and suffering. Lowering the aspiration level to the least preferred outcome guarantees success. Raising one's appreciation so that all outcomes are as desirable as the most preferred outcome guarantees happiness. The highest happiness can thus be guaranteed by having no preferences and having the highest appreciation for everything (Becker, 1990, 1991), yet hardly anyone does this (Csikszentmihalyi, 1990). The prescriptions (often irrational) that people learn significantly determine their behavior. Our descriptive models, based on observed behavior, are thus significantly determined by such prescriptions. It is important that we give more attention to describing and improving the prescriptions underlying observed behavior.

REFERENCES

Becker, G. M. (1990). *Optimal utilities.* PSYCOLOQUY 1 (16) December 4, 1990 (electronic journal retrievable by anonymous ftp in directory pub/harnad on princeton.edu [telnet number 128.112.128.1] as file psyc.arch.90.1.16).

Becker, G. M. (1991). *Optimal utilities.* In R. Frantz, H. Singh, & J. Gerber, (Eds.), *Handbook of behavioral economics: Vol. 2B. Behavioral Decision Making* (pp. 439–451). Greenwich, CT: JAI.

Csikszentmihalyi, M. (1990). *Flow: The psychology of optimal experience.* New York: Harper & Row.

Simon, H. A. (1957). *Models of man: Social and rational.* New York: Wiley.

Simon, H. A. (1982). *Models of bounded rationality.* Cambridge, MA: MIT Press.

Parents' Influence on Children's Decision-Making: A Comparison of Decision Process and Decision Outcome

A. K. Ganzel, University of Nebraska–Lincoln

Parents' influence on the decision making of their pre- and early-adolescent children was investigated by coding family conversations for parent-to-child ratios of agreements, statements, questions, and disagreements (which collectively represent the decision process). Parents used many more questions than did children. There were few relationships between decision process and decision outcome (e.g., parent's choice vs. child's choice vs. new choice); however, higher child disagreement in single-parent families predicted child's choice outcome; higher child disagreement in two-parent families predicted parent(s)' choice outcome. Mothers in both single- and two-parent families used more questions with preadolescent than with early-adolescent children.

An Integrated Theory of Motivation from *A Portrait of the Person; A Personality Theory for the Clinician*

Zoltan Gross

When the brain's hypothalamic-limbic (H-L) system is disequilibrated by internal and/or external sources of information, goal-directed (motivation) behavior occurs. Sensory information is the external source of motivation.

The need for invariant stimulation to maintain the integrity of biological systems is affect hunger. Affect-hungry and/or informationally disequilibrated H-L systems activate emotionally.

The person is an equilibratory system of cognitions about the H-L system. Developmentally generated incongruent personal systems also disequilibrate the H-L/person system. The person and action programs generating behavior are activated to restore disequilibrated H-L/person systems to their steady-state condition. These underlie internally activated motivation.

Why Do They Drink?

C. J. Krauskopf, Ohio State University
D.R. Saunders, MARS Measurement Associates

Using the Gittinger Personality Assessment system that was presented to the Nebraska Symposium on Motivation by Bem in 1982, several groups of alcoholics were identified that the theory suggests drink for quite different reasons. The theory begins with the motivational construct that people act to minimize the significance of their weaknesses and exploit their strengths. Operationally, patterns of Wechsler scales are used to infer cognitive styles and motivations. For example, one group drinks to dampen the effects of anxiety, another to avoid symptoms of depression, and another to improve on their internal fantasy world. Hypotheses are suggested for confirmation studies or for treatment studies.

Female Prisoners' Conceptions of AIDS: Cognitive-Developmental Level of Understanding, Factual Knowledge, and Prejudice against People with AIDS

David K. Marcus, Sam Houston State University

Female prisoners' reasoning about the causes and transmission of AIDS was examined. At two women's prisons in Texas 113 inmates were administered the Concepts of AIDS Protocol, an AIDS information test, and a measure assessing prejudice against people with AIDS. Subjects' developmental level of understanding AIDS was moderately correlated with their knowledge about AIDS and their reported acceptance of people with AIDS. Apparently individuals who are more knowledgeable about AIDS are less fearful of and prejudiced against people with AIDS.

Emotions and Cognitions as Predictors of Post-hospitalization Health Behavior Change

Chloe D. Martin, Deborah Bowen, Mauren Carney
Fred Hutchinson Cancer Research Center

Theoretically, the period after a cardiac event is motivating for health behavior changes, yet rates of behavior change after myocardial infarction are not high. Leventhal has proposed that both emotions and cognitions are critical in motivating decisions about health-related behavior change. This study applied Leventhal's model to patients admitted to a hospital with a cardiac event. Lack of positive emotions and beliefs that condition was preventable and stressful predicted intent to change behaviors at baseline. Additional analyses delineated the role of emotions and cognitions in long-term change.

The Effects of Task Complexity and Goal Difficulty on Task Strategy and Performance over Time

Mark A. Mone, University of Wisconsin–Milwaukee
Christina Shalley, University of Arizona

A 2 (specific difficult, do-your-best goal) by 2 (simple, complex) by 3 (performance trial) experimental design was employed to examine whether task complexity interacts with goal difficulty over multiple performance periods. Results indicated that do-your-best goals led to higher quantity of performance on a complex task, whereas specific difficult goals led to higher quantity of performance on a simpler task. Additionally, goal difficulty and task complexity led to continued strategy search, with those in the complex, specific difficult condition exhibiting the highest amount of search. Finally, quality of performance was higher for the complex task.

Self-Discrepancies: Motivation to Pursue Life Tasks

Ethel D. Moore, Swarthmore College

In this experimental time-sampling study, we examined the relationships between first year college students' self-concept discrepancies, their selected daily activities, and accompanying affective experiences. For a period of 10 d, responding to the random signals of electronic beepers, the students systematically reported what they were doing and their associated feelings and thoughts as they engaged in the business of the day. We found that these students were motivated to pursue their self-articulated life tasks or goals and that this motivation was reflected in the finding of their devotion of larger chunks of time to activities related to those life-task domains in which they had reported discrepancies between their actual and ideal self-concepts than they had devoted to activities not related to those discrepant life-task domains. We also found that students experienced greater stress while performing activities related to their self-discrepant task activities than they experienced in the performance of activities not associated with their discrepant life tasks.

The Role of Satisfaction, Commitment, and Values in Motivating Resource Allocation

Taryn Reeder, G. Kenneth Koves, Michele I. Mobley, Jacqueline R. Idaszak, Georgia Institute of Technology

Research concerning time allocation issues have produced inconclusive results; therefore, we attempted to further understanding of the role of motivation in resource investment by exploring value, satisfaction, and commitment profiles of persons who differentially allocate their time. Questionnaires were completed by 53 female and 86 male college students. Results of profile analyses indicate that commitment to a situation is related to allocation decisions, but satisfaction with the situation is not related to allocation processes. While value profiles do not differentially predict allocation, levels of value importance vary depending on whether individuals allocate their time to work, nonwork, or leisure activities.

Adolescent Drinking Motives: Longitudinal Relations with Stressful Life Events, Social Support, Personality, and Alcohol Consumption

Alan Reifman and Michael Windle, Research Institute on Addictions

Two general motives for consuming alcohol are to cope with negative affect (coping motive) and to facilitate social interaction (social motive). We analyzed longitudinal data from 434 high school students. Social motivation predicted alcohol consumption 1 yr later when earlier consumption was controlled for. Cross-sectionally, alcohol consumption was predicted by both motivations, occurrence of stressful life events, and low social support from family. Low family support was also related to endorsement of coping motives. Adolescents with a history of shyness in childhood reported low levels of family support and alcohol consumption, although shyness was positively related to coping motivation for drinking.

The More You Suppress, The Less You Rebound: A Within-Subjects Investigation of the Wegner Rebound Effect

Patricia C. Rutledge, Robert A. Hancock, and Dene Hollenberg
Jefferson City, Missouri

We examined thought rebounding, increased thought preoccupation after thought suppression, in a unique within-subjects research design. The purpose of this design was to measure the degree of thought rebound after suppression in *individual* subjects to allow for the examination of potential correlates of the rebound effect. Eighty-four subjects expressed (baseline period), suppressed (suppression period), and then expressed (expression period) thoughts of a white bear. The number of thought tokens about the bear were calculated for each period. Measures of thought rebound and thought suppression were calculated and were found to be significantly correlated, $r_s = .256$, $p < .02$, but in an unexpected direction. Increased suppression coincided with less, not more, rebounding.
Supported by NIH/NIGMS/MBRS 08202.

Measures of Time Perspective: A Comparison of Cognitive, Affective, and Motivation Approaches

Cathryn L. Savage, Brian P. V. Sarata

Ninety-two subjects completed three instruments for measuring time perspective: the *time line* procedure taps cognitive representations of important life events. The *time reference inventory* samples affectively salient events. The *motivation induction method* samples motivational goal objects. Indices of central focus, future time perspective, and past extension were derived from each measure. Additional items were written for the motivational induction method in order to complete past extension. Initial data analysis revealed substantial variation among indices derived from different instruments. However, differences stemming from methodological variations must be eliminated before it can be concluded that motivational time perspective differs from other indices.

The Role of Cognition in Goal Setting: An Attributional Perspective of Contextual Effects on Intrinsic Motivation and Goal Attainment

Christina E. Shalley and Deborah E. Adair, University of Arizona

Effects of task type, goal-setting method, and experience on intrinsic motivation and goal attainment were examined with attributions as an explanatory mechanism. The highest goal attainment was obtained on the simple task. A significant two-way interaction on intrinsic motivation was observed, in which those who had experience and worked on the complex task had the highest levels of intrinsic motivation. The effects obtained supported an attributional explanation. Implications of these findings are discussed.

Cross-cultural Recognition of Emotions in East-Central Africa

Catherine C. Tikiwa, University of Malawi
Stephen E. Buggie, Presbyterian College

Previous research (Boucher and Brandt, 1981) reported that American subjects recognized and classified emotional antecedent situational descriptions accurately regardless whether the descriptions were generated by Malaysians or by other Americans. A replication was conducted in Malawi, located in east-central Africa. Fifty-six fluent English-speaking African college students classified each of 48 written emotional situations into six stated categories. Descriptions were generated in English by either Malawian or foreign college professors. The results showed that subjects were more accurate at classifying locally generated emotional situations than those by foreigners, especially when the emotion portrayed was a negative hedonic one (e.g., anger, pain, and fear). It was concluded that subtle culture-specific cues help in the classification of emotional situations.

The Connections between Music, Cognition, and Emotion

Sandra K. Webster, Lara Redjenovic, and Aimee M. Woods,
Westminster College

Experiment 1 tested the hypothesis that the musical induction of mood (Pignatiello et al., 1986) can influence cognitive performance. However, the effects of music on emotion were only as predicted for male subjects. Experiment 2 more precisely manipulated music by varying the complexity of rhythm. Moderately complex rhythms played in an adjacent room increased hostility for both women and men, while very simple and very complex rhythms reduced hostility levels. These studies suggest that further research in the roles of music on cognition and emotion recognize that music has both cognitive and emotional components.

Subject Index

Author Index